W9-ALX-387

ADAPTER KIT

BELIZE

a traveler's tools for living like a local

Lan Sluder

AVALON
TRAVEL

ADAPTER KIT: BELIZE
First edition
Lan Sluder

Published by Avalon Travel Publishing
5855 Beaudry Street, Emeryville CA 94608, USA

Please send all comments, corrections, additions, amendments, and critiques to:

ADAPTER KIT: Belize
AVALON TRAVEL PUBLISHING
5855 BEAUDRY ST.
EMERYVILLE, CA 94608, USA
email: info@travelmatters.com
website: www.travelmatters.com

Text and Photographs © 2001 by Lan Sluder unless otherwise noted.
Cover, illustrations, and maps © 2001 by Avalon Travel Publishing, Inc. All rights reserved.
Some photos and illustrations are used by permission and are the property of the original copyright owners.

Printed in the United States of America by R.R. Donnelley

ISSN 1534-5882
ISBN 1-56691-350-0

Printing History
1st edition — August 2001
5 4 3 2 1

Editor: Kate Willis
Series Manager: Kate Willis
Copy Editor: Jean Blomquist
Graphics: Melissa Sherowski
Design: Amber Pirker
Production: Marcie McKinley
Cartographers: Chris Folks, Kat Kalamaras, Mike Morgenfeld
Map Editor: Michael Balsbaugh
Index: Kate Willis

Front cover photo: Graeme Teague
Back cover photos: Lan Sluder (jaguar), Leo de Wys

photo on page 1: Lan Sluder; photo on page 3: Marty Casado; photo on page 13: Lan Sluder; photo on page 27: Lan Sluder; photo on page 55: Fran Dwight; photo on page 69: Lan Sluder; photo on page 77: Lan Sluder; photo on page 79: Lan Sluder; photo on page 95: Lan Sluder; photo on page 109: Lan Sluder; photo on page 123: Lan Sluder; photo on page 125: Lan Sluder; photo on page 137: Lan Sluder; photo on page 157: Marty Casado; photo on page 177: Lan Sluder; photo on page 219: Lan Sluder; photo on page 231: Lan Sluder; photo on page 233: Marty Casado; photo on page 243: Fran Dwight

Distributed in the United States and Canada by Publishers Group West

All rights reserved. No part of this book may be translated or reproduced in any form, except brief extracts by a reviewer for the purpose of a review, without written permission of the copyright owner.

Although every effort was made to ensure that the information was correct at the time of going to press, the author and publisher do not assume and hereby disclaim any liability to any party for any loss or damage caused by errors, omissions, or any potential travel disruption due to labor or financial difficulty, whether such errors or omissions result from negligence, accident, or any other cause.

Contents

DAILY LIFE

MOVING IN

EARNING A LIVING

APPENDIX

PART I
Introduction

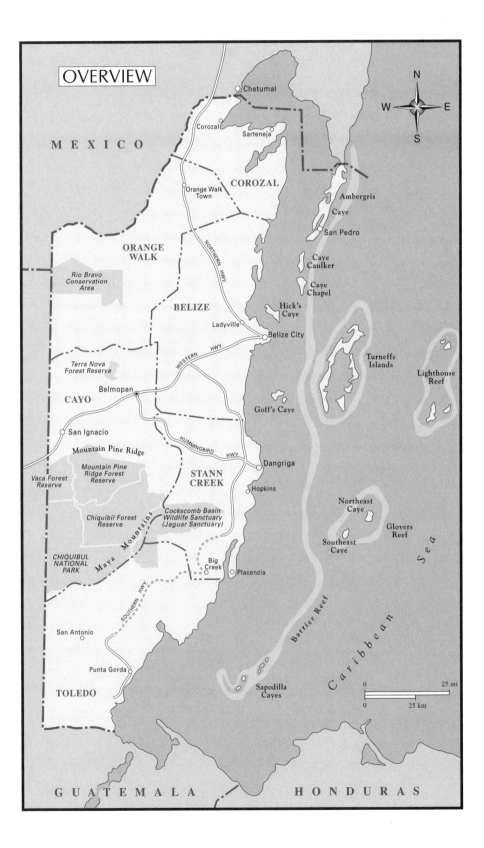

1 Welcome to Belize

Hold on! You're about to experience Belize, and I guarantee it will be one of the most surprising, exasperating, fascinating, and frustrating experiences of your entire life.

To start with, Belize is simply beautiful. It is a place of incredible natural beauty, with mint green or turquoise seas and emerald forests, the longest barrier reef in the Western or Northern hemispheres, and more kinds of birds, butterflies, flowers, and trees than in all of the United States and Canada combined. Massive *ceiba* trees and exotic *cohune* palms stand guard in rainforests where jaguars still roam free and toucans and parrots fly overhead. Rivers and lagoons are rich with hundreds of different kinds of fish. Belize is one of the world's wild frontiers, a kind of pint-sized, subtropical Alaska.

Belize is also a steaming gumbo of cultures, ethnicities, and heritages. It's a dilemma, an enigma, an exception to most of the rules of its region: an English-speaking country in a Spanish-speaking world, a British colony in a Hispanic area, a Caribbean culture in a Latin society.

Belize is a great place for adventure.

Belize is usually safe and friendly, but it also can be dangerous. There are sharks on land as well as in the sea. Belize is a little country with big problems to face. It has both corrupt politicians and proud bureaucrats who expect respect, not bribes. It's a poor, developing country, but even so it

3

CHECKLIST: IS BELIZE FOR YOU?

Belize may be for you if you want. . .

☐ To live on or near the Caribbean Sea where you can enjoy world-class diving, snorkeling, fishing, beachcombing and boating year-round.

☐ To live where English is the official language.

☐ A subtropical, frost-free climate similar to South Florida, ideal for those who wish to garden and enjoy an active outdoors lifestyle.

☐ To escape pollution, turnpikes, and large cities and want to return to a simpler way of life.

☐ To live better on a small to moderate income from investments, Social Security, pension, or other sources than is generally possible in the United States, Canada, or Western Europe.

☐ To live where a seaside house still rents for US$100 to $250 a month, land (in larger tracts) sells for US$500 or less an acre, a sea-view building lot is US$10,000, and full-time household help costs US$10 a day.

☐ To be a part of a fascinating multicultural society combining ancient Maya, African, Hispanic, Caribbean, and European influences.

☐ To live in stable, democratic country, a member of the British Commonwealth, with a familiar English common law tradition.

☐ To enjoy wide-open spaces with large parts of the country devoted to national parks and reserves.

☐ A place that welcomes new residents and retirees, with a new Retired Persons Incentive Act offering tax-free advantages for those age 45 and over who qualify.

☐ Friendly, laid-back lifestyle.

☐ A country where noncitizens can own real estate, including seafront land, with few if any restrictions.

☐ To have modern conveniences such as fiber optic telecommunications, Internet connections, air-conditioning, and North American–style houses, but without franchised fast-food restaurants, chain stores, or frenetic consumer culture.

☐ The convenience of being two hours by air from gateways in Texas and Florida.

seems to pay more attention to the environment than do its richer neighbors to the north. Belize is a nation in the making, but it's also a land with a four-thousand-year history of achievement. When Europe was huddling in ignorance in the Dark Ages, Belize was the center of an empire of wealth and sophistication, a land of a million people, four times the population of the country today. The Maya, who were mathematicians, architects, and theologians of great skill, erected buildings that remain today the tallest in the region.

Belize is not St. Petersburg, Florida, or Myrtle Beach, South Carolina, or Flagstaff, Arizona, or indeed like any other place you've likely ever been. It's not a place where the living is always easy. It can be cheap, or expensive,

Belize may NOT be for you. . .

☐ If you aren't comfortable sharing life with people of every color, background, and heritage. Belize is not for bigots or for those who think the world is run by White Anglo-Saxon Protestants.

☐ If you love opera, the theater, bookstores, and art and must be a part of a vibrant cultural scene. Belize is a long, long way from the Upper West Side.

☐ If you're a shop-til-you-drop kind of person. Belize doesn't even have a Wal-Mart.

☐ If you like things done in a certain way, fast and efficiently and just to your liking. "Belize time" is different.

☐ If you're on the financial edge and are looking for the cheapest place to live— Belize is definitely not the cheapest spot in the world.

☐ If you're a hard-driving entrepreneur and are looking for a way to make big bucks fast—the good old USA can't be beat. As the old saw goes, the easiest way to end up with a small fortune in Belize is to start with a large one.

☐ If you have a serious chronic illness and need state-of-the-art medical care. You can get caring and inexpensive medical services in Belize and neighboring Guatemala and Mexico, but the latest health-care technology and power pills may be not be available.

☐ If you're looking to escape personal, business, or social problems back home. Those types of problems have a nasty way of following wherever you go.

☐ If you're a political animal and you think your voice is as important as the next guy's. Unless you're willing to become a Belizean citizen, your impact on Belize politics will be slim to none. Politicians will listen politely and then totally ignore what you say.

depending on how you choose to live. You can't just move to Belize and vegetate in comfortable retirement. It's not a place in which to make easy money, and it's all too easy here to lose the money you have.

Take a little bit of Africa, a little of Europe, a little of the Caribbean, a little of Mexico and Guatemala, a little of the United States, and you almost have Belize. Yet Belize is more than that.

You've probably heard someone, talking about a certain part of the world, say, "I like it, but it is not for everyone." Of course not. Not everyone likes New York City, not everyone likes London, or Montana, or New Zealand, or any other place on the map.

No place is for everyone. But Belize is *really* not for everyone. More people will dislike Belize than will like it. Far more will feel uncomfortable here than at home.

Some years ago, I was a business newspaper editor in New Orleans. A real estate agent I interviewed one time told me he could tell within minutes of meeting a prospective new resident at the airport whether that person would like New Orleans. He said that people either got off the plane complaining about the heat and humidity, swatting bugs and yelling at workers to hurry up with their bags, in which case they immediately hated New Orleans, or they were enchanted by this most storied and eccentric of American cities and fell in love with it right from the moment they stepped off the plane.

Coming to Belize the first time is a little like that. You arrive at a little airport on the edge of nowhere. The hot, humid air hits you like a steaming blanket. Inside the airport is a confusing mélange of people of every color and station in life, speaking a language that sounds only vaguely familiar, and everywhere there's a mix of anxious tourists and laid-back locals. En route to wherever you're off to, you soon pass a wide dark river that looks like something out of a Joseph Conrad novel. You see run-down pastel-colored shacks like those in Jamaica, unfinished concrete houses such as you've seen in Mexico, and new homes with chain-link fences and signs in Chinese. You go through a bit of Greeneland, passing by bars and brothels, through streets jammed with rickety wood-frame buildings that could, just like the 1981 film *Dogs of War,* have been the setting for a long, bad afternoon in West Africa. Just when you think you're ready to turn around and go back to where you came from, you catch a glimpse of an unbelievably blue sea, a group of friendly schoolchildren in khaki uniforms who wave and shout, or, perhaps, in the far distance the mysterious Maya Mountains.

Belize may not be for you. But, then, maybe you *are* that one person in a hundred who will fall in love with Belize, for all its failings and frustrations. You won't find it paradise. You won't find it perfect. But you'll wish you'd found it sooner.

The Appeal of Belize

Here's what many foreign expatriates in Belize say they like about the country. These qualities may appeal to you too.

Life on a human scale: Belize operates at 98.6 degrees. It's about people. Belize is a culture of relationships. Belize is still a country of villages and small towns where people know each other. The only city, Belize City, is hardly more than an overgrown town. That most American of places, the suburb, with big houses separated by automobiles, barely exists at all in Belize.

United States Postal Service

Sorry We Missed You! We ☑ Deliver for You

		Today's Date	Sender's Name

Item is at:
— Post Office (See back)

Available for Pick-up After

Date:

Time:

☐ **If checked, you or your agent must be present at time of delivery to sign for Item**

We will redeliver or you or your agent can pick up. See reverse.

Article Number(s)

Dr. Bell 3:15

June 14

Notice Left Section

Customer Name and Address

— Letter
— Large envelope, magazine, catalog, etc.
— Parcel
— Restricted Delivery
— Perishable Item
— Other:

For Delivery: *(Enter total number of items delivered by service type)*

For Notice Left: *(Check applicable item)*

— Express Mail *(We will attempt to deliver on the next delivery day unless you instruct the post office to hold it,)*
— Certified
— Recorded Delivery
— Firm Bill

— Registered
— Insured
— Return Receipt for Merchandise
— Delivery Confirmation
— Signature Confirmation

Amount Due

Article Requiring Payment

☐ Postage Due ☐ COD ☐ Customs $

☐ **Final Notice:** Article will be returned to sender on

Delivered By and Date

Delivery Notice/Reminder/Receipt

PS Form **3849**, November 1999

We will redeliver OR you or your agent can pick up your mail at the post office. (Bring this form and proper ID. If your agent will pick up, sign below in item 2, and enter agent's name here): _____

1.

▼

   a. Check all that apply in section 3;

   b. Sign in section 2 below;

   c. Leave this notice where the carrier can see it.

2. Sign Here to Authorize Redelivery or to Authorize an Agent to Sign for You:

3. ☐ Redeliver (Enter day of week,):

(Allow at least two delivery days for redelivery, or call your post office to arrange delivery.)

☐ Leave item at my address

(Specify where to leave. Example: "porch," "side door". This option is not available if box is checked on the front requiring your signature at time of delivery.)

☐ Refused ☐ Forward ☐ Return

PS Form 3849, November 1999 (Reverse)

	Delivery Section	
Signature	X	
Printed Name		
Delivery Address		

MURFREESBORO   TNPOSTMAST
825 S CHURCH ST
MURFREESBORO TN 37130-9998
PHONE: (615) 217-0596
M-F 8:00-4:30 SAT 9:00-12:00

USPS

5293 0164 5969 8234

Belizeans are usually remarkably friendly and open, but that does not mean they don't hold a grudge. Money is often secondary to respect in relationships, and disrespect can get you in serious trouble with Belizeans. They take people one at a time. You'll often be amazed at how welcoming they are to foreigners, but that doesn't mean they won't grumble about wealthy foreigners buying up their country.

Reasonable cost of living: Living as some do in America or Canada, with a big SUV in the driveway, the air conditioner turned to frigid, and three fingers of Jack Daniels in the glass, will cost more than back home. But if you live as a local, eating the same foods Belizeans do, drinking Belizean

> *Belize is still a country of villages and small towns where people know each other.*

rum, using public transport, and living in a Belize-style home with ceiling fans and cooling breezes, you can get by on a few hundred dollars a month. In between, combining some elements of Belizean life and some from your former way of doing things, you can live well for less than you would pay in the United States, Canada, or Europe.

Health care, the cost of renting, buying, or building a home in most areas, personal and auto insurance, property taxes, the cost of heating (who needs a furnace in Belize?), household labor, and most anything produced in Belize are less expensive than what you're used to paying. Real estate and rental costs in popular areas such as Ambergris Caye are near those you'd pay in Florida, but in rural areas and low-cost towns such as Corozal, you can find nice rentals for US$200 or less a month, build for US$30 to $60

Tourist shops on Barrier Reef Drive, known locally as Front Street

Lan Sluder

10 COMMANDMENTS OF EXPAT LIVING

1. Test drive the country *before* deciding to move there permanently—rent before you even think about buying.

2. Keep a financial and legal lifeline to your home country—the United States and Canada are islands of stability in a world where currencies can devalue overnight and where laws and politics can change just as fast.

3. Learn the local lingo—even in Belize, where English is the official language, a knowledge of Spanish or Creole is an asset.

4. Understand that as a foreigner with a totally different background and set of experiences you probably will never be 100 percent accepted as a part of the local community, or you may experience some resentment.

5. Even so, work to become accepted by volunteering your talents and becoming involved in the daily life of your new community.

6. Do not try to duplicate your lifestyle as it was "back home"—in many cases that will cost more and certainly doing so will not let you benefit from the local ways of doing things.

7. Be prepared for culture shock to hit, usually after a year or so in the new setting.

8. Be aware that as a "wealthy" foreigner you may be the target of all kinds of scams and thefts, from real estate rip-offs to squatters occupying your land to legal problems to burglaries and robberies, and that you must protect yourself from such problems.

9. Don't limit yourself to the local expat community—get to know the local folks.

10. Enjoy the wonders of your new home to the fullest—life is not a dress rehearsal.

a square foot, or buy an attractive modern home for US$50,000 to $100,000. Land in large tracts is available for US$200 an acre or less and farmland with good access by road is US$500 to $1,000 an acre.

Unspoiled nature and wildlife: Most of Belize remains lightly populated by humans and untouched by developers, so it is a paradise for wild critters and birds. More than 500 species of birds have been spotted in Belize. The country has as many as 700 species of butterflies. Animals rare elsewhere still thrive in Belize's bush.

Land of water: Regardless of your level of ability or physical condition, you can enjoy activities on Belize's Caribbean Sea, rivers, and lagoons. Diving around the atolls is world-class, excellent on the reef off Stann Creek and Toledo districts, and not bad even around the more frequently visited parts of the Belize barrier reef. Snorkeling, fishing, boating, kayaking, canoeing, and other water activities all are excellent. And, for most Americans, the best part is that property on or near the water is affordable. Not cheap, but compared with prices for beachfront land in the United States, affordable.

Fascinating history: Belize was the heart of the Maya world, and today you can visit dozens of ruins without the hordes of tourists common in Mexico and elsewhere in the region. Among the most interesting ruins in Belize for the nonarchaeologist are Lamanai, Caracol, Xunantunich, Cahal Pech, El Pilar, and Lubaantun. In nearly every pasture or backyard are signs and relics of the Maya past, just waiting to be discovered.

Exciting adventure: Belize is a great place for adventure, soft or otherwise. Enjoy hiking, canoeing, kayaking, windsurfing and caving. Indeed, Belize offers some of the best spelunking anywhere, with huge cave systems, some yet unexplored, in the Maya Mountains and elsewhere.

Diverse and rich culture: Belize offers a laboratory of human culture, all in a small and accessible space. Belize is a truly multiracial, multicultural, multilingual society. Far from perfect, Belize is a continuing education. Belize does not have many museums or art galleries. It has few bookstores and theaters. But something is always going on, and there's always something new to discover about people and about the world. If you're bored in Belize, shame on you.

Frost-free climate: If you tire of cold Northern winters, Belize is for you. It never snows in Belize, and the temperature never drops even close to freezing. The weather is a bit like what you find in South Florida—humid, warm to hot, but tempered on the coast and cayes by prevailing sea breezes. Subtropical fruits and vegetables such as mangoes, papaya, bananas, and citrus grow almost like weeds.

I discovered Belize (formerly British Honduras), at least in my imagination, some two decades ago. Backwaters appeal to me, and I was attracted by Aldous Huxley's oft-quoted comment: "If the world had any ends, British Honduras would surely be one of them."

Aerial shot of San Pedro Town on Ambergris Caye

Marty Casado

Living then in New Orleans, once the gateway to Central America, I visited Costa Rica in 1982 but didn't get to Belize until 1991. I've been banging around the country ever since, poking my nose into all its obscure corners and a few of its secrets, making friends and, here and there, an enemy.

What I've tried to do in this book is to share with you my understanding of the country, which is as incomplete as anyone else's. Belize is a small country, but it is incredibly complicated. I've found that even many Belizeans know only a little about their country, or rather they know a lot but only about a little part of it. Living, say, in Belize City, they know all the crannies and grannies of that port town, but Punta Gorda or Sarteneja is as foreign to them as Peoria is to a New Yorker, or as Iowa is to a South Carolinian, or as Belize City is to a Corozaleño.

My goal is to provide you with information that will help you decide if Belize is for you, and if so, what options you will have in the country. This is not a guide to daily living in Belize, because that would take many thousands of pages, but a guide to making your first decisions about living in Belize. You'll learn about the history of Belize, its culture and people, about how to get good health care and how to find affordable housing, about how to travel around the country, where to find more information about it and, if it comes to that, how to move to Belize. Beginning with chapter 13, you'll find specific information on the areas of Belize that are likely to be the most attractive for an extended stay, relocation, or investment, including Ambergris Caye, Corozal, Cayo, Placencia, and Punta Gorda. Throughout the book, I've been as candid as I can be, sharing with you the bad in Belize as well as the beautiful.

Seafront on the south end of Ambergris Caye

Lan Sluder

Reader Feedback

Now you can do something for me. Tell me what you discover in Belize. If you find a great bargain, or a bad egg, or if you come across a better way of doing things than I've described here, drop me a note, care of the publisher, or email me at BZEFIRST@aol.com or Lan@BelizeFirst.com. Belize is changing rapidly, and only one thing is certain: Before the ink is dry on these pages, prices will have changed, people will have moved on, and places will be a little different than when I was last there. Let me hear from you.

2 An Overview of Belize

The most important thing to understand about the country of Belize is this: Belize is like a little kid trying to survive in a grown-up world where almost all the adults are bigger, richer, and more powerful.

Imagine a country about the size of the state of Massachusetts. But instead of having the population of Massachusetts, about six million, this country has only 240,000 people, about the population of Savannah, Georgia. Instead of having the resources of Savannah, this country has the resources of a town of 25,000 people. With a per capita income of just US$2,600, about one-tenth that of the United States, Belize has the financial, educational, and structural resources of Tinyville, USA.

Now imagine trying to run an entire country with the resources of a small town—establish and maintain the national government; raise an army; staff embassies around the world; participate in the U.N.; have your political leaders travel the world and meet with the president of the United States, with the heads of other countries, and with the Pope in Rome; provide health care, police, and all the other services of a modern state; build a road system; educate the two-thirds of the population who are under age 20—and do it all with the economic base of Mayberry.

Whenever you have a problem in Belize, chances are it can be traced back to the fact that Belize is just a little guy struggling to make it in a big, big world.

Where the Heck is Belize?

Belize is that little spot on the map just to the right of Guatemala and just below Mexico.

The Rio Hondo separates Mexico, a country with 100 million people and an area of about three-quarters of a million square miles, from Belize, with its area of 8,866 square miles. Its neighbor to the west, Guatemala, has long claimed *Belice,* as it's known in Spanish, as a province. Belize and its allies—Britain, the United States, and most of the rest of the world—have successfully denied this claim.

By air, Belize is a little over two hours from Miami or Houston. Driving through Mexico from Texas takes three or four days.

The Lay of the Land

Mainland Belize has three distinct topographies. A low-lying coastal plain, much of it covered with mangrove swamp, stretches 190 miles along the sea. As you go inland from the coastal plain, the land gradually rises, though not to the towering heights of its Central American neighbors Guatemala, Honduras, and Costa Rica. The Maya Mountains and the Cockscomb Range form the backbone of the southern interior of the country, the highest point being Doyle's Delight, 3,700 feet above sea level, in the Cockscomb Range. The Cayo District in the west includes the Mountain Pine Ridge, ranging from around 1,000 to 3,000 feet. Northern Belize is flatter, with many rivers.

Belize has six districts, which are similar to American counties: Belize, Corozal, Orange Walk, Cayo, Stann Creek, and Toledo.

The inner coastal waters are shallow, protected by a line of coral reef called the Belize Barrier Reef, the fifth longest in the world, and the longest in the Western and Northern hemispheres. Belize's Caribbean coast is dotted with small islands called *cayes* (pronounced "keys"). Of the 400 or so islands, Ambergris Caye is the largest, followed by Caye Caulker. These two islands are the most populated of Belize's cayes, together having around 13,000 people; they are also the primary destinations for island tourism.

Belize has six districts, which are similar to American counties: Belize, Corozal, Orange Walk, Cayo, Stann Creek, and Toledo. Population density is only about 27 people per square mile, one of the lowest figures in the Western hemisphere. It's even lower than the statistics suggest, since population is mostly concentrated in Belize City (population 80,000) and a few district towns, including Corozal Town, Orange Walk Town, San Ignacio, Dangriga, and Punta Gorda, none with a population of more than 20,000. About 40 percent of the country's land is devoted to parks and reserves.

Politics and Government

Belize is a stable democracy, a member of the British Commonwealth, with an English common law tradition. The Westminster-style system has a prime minister, an elected house of representatives, and an appointed senate. The current prime minister is Said Musa, a British-educated lawyer of Palestinian and Belizean heritage. He heads the People's United Party (PUP), which swept the last national elections in 1998. The main opposition party is the United Democratic Party (UDP). The two parties are centrist, and their policies and ideologies are not very different. Belize politics, however, are often intensely personal. Everyone seems to know everyone else, and party loyalties are rewarded and long remembered. Some villages traditionally are "blue" (the PUP colors) and others "red" (UDP).

Society and Culture

Belize is a true multiethnic, multicultural society. About four in ten Belizeans are Mestizos, people of mixed Indian and European heritage, most originally from neighboring Latin countries, and most living in northern and western Belize; three in ten are Creoles, of mixed African and European, concentrated in and around Belize City; one in ten is Maya, and another one in ten Garifuna, of mixed African and Carib Indian descent. The Garifuna live mainly in southern Belize along the coast. Kek'chi and Yucatec Maya are in southern, western, and northern Belize. The rest are Americans, Europeans, and other Anglos, Chinese, East Indians, and others.

As a multicultural society, Belize cannot be understood through generalities. What may be the case in Mestizo culture in northern Belize may not apply at all among the Garifuna at the other end of the country. However, it's fair to say that Belize does not share with its Latin neighbors the same culture of *machismo*. It's present, especially among Mestizos, but it is not a dominant part of the culture. Women play an increasingly important role in Belize, and quite a few Belizean women from all backgrounds run successful businesses. With the breakup of traditional family structures and more single mothers raising children, women are helping hold a fragile society together in changing times. Still, at least on the surface, it's a

> *Belize is a true multiethnic, multicultural society.*

man's world in Belize, especially in politics and romance. Many Belizean men think it is perfectly acceptable, even expected of them, to have lovers outside of marriage.

The ethnic pecking order in Belize is changing with demographic shifts, but Creoles, especially those from old-line Creole families—so-called "royal Creoles"—from Belize City still dominate politics and professions. Mestizos, thanks to their growing numbers, are fast gaining political and economic clout. Garifuna and Maya seem to get the short end of the stick in modern Belize society, typically living in rural areas or in poor villages at the edges of the country. Gringos are not so much on the social ladder in Belize as beside it. Despite money or education, gringos typically have few political or family connections, they don't have the right to vote, and in the overall power frame in Belize they simply don't much matter. That's a tough thing for many Americans to accept, coming as we do from a culture where white, middle-class males tend to run things.

The exact number of foreign expatriates from the United States, Canada, Asia, and Europe in Belize is unknown. Estimates range from around a thousand to several thousand. Most foreigners living in Belize are not in the country as official residents. Either they are in the country illegally, as is the case with many Guatemalan and Honduras refugees, or are in Belize for only part of the year, as in the case of American and Canadian snowbirds. In any case, the number is as yet small, although interest in Belize as a relocation or retirement destination, or as a second home, has been growing by leaps and bounds in recent years. Given the

April, the tapir at the Belize Zoo

Lan Sluder

millions of baby boomers soon to reach retirement age, the increased awareness of Belize due to expanded tourism promotion (no doubt helped by the widely watched and publicized *Temptation Island* television show, filmed in Belize, that aired in early 2001, although the sequel is being shot in Honduras), and the increased efforts by the Belizean government hoping to attract foreigners and investors, it is reasonable to expect, in coming years, a significant increase in the number of North Americans and Europeans living, investing, and retiring in Belize.

Attitude toward Foreigners

Most people who have spent any time in Belize realize that by and large Belizeans deal with non-Belizeans the same way they deal with other Belizeans—on a case-by-case basis.

From time to time, Belizeans do voice concern when they see land being bought by foreign investors, or worry that one group or another—sometimes it's Chinese from Taiwan, and another time, illegal immigrants from Guatemala—are taking over. But Belizeans soon revert to their live-and-let-live philosophy.

As one Ambergris Caye expatriate, Diane Campbell, puts it: "This is the friendliest place I have ever been, and I have traveled a lot. Belizeans take people one at a time—foreign or local is not the issue. How you behave and how you are in your heart is what makes the difference. If you are nice, kind, and honest you will be well loved and respected here. The resident foreigners who live here long term are basically good people. They show respect and decency. . . and therefore they too take people one at a time. If you get used to living here you won't be able to imagine living elsewhere."

Language

Although English is the official language in Belize, Spanish also is widely spoken. In the far north and west near the Mexican and Guatemala borders, Spanish is the first language. Even in those areas, most people speak at least some English, and it's rare that you would have a problem getting by with only English. All official government documents, deeds, and papers are written in English.

If there's a *lingua franca* in Belize, it's Creole, a mixture of English and other languages with West African grammar and syntax. Even Chinese shopkeepers and American ranchers, if they've grown up in Belize, speak Creole. As an English speaker, you can almost, but not quite, understand it.

Garifuna and several Maya languages also are spoken in Belize. Many Belizeans are trilingual—speaking English, Spanish, and Creole—and an effort is underway in Belize to teach Spanish to all students, so that Belize can better coexist with its Spanish-speaking neighbors.

Money

The good old greenback is the national currency of Belize. Almost. Belize does have its own currency, the Belize dollar. But it's pegged at two Belize dollars to one United States dollar, and it's been that way for decades. Belizean stores accept either one and often give change in a mix of the two currencies. While the peg could change—there are rumors to that effect from time to time—the watchdogs at the International Monetary Fund regularly recommend that the two-to-one peg be maintained. As it's not always easy to exchange Belize dollars back into U.S. dollars or other hard currencies, expatriates in Belize usually keep most of their funds in a bank in their home country, transferring just what they need for living expenses to their Belize bank account.

Cooking

Belize cooking is hardly one of the world's noted cuisines, and indeed it has borrowed almost every dish from its neighbors and from immigrants to the country. Still, with a wealth of fresh seafood easily at hand, spicy dishes from Mexico and Guatemala, fresh fruits and vegetables from local gardens and Mennonite farms, and earthy cooking from the Caribbean and Africa, you can eat well and inexpensively in Belize.

Rice with beans is the national dish, usually served with stewed beef, chicken, or fish. What makes rice and beans so delicious are the seasonings. *Recado*—a paste of ground annatto seed and a variety of herbs, which is made into a cake and is available in either red or black versions—is used liberally in this and many other Belizean dishes. Coconut milk also is a common seasoning for rice and beans and other dishes.

The sweet, succulent spiny lobster caught by the thousands off Belize's coast is a treat for many visitors to Belize.

On the coast and cayes, seafood is the way to go. Catch snapper or grouper and cook it the same day. Douse it in lime juice and serve it with fried *plantains* (cooking bananas) and beans and rice. That's heaven. The sweet, succulent spiny lobster caught by the thousands off Belize's coast is a treat for many

Iguana Stew, Cowfoot Soup, The Royal Rat, and Other Belizean Taste Treats

Belizeans will eat almost anything. At least, it seems that way sometimes. Among the taste treats you can enjoy in Belize:

Stewed Iguana: Start by catching, skinning, and cleaning a green iguana. Wash it thoroughly in vinegar and lime. Add carrots, onions, pepper, red recado (achiote or annatto with herbs), and other seasonings. Tastes like—you guessed it—chicken.

Roast Gibnut: The paca, or gibnut in local parlance, is a brown rodent about the size of big rabbit. It got its nickname, the Royal Rat, because it was served to Queen Elizabeth when she visited Belize. It tastes a little like venison.

Cowfoot Soup: To make cowfoot soup, you start with, yes, cow's feet. You boil them for as long as you can stand it, add potatoes, okra, carrots, and seasonings. It's served with white rice. If you try it, let us know how it tastes.

visitors to Belize. It's in season from mid-June to mid-February. When lobster is out of season, you can enjoy *conch*. Whether it's fried, broiled, as a *conch* burger, or in fritters or in soup, *conch* is delicious.

Many of Belize's best dishes are imports from Latin America: *escabeche* (hearty chicken and onion soup), *salbutes* (corn tortillas with chicken), *panades* (corn tortillas with cabbage and beans), and other Mexican items are mainstays of Mestizo cooking in Belize. From the United States, Belizeans imported fried chicken, another national dish. It's usually served with salad, which in Belize means cole slaw. The Garifuna have many dishes of their own, including *serre,* which is fish or other seafood cooked with coconut milk, plantains, and seasoning. The best-known Maya dish, served at a number of restaurants, is *pibil,* seasoned pork wrapped in banana leaves and cooked in hot coals buried in the ground.

For breakfast, try *fry jacks* (fried bread dough) or *johnny cakes* (baked bread with coconut milk). A variety of mangoes, papaya, pineapples, *soursop,* and other tropical fruit grow easily in Belize, and they make a delicious breakfast. The only eggs that are legal in Belize, by the way, are brown eggs. If you see a white egg, it's been illegally imported. Nothing tastes better on fried eggs than Marie Sharp's, the orange-colored hot sauce you'll find on every Belizean table.

The beverage of choice in Belize is Belikin beer, available in regular or stout, brewed by Bowen & Bowen near Belize City. Red and orange Fantas also are national drinks, and they too are from the Bowen bottling dynasty. Local rum is cheap and generally good, with Duurly's gold Parrot Rum and Traveler's One Barrel being favorites. Coffee is usually awful in Belize, except in Cayo where you can get rich Guatemalan beans. Gallon Jug Estates coffee—from the farm of, guess who, Barry Bowen—isn't bad, although the best coffee is grown on mountainsides at altitudes higher than exist in Belize.

Climate and Weather

The climate of Belize is subtropical, similar to that of South Florida. Daytime temperatures generally are in the 80s or 90s most of the year, with nighttime temps in the 60s in winter, 70s in the summer. In higher altitude areas such as the Pine Ridge and Maya Mountains, winter temperatures may occasionally fall into the 40s or low 50s. Humidity is high year-round, tempered on the coast and cayes by prevailing breezes from the sea. Rainfall varies from 150 to 200 inches a year in the far south, feeding lush rainforests and jungle, to 50 inches in the north, similar to most of the Southeastern United States. The so-called "rainy season"—late June through early November for most of the country—means not monsoons but a couple of hours rain, often at night, followed by hours or days of sunshine.

Coco palms

Lan Sluder

Inland, the "dry season" in the late spring is hot (temps may reach 100°F), and forest fires are common.

The Western Caribbean does not get as many hurricanes as the Southeastern U.S. Atlantic Coast or the Gulf Coast of Texas, but, yes, Belize is in the hurricane belt. On average, Belize is visited by a hurricane about once every ten years. Tropical storm and hurricane season in Belize is June through November, with most storms coming late in the season, particularly September through early November.

Only four storms in the past 100 years have done significant damage. An unnamed hurricane in 1931 killed 2,500, Hurricane Janet did massive damage in northern Belize in 1955 but loss of life was limited, and Hurricane Hattie in 1961 killed about 300 and badly damaged much of Belize City. In late September and early October 2000, Hurricane Keith slammed Ambergris Caye and Caye Caulker with 125 mile-per-hour winds, destroying hundreds of houses and killing three people on Ambergris. Posthurricane flooding on the mainland and other effects of Keith resulted in some US$275 million in damage. However, by early 2001 things were back to normal in Belize, and visitors, except for noting a lot of downed trees and palms stripped by the storm, might not even know a big hurricane had blown through the country.

Bugs and Creepy Crawlies

Belize is subtropical, and that means you have to coexist with a lot of life-forms, including bugs and various nasties. Mosquitoes are not a big problem in Belize City or in most towns, thanks to mosquito control efforts. When a breeze is blowing, which is most of the time, they're also not a problem on the coast or cayes. Inland, especially in the far south and around standing water, they can be ferocious. Bug juice with up to 30 percent DEET helps. Mosquitoes in Belize (two different species) can carry malaria and dengue fever. *(See chapter 9, Staying Healthy.)*

Even worse are sand flies, also called sand fleas or *no-see-ums*. These little monsters are common on some beaches and in grassy areas near the coast. They affect some people worse than others. Many people eventually build up a resistance to them, although some lifelong Belize residents still get badly bitten. Baby oil, Avon Skin-So-Soft, or other oily lotions drown 'em, and DEET also helps.

The bot fly is a noxious creature, though not deadly. With the help of a mosquito, it lays an egg under your skin. The worm-like larva then digs its way out of your body. You can kill it by putting petroleum jelly over the opening in your skin. This suffocates the larva, and you can then remove it. Another treatment favored by many Belizeans is to put damp cigarette tobacco or snuff on the opening in your skin. In many cases, this either draws the larva out or kills it.

For skeeters and other kinds of bugs, some people also swear by Vitamin B6, in doses of 100 mg/day.

Killer bees are a common problem, especially if you're out clearing land. All honey bees in Belize are now Africanized. The sting of an Africanized bee isn't any worse than a regular bee, but when disturbed the bees tend to be very aggressive and can kill cattle and other livestock—and you. If attacked, try to get into water or under a shed. Some people advise standing dead still.

Say Hello to a Jaguar

You turn a corner on the trail. Suddenly you're face to face with the biggest wild cat in the hemisphere. *Panthera onca. El Tigre.* Jaguar. You're two feet from 250 pounds of rippling muscle and raw power. Up close, the big cat's teeth look as big as Michael Jordan's shoes. The jaguar growls, a deep rumbling cough. Involuntarily, you jump back, thankful a strong but inconspicuous fence separates you and the jaguar.

You're at the Belize Zoo, at 29 acres one of the smallest zoos in the world, but arguably one of the best. Travel writer Peter Eltringham, author of guidebooks to Belize, Mexico, and Guatemala, says the Belize Zoo is "the finest zoo in the Americas south of the U.S."

Here, less than half an hour from Belize's unprepossessing capital of Belmopan, you can see more than 125 species of wild things native to Belize, including the jaguar. The zoo has both the spotted and the rarer black versions of the jaguar; they look very different but are the same species.

The spotted jaguar, a male, has been nicknamed C. T. Katun; the black jaguar is called Ellen. The jaguar once roamed much of Central and South America, but today it is endangered. Belize is one of the few remaining places where the jaguar still exists in sizable numbers. Estimates are that as many as 600 to 1,000 jaguars are in Belize's jungles, primarily in the Maya Mountains and the Cockscomb Jaguar Preserve in southern Belize and in Orange Walk District in northwestern Belize.

At the zoo you'll also see the four other wild cats of Belize: the puma, margay, ocelot, and jaguarundi. Most of the animals are behind wire barriers, under a canopy of subtropical trees. The zoo does not capture wild animals but instead provides a home for animals that were orphaned, injured, born at the zoo, or sent to it from other zoological institutions. The black jaguar, for example, came from a zoo in Texas, and the spotted one from Guatemala.

Scorpions and tarantulas are common. (Belizean school kids sometimes keep them as pets.) Neither is deadly, though their bites can be painful.

Belize has about two dozen species of poisonous snakes. The good news is that only nine are deadly to humans, and Belize hospitals usually have antivenin for *fer-de-lance* and other snakes. Bats are the most prevalent mammal in Belize, and among the ones present are vampire bats. Unless you make it a practice to sleep naked outdoors, you shouldn't be bothered by them.

Frankly, though, none of these pesky critters is even remotely as dangerous as commuting on the New Jersey Turnpike.

Economy

Belize has a small and inefficient economy. Belize's gross domestic product (GDP) is around US$750 million annually. Microsoft gets that much revenue *every two weeks.* Per capita GDP in Belize is around US$2,600, about one-tenth of that in the United States. Economic growth declined from an average of more than 9 percent a year during 1987-92, to around 3 percent during 1993-98, but growth recovered to 6 percent in 1999 according to the World Bank.

The country's small population and low population density mean that it's difficult for domestic industries to operate efficiently. You can't build cars, or even bicycles, for a population of a quarter of a million with little disposable income. Only products with export potential can be produced with real economies of scale. There are no big discount stores—no Wal-Marts, and no blue light specials.

Agriculture—mainly sugarcane, citrus, and bananas—is the number one industry in Belize, contributing about one-fifth of total gross domestic product. Shrimp farming is the latest thing. It's controversial, though, because shrimp farming can have a strong environmental impact on lagoons, due to the use of antibiotics and chemicals.

Tourism is the fastest-growing sector, and by the time you read this it may have moved into the number one spot, surpassing agriculture. However, by most measures Belize remains an off-the-beaten path destination, with fewer than 200,000 international visitors a year. Cancun gets more tourists in a month than the whole country of Belize does in an entire year.

Belize imports more than it exports. Belize's largest trade partner is the United States. Belize is hardly a haven for free trade, as import taxes are high. Workers earning under US$10,000 annually, and that's most Belizeans, pay no income tax, so import taxes and fees, along with the national sales tax of 8 percent, are an important source of government revenue.

Tika, a jaguar who lives at Banana Bank near Belmopan

Lan Sluder

Annual inflation rate in Belize has been low in recent years. The rate has been under 2 percent per year since the mid-1990s, though it was creeping up in 2000 and early 2001. Unemployment is estimated at 14 percent or more of the total work force of about 75,000, and underemployment is a serious problem in some areas. In many remote villages in Belize, few if any of the residents have ever worked outside the home or subsistence farm. Paradoxically, however, skilled workers are in short supply in some areas, and employers worry about getting and keeping good employees.

Education

Belize's educational system is based roughly on the English system (since it used to be a British colony). Students move through *forms* rather than grades. The Catholic Church, through an agreement with the government, operates many of Belize's public schools. Nearly two-thirds of Belize's population are teenagers or younger, so in every part of Belize you'll see schoolkids in their khaki or blue school uniforms. In Belize City and elsewhere, there are both Catholic and government-run high schools. A few private or parochial schools run by Protestant denominations also exist. The best schools are in Belize City and in larger towns, and many of the worst schools—with untrained teachers and few books or equipment—are in the far south.

Education is compulsory and free through elementary school. Books and other costs of going to school keep many students out of school past this level.

Brahma cattle

Lan Sluder

HAVE YOU BEEN TO DOG FLEA CAYE OR PULL TROUSER SWAMP?

Many place names in Belize tell a story. What story, we're not sure, but the names make fascinating conjecture. Pull out a map and check out some of these fascinating places:

Go-to-Hell Camp
Pull Trouser Swamp
Never Delay
Dog Flea Caye
Meditation

More Tomorrow
Condemned Point
Good Living Camp
Double Head Cabbage
Bound to Shine
Pork and Doughboy Point
Hen and Chicken Cayes
Black Man Eddy
Cowboy Camp
Baking Pot

The literacy rate in Belize has been touted as being in the 90-plus percent range, but this is misleading, as a large number of Belizeans, especially recent immigrants from Honduras and Guatemala, are functionally illiterate. A more accurate number is about 70 percent. Still, compared with neighboring countries, Belize has a high literacy rate and a well-educated population.

Until recently, Belize did not have a true four-year university system. The colleges in Belize City and elsewhere were more like American high schools. However, in 2000, provisions were made for the development of the University of Belize, which combines several existing Belize educational facilities and which offers baccalaureate degrees in engineering, nursing, and other disciplines, along with other training programs at its campus near Belmopan and at satellite campuses. Belizean citizens and residents can attend at modest rates, as low as US$10 per credit hour.

Many Belizeans who pursue advanced education do so at universities in Cuba and elsewhere in the Caribbean, in Guatemala, the United States, and England. Many lawyers in Belize have been trained in England, and many physicians in Guatemala or the United States.

Crime

Crime is one of Belize's puzzling dilemmas. On the one hand, most who visit Belize feel safe, and visitors and expatriates rarely are affected by serious crime. Crimes that would pass almost unnoticed in some countries such as Honduras or Guatemala, or in Mexico where there are an estimated one million muggings every year in Mexico City alone, get big headlines in Belize. Belizeans expect their police to solve crimes, and the police try, even if they are undertrained and underpaid. On the other hand, the statistics—such as they are, and they aren't very complete—suggest that the entire country of Belize, and not just Belize City, has a serious crime problem, albeit one affecting mostly the lower strata of society. For example, in a recent year, Belize had more murders than Ireland. In 1998 there were more than 50 murders in Belize compared with just 39 in Ireland, despite the fact that Ireland has a population more than 14 times larger, some three and a half million compared with 240,000 in Belize.

Muggings, shootings, and knifings are sadly common on the rougher streets of Belize City and, to a lesser degree, in Orange Walk Town and Dangriga. Hardly a weekend goes by when the newspapers and television news aren't filled with news of people being injured or killed in robbery and burglary attempts. Machete choppings and knifings are fairly common, and ride-by shootings (usually on bicycles) are a fact of life as well. In 1999, at least four Chinese shop owners were murdered in holdups in Belize City, and there were at least two multiple killings on remote cayes, apparently related to drug dealing. Too many of these crimes remain unsolved.

As in the United States, most of these crimes are by poor people against poor people, are drug-related, or are a result of family squabbles. However, if you're planning to live in Belize, even in a rural area or small village where crime is not routine, you will have to take crime prevention measures. Many expats keep a large dog. Local wisdom is that a big, black, barking dog is the best deterrent to theft and other crimes. Walls, fences, and burglar bars on windows may be a good idea. When you leave on a trip, someone needs to watch your property. Bicycles, construction supplies, and movable equipment of any type are likely to disappear if you don't have a security guard, housekeeper, or dog keeping an eye on it. Even then, you'll suffer plenty of shrinkage.

There's no need to be paranoid, but crime is a fact of life in Belize, as it is in many poor, developing countries, and when buying, building, or renting you should budget for security. Most Belizeans are law-abiding and fear crime as much as you do, but the tiny minority of bad guys in Belize can do a lot of damage to you and your property, unless you prepare for it in ways that you probably don't have to do in America or Canada, where your high taxes pay for a professional police force and other anticrime measures.

In future years, we'll probably see more gated housing developments for retirees and expatriates in Belize, with security provided as part of the living package.

3

Planning Your Fact-Finding Trip

nly one thing will tell you for sure whether Belize is right for you, and that is a personal visit. If you've never been to Belize before, it is essential you make an initial scouting trip to learn firsthand about the country and to gauge your personal reaction to it. Then, as your time and budget allow, return to Belize at least twice more before making any decision about living or investing here. Ideally one of these follow-up trips should be an extended stay of at least a few weeks, preferably in a rented apartment, condo, or house. This will give you a feel for the nitty-gritty of daily life as opposed to a vacation trip where bumpy reality is smoothed over by solicitous hotel and tour operators.

Independent Travel or Group Tour?

With the possible exception listed below, it's best that you plan to travel on your own in Belize rather than going on a group tour. If you feel uncomfortable traveling on your own on a brief exploratory trip, you may have real problems living long-term in Belize.

It's easy to travel independently in Belize. Since English is widely spoken, you won't have a language problem. Most of Belize is wired, so you can quickly make hotel and other reservations via the Internet or by fax. You'll probably also save money by traveling on your own. Package tours to Belize are rarely a real bargain, though sometimes they offer the easiest option for those with special travel interests such as diving or caving. Even if you save a few bucks, you're locked into a fixed itinerary or to a few of the larger resorts. As most hotels in Belize are family-run places with only a few rooms, owners generally prefer that you book direct with them, if possible via the Internet, saving them 15 to 40 percent in travel agent and wholesaler commissions, plus expensive long-distance telephone charges. Usually some of the savings are passed on to you in the form of lower direct-booking rates. (Belize hotel owners are reluctant to admit in public that they prefer to bypass travel agents and packagers, but in fact they do.)

The major exception to independent travel may be if you want to take a retirement or real estate tour to Belize, such as those occasionally offered by *International Living* (Contact: International Living, Agora Publishing, P.O. Box 1936, Baltimore, MD 21203, 410/223-2600, www.internationalliving .com). While usually more expensive than independent travel, these tours do provide a lot of relocation information in a short period. Typically you visit three or four areas in a week's time—usually Ambergris Caye, Cayo, Placencia, and either Corozal or Punta Gorda—and hear speakers in each area representing real estate companies, law firms, and Belize government agencies. The disadvantages are that it's a whirlwind visit, and some of speakers you hear may have a vested, if perhaps hidden, interest in getting you to buy something.

Street scene of Belize City's narrow streets and ramshackle buildings

BETO'S MINI MART

Lan Sluder

The Scouting Trip

How long should you plan to stay on your initial scouting trip? A week is not really long enough to see the highlights of the country; 10 to 14 days is recommended. Belize is a small country, but getting from one place to another almost always takes longer than you think it will due to bad roads, transportation delays, and in many cases the Belizean "go slow" attitude. Figure that a trip of 100 miles in Belize will take at least as long as a trip of 200 miles in the United States.

Where you go in Belize and how long you stay in each area depends in part on your preferences for a place to live. If, for example, you're dead set on living on or near the sea, you'll want to spend most of your time on the coast or cayes. On the other hand, if you're looking for a sizable tract of land, you'll want to allocate more time to inland areas such as Cayo District.

In any case, before you go gather as much information about Belize as you can. Get the ITMB *Belize Traveller's Map*, available from the larger bookstores in the United States and Canada, and several good Belize guidebooks. Also, spend some time on the many excellent websites devoted to Belize, (see sidebar in *chapter 7, Keeping in Touch*).

Suggested Basic 10-Day Itinerary

Day 1: Fly into Belize City and spend the night. Most visitors think Belize City is the least appealing part of Belize. If you can put up with Belize City, you'll probably love the rest of Belize.

Day 2: Fly (20 minutes) or take a water taxi (1.25 hours) to Ambergris Caye. Relax and get on Belize time.

Day 3: Continue explorations of San Pedro and the rest of the island.

Day 4: Return to Belize City and pick up a rental car. Drive to Corozal Town (2 hours).

Day 5: Continue exploration of Corozal and northern Belize.

Day 6: Drive to San Ignacio (about 3.5 hours from Corozal Town via the Barrel Boom shortcut).

Day 7: Continue exploration of Cayo District.

Day 8: Drive to Placencia via Hummingbird Highway, Belize's most scenic route (about 3.5 hours).

Day 9: Continue exploration of Placencia.

Day 10: Drive back to Belize City, turn in rental car, and fly home from Philip S.W. Goldson International Airport.

OPTIONAL EXTENSIONS:

2–3 Days: Punta Gorda and southern Belize (in the rainy season, it's best to fly).

1–2 Days: Hopkins/Sittee Point (can be added between Cayo and Placencia stops).

2–4 Days: Visit to Caye Caulker or to a remote caye such as South Water, Little, Water or Ranguana to see an atoll such as Glover's or Lighthouse.

Transportation

Only three major international airlines fly to Belize: **American** (800/624-6262, www.aa.com), with daily nonstop flights from Miami and Dallas–Fort Worth; **Continental** (800/231-0856, www.continental.com), two daily nonstop flights from Houston; and **TACA** (800/535-8780, www.grupotaca.com), flights, some with stopovers, from Houston, Los Angeles, Miami, New York, and San Francisco. There is no direct scheduled service from Canada or Europe. Flying time nonstop from the Houston, Miami, and Dallas–Fort Worth main gateways is a little over two hours. Commuter service is available from Cancun, Mexico; Flores and Guatemala City, Guatemala; and San Pedro Sula, Honduras.

All international flights arrive at **Philip S. W. Goldson International Airport** in Ladyville about nine miles north of Belize City, perhaps the only airport in the world with a mahogany ceiling. This airport also has domestic flights to all parts of the country, but you'll save up to one-half on domestic fares by flying from the old **Municipal Airport** in Belize City. Taxi fare from the international airport to any point in Belize City including the Municipal Airport is US$17.50 for up to four people. Ride only in official taxis with green license plates. There is no bus service from the international airport to Belize City.

In Belize, your visit probably will involve a combination of types of transportation. You'll fly or take water taxis to island destinations. For your mainland destinations, bus travel is the cheapest option, but having your own rental car is the best way to see the most in the least time.

The two domestic air carriers in Belize are **Tropic Air** (tel. 501/2-45671 or 800/422-3435 in the United States, www.tropicair.com) and **Maya Island Air** (tel. 501/2-31140, www.mayaairways.com). Tropic Air is a little larger, but the two airlines are about equal in service, price, and reliability. They each offer service to Belize City (International and Municipal), San Pedro, Caye Caulker, Corozal Town, Placencia, and Punta Gorda. You can book flights on these carriers by phone or via the airlines' websites, or your hotel in Belize can do it for you.

Expect to pay more for a rental car in Belize than you would in the United States or Canada. A small four-wheel drive Suzuki is around US$70 a day or US$400 a week, and a full-size Isuzu Trooper or Jeep Cherokee can run US$100 a day. Some discounts are available off season, which is roughly between Easter and Thanksgiving. A favorite rental car company in Belize is **Budget** (locations at the International airport and at 771 Bella Vista, Northern Highway, Belize City; tel. 501/2-32435, fax 2-30237, or 800/527-0700 in the United States; email jmagroup@btl.net, www.budget-belize.com). The local Budget agency is owned by the same people who own the Suzuki and Mitsubishi new car dealership, so the vehicles are usually in good shape with low mileage. Other recommended car agencies, all with locations at the international airport, include **Hertz** (tel. 501/2-35395 or 800/654-3131; email safarihz@btl.net) and **Crystal** (tel. 501/2-31600; email crystal@btl.net).

The good news about Belize's roads is that they are being improved, and most are well-signed; the bad news is some of them are still pretty awful. Only the **Northern Highway** to Orange Walk, Corozal, and the

CALLING BELIZE

When dialing telephone numbers in Belize from the United States or Canada, add the prefix 011. The Belize country code is 501. Phone numbers in Belize have six digits. Thus, to call Belize from the United States you dial 011-501-5-55555. When calling within the same town or village in Belize, usually you need only dial the last four digits. You may see some Belize telephone numbers prefixed with a 0, as in 05-55555. The 0 is used only when calling a long distance number *within* Belize, for example from Belize City to Dangriga.

Mexican border; the **Western Highway** to Belmopan, San Ignacio, and the Guatemala border; and the **Hummingbird Highway** from Belmopan to Dangriga are fully paved. A 25-mile section of the **Southern Highway** at Punta Gorda and another section just south of Dangriga are paved, but the 50 or so miles in-between are dusty or muddy, depending on when it has rained. Off the main paved roads, conditions vary, and a four-wheel drive vehicle is often necessary, especially after a heavy rain. Gasoline costs about US$3 per gallon for unleaded. Modern Texaco, Shell, and Esso stations are found in most areas of Belize.

Belize has no railroads, but it has good and very inexpensive bus service, at least to larger towns and villages. A few coaches are deluxe Mercedes liners, but many are recycled American school buses. There are four main companies: **Novelo's** (W. Collet Canal, Belize City, tel. 501/2-77372) **Batty Bros.** (15 Mosul St., Belize City, tel. 501/2-72025), purchased in 2000 by Novelo's but still operating independently, both with frequent service on the Western and Northern highways; **Venus** (Magazine Rd., Belize City, tel. 501/2-77390) concentrating on the Northern Highway routes; and **Z-Line** (Magazine Rd., Belize City, tel. 501/2-73937), which goes south to Dangriga, Placencia, and Punta Gorda. For schedules and prices on most bus routes in Belize, see www.belizecentral.net/bus_schedule/schedule.html.

Entry Requirements

To enter Belize, you MUST have a valid passport, with at least six months before expiration. Visas are not required for U.S. and Canadian citizens, nor for citizens of the United Kingdom and those from most European Union countries.

Entry is granted for up to 30 days. The immigration officer usually will ask how long you are staying. The best answer is "about a month," because if you state a shorter period the officer may grant only that shorter stay. Extensions can be obtained at government offices in Belize City, Belmopan, Dangriga, and elsewhere for up to six months, for a fee of US$12.50 per month.

When leaving Belize by air, there is a US$18.75 exit fee, which must be paid in cash, either in Belize or U.S. dollars. A US$10 border-crossing fee was introduced in mid-2000, which applies if you go into Guatemala from Benque Viejo or into Mexico from Corozal. Save your receipt as the border fee can be used to reduce your air exit tax.

Packing

Belize is a very casual country. You don't need evening clothes or even a coat and tie or other U.S.-style business dress. You'll live in T-shirts, shorts, loose-fitting slacks, and shirts. A really dressy occasion for men might require a *guayaberra* (a loose-fitting shirt worn not tucked in) or long-sleeved shirt and long pants, and for women a simple skirt or dress.

> *Leave all your fancy jewelry and Rolex watches at home. They will impress only a thief.*

Leave all your fancy jewelry and Rolex watches at home. They will impress only a thief. Also leave your rain gear at home. It probably will rain, but raincoats will just make you sweat.

Here are ideas for your packing list:

- Light-weight cotton clothes or quick-drying cotton/synthetic blends such as those sold by Ex Officio (800/644-7303, www.exofficio.com) and other travel stores.
- Comfortable walking shoes. Consider light boots for hiking and sandals for the beach.
- An extra swimsuit.
- Maps, guidebooks, and reading material. If available at all in Belize, these will cost more than back home and may be old editions.
- Cap or hat—be sure it's one that won't blow off in windy conditions on the water. You can't beat a Tilley Endurables hat (800/363-8737, www.tilley.com).
- Sunglasses—the darker the better.
- Small flashlight, baggies in various sizes, a roll of duct tape, a large garbage bag, pen and writing pad, and Swiss Army–style knife—with these you can go anywhere and do anything.

- Your favorite snacks—many American brands are available in Belize, but they are expensive.
- Extra film, camera battery, or the digital equivalent—you'll shoot many more photos in Belize than you think you will. Film is readily available in Belize, but it's expensive.
- Health kit consisting of your prescription medicines, plus aspirin, insect spray with 30% DEET, sunscreen, Pepto-Bismol or other tummy medicine, bandages, sunburn lotion, toilet tissue, moist wipes, seasick pills, and other over-the-counter medicines you think you'll need.

Optional:
- Battery-operated radio if coming during tropical storm/hurricane season (June–November).
- Snorkel mask—you can rent snorkel and dive gear in Belize, but rental masks often don't fit well.
- Fishing gear.
- Headlamp if you are going caving or river-cave tubing.
- Cotton sweater or light jacket may be needed in the winter, especially on the water or in the higher elevations of the Mountain Pine Ridge.

Money

Bring a combination of credit cards, cash in U.S. currency (mostly $20 bills and smaller), and traveler's checks. Visa and MasterCard are accepted at most hotels and some restaurants, shops, and tour operations. American Express is accepted but not as widely; Discover is accepted almost nowhere. Some places levy a surcharge for credit-card use, usually 5 percent. There are ATMs in Belize City and elsewhere, but most do not work with non-Belize issued ATM cards. Banks will provide a cash advance on your Visa or MasterCard, for a fee of US$3 to $15 plus any fees or interest charged by your bank.

You don't need to exchange money. U.S. dollars are accepted everywhere at the rate of two Belize dollars to one U.S. dollar. Money changers at border areas may give a little more—up to 2.15 Belize to 1 U.S. dollar. When paying in U.S. dollars, you often will get change in a combination of U.S. and Belize currencies. When quoted a price, be sure it's clear whether it's U.S. or Belize dollars. Ask: "Is that 20 *Belize* dollars?" Most hotels, car rental companies, and tour operators post rates in U.S. dollars. Restaurants and shops almost always price in Belize dollars.

Traveler's checks are accepted at most hotels and at businesses frequented by visitors. You may get a slightly lower rate on traveler's checks than for cash, around $1.98 Belize to US$1.

Taxes and Tipping

Belize has a national sales tax of 8 percent on all purchases except some medicine and food items. The tax applies to restaurant meals, car rentals, dive and tour trips, and most other purchases you'll make in Belize. There is a hotel tax of 7 percent of the room rate.

Belizeans rarely tip, but they usually expect visitors to do so. At better restaurants, 10 percent is usually sufficient; at small local restaurants, you can leave loose change. Many hotels add a service charge of 5 to 15 percent, in which case there's no need to tip anything extra. Tip tour guides 5 to 10 percent of the tour amount. Don't tip taxi drivers or gas station attendants.

Safety Precautions

Most visitors to Belize feel quite safe. Unlike in some other countries in the region, the police in Belize, though not always well trained, make an effort to control crime and to bring criminals to justice. Thanks to the British heritage, most Belizeans expect police to solve crimes and are outraged when they don't.

Belize City has a reputation, probably worse than the reality, as a crime center. While street crime, gangs, and drugs are real problems for the city, visitors rarely are affected. The Belize government works hard to stop crime against tourists. Thanks to a rapid justice program, anyone caught committing a crime against a tourist can expect to be tried, sentenced, and, if convicted, sent to jail the same day. Nonetheless, in Belize City, with the exception of the Fort George section where tourist police regularly patrol, at night take cabs and avoid walking around alone or even in small groups.

Petty thefts do occasionally occur, especially in resort areas where "rich" tourists are magnets for thieves. Use standard travel precautions such as putting your valuables in the hotel safe or keeping your cash and passport in a hidden pocket.

Some Belizeans do smoke "Belize breeze"—marijuana—and use other drugs, but visitors are well advised not to experiment. Belize's drug laws are strict, and the Hattieville Prison (the national jail known locally as the Hattieville Ramada), has been called one of the worst prisons in the world.

Do You Need Reservations?

If you're traveling in the high season (roughly Thanksgiving through Easter), it's a good idea to book ahead. That's especially the case for travel during the peak Christmas–New Year period, Easter week, and late January through March. Even during the busiest periods, you can almost always find *some* place to stay in Belize without advance reservations, but the best—and best-value—places often will be fully booked. You don't want to spend all your time hunting for a room. Sleeping on the beach may sound romantic, but remember the sand fleas got there first.

In the off-season, you usually don't need advance reservations. Indeed, walk-in rates in resort areas such as Ambergris Caye are often lower than even direct-booked Internet rates. Beachfront rooms that go for US$125 a night in-season and US$85 off-season may cost you just US$65 or $70 as a walk-in. Of course, you run the risk that on a given night rooms may be in tight supply.

Recommended Hotels, Restaurants, and Activities

Here are my top picks in each area of Belize, for accommodations, dining and activities. I've listed hotels in three categories, for an in-season double without meals, not including taxes and service charge:

    Expensive—over US$125
    Moderate—US$50–125
    Budget—under US$50

Here also are recommendations for restaurants, in three price categories. Costs are per person, not including tip, tax, or drinks:

    Expensive—over US$30
    Moderate—US$10–30
    Budget—under US$10

Belize City

Belize City is Belize's business, transportation, and cultural hub. It's really not as bad as you've heard.

LODGING:

Radisson Fort George 2 Marine Parade, tel. 501/2-33333, www.radissonbelize.com. (Expensive): Belize's best international-style hotel, with friendly staff and doormen gussied up in pith helmets. Emory King, Belize's best-known expatriate, has breakfast here most mornings. Two pools.

Villa Boscardi 6043 Manatee Dr., tel. 501/2-31691, www.villaboscardi .com. (Moderate): If you're nervous about staying in the city, consider overnighting at this new B&B in a lovely home in the suburbs, about half way between the international airport and the city center. Free airport pickup and full breakfast included for $65 double.

Colton House 9 Cork St., tel. 501/2-44666, www.coltonhouse.com. (Moderate): In a safe area across the street from the Radisson. Alan and Ondina Colton cherish their 1920s West Indian bungalow and make guests feel welcome. Great selection of books and videos on Belize.

Seaside Guest House 3 Prince St., at Regent St., tel. 501/2-78339, email friends@btl.net. (Budget): Belize City's safest and most popular budget spot, with dorm beds for US$10 and double rooms for US$25.

RESTAURANTS:

Four Fort Street Guesthouse 4 Fort St., tel. 501/2-30116. (Moderate): In an old colonial mansion, this is the most atmospheric restaurant in Belize and a great place to enjoy a rum and tonic on the veranda.

Macy's 18 Bishop St., tel. 50/-2-73419. (Budget): Harrison Ford ate here when filming *The Mosquito Coast*. The menu includes stewed iguana and gibnut, but most people order the fresh fish or Creole dishes.

ACTIVITIES:

Casino gambling, city tour.

Cayo District

Cayo District is Belize's "Wild West" and ideal for those who relish outdoor activities such as caving, tubing on a river, hiking, horseback riding, and climbing Mayan temples. San Ignacio and Benque Viejo del Carmen are the main towns.

LODGING:

Chaa Creek, tel. 501/9-22037, www.chaacreek.com. (Expensive): One of the top jungle lodges in Belize. You'll love the Maya-inspired thatch cottages in a beautiful setting on the Macal River west of San Ignacio. New spa. For budget travelers, there's a safari camp with meals and lodging in small A-frames on raised platforms for US$50 per person.

Ek' Tun, fax in the United States 303/442-6150; www.ektunbelize.com. (Expensive–Moderate): If you want a personalized, B&B-style experience in the jungle, Ek'Tun is for you. This lodge, run by a couple from Colorado, has only two cabañas on 600 acres along the Macal River. The home-cooked food is delicious, and you can swim in a mineral pool, go horseback riding, or explore this wild, beautiful area about 12 miles from San Ignacio.

Mopan River Resort, Benque Viejo del Carmen, tel. 501/9-32047, www.mopanriverresort.com. (Expensive–Moderate): New all-inclusive with lovely thatch cabañas and pool offers excellent value, at under US$125 a day per person including lodging, meals, tours, tips, taxes, and transfers.

Clarissa Falls, tel. 501/9-23916. (Budget): Belizeans flock to this little cabaña colony on a cattle ranch by the Mopan River. Cheap and cheerful, with good Mestizo food at the restaurant.

Aguada Santa Elena, tel. 501/9-23609, www.belizex.com/aguada.htm. (Budget): With air-conditioning, pool, and nice rooms with private bath, at US$25 double this is the best deal in Cayo. New, second-floor rooms are larger, with vaulted ceilings.

RESTAURANTS:

Sanny's, off Benque Rd., tel. 501/9-22988 (Moderate–Budget): Delicious, spicy grilled chops, shrimp, and chicken at "prices anyone can afford."

Eva's, 22 Burns Ave., tel. 501/9-22267. (Budget): Get tourist info, check your email, and grab a taco at this meeting place and traveler hangout in downtown San Ignacio.

ACTIVITIES:

Maya sites (Xunantunich, Cahal Pech, El Pilar, Che Chem Ha), butterfly farms (Green Hills, Chaa Creek, Tropical Wings), Belize Zoo, horseback riding, caving, canoeing, hiking.

A simple Belizean-style thatch house can be built for a few thousand dollars.

Lan Sluder

Mountain Pine Ridge

With elevations up to around 3,000 feet, the Pine Ridge—"ridge" in Belizean use is a type of forest and does not refer to topography—looks something like the southern Appalachians, except with orchids and fer-de-lances. In winter, temperatures can drop into the low 50s, fireplace weather for Belize. In 2000–2001, pine beetle infestation has killed many mountain pines, and dead trees have increased the danger of forest fires during the dry season.

LODGING:

Blancaneaux, tel. 501/9-23878, email blodge@btl.net. (Expensive): Director Francis Ford Coppola's lodge has manicured grounds, the most deluxe (and pricey) villas in Belize, complete with 20-ft. vaulted thatch ceilings and Japanese baths. Good Italian food with wines from Coppola's own vineyard. To complete the surf 'n' turf package, in 2000 Coppola bought a beach resort in Placencia and renamed it Blancaneaux's Turtle Inn.

   Five Sisters, tel. 501/9-23641, email fivesislo@btl.net. (Moderate): If Blancaneaux is above your budget, this Belizean-owned lodge is in the same area, in an even more spectacular natural setting.

ACTIVITIES:

Maya sites (Caracol), Rio Frio caves, Rio On, waterfalls, hiking, caving, horseback riding.

Northern Belize

The north is one of the least-visited parts of Belize, which is a shame because it offers some of the lowest prices, friendliest people, and most interesting sights in the country. Orange Walk Town, Corozal Town, and Sarteneja on the Shipstern peninsula are among the main settlements.

LODGING:

Chan Chich Lodge, Gallon Jug, tel.501/2-34419, www.chanchich.com. (Expensive): One of the best jungle lodges in Central America, with fantastic birding and the chance to see a jaguar. Owned by Belikin beer impresario Barry Bowen, built directly on a Maya ruin, and surrounded by thousands of acres of bush.

   Lamanai Outpost, near Indian Church Village, tel. 501/2-33578, www.lamanai.com. (Moderate): Fabulous setting on the New River Lagoon (watch out for crocodiles!), near the Lamanai ruins.

   Corozal Bay Inn, Corozal Town, tel. 501/4-22691, www.corozalbayinn .com. (Moderate): For a longer stay while shopping for real estate, this new

A Day in the Jungle, a Night at the Bar: Belize's Top Jungle Lodges

At Belize's jungle lodges, you can stalk the wild jaguar, the neon blue morpho, and the rare scarlet macaw by day, then enjoy a hot shower, a good meal, and a cold Belikin or Lighthouse beer afterward. Here are the 10 best jungle lodges in Belize:

1. Chan Chich, Gallon Jug, Orange Walk District
2. Chaa Creek, near San Ignacio, Cayo District
3. Ek' Tun, near San Ignacio, Cayo District
4. Blancaneaux, Mountain Pine Ridge, Cayo District
5. Lamanai Outpost, near Indian Church Village, Orange Walk District
6. duPlooy's, near San Ignacio, Cayo District
7. Jaguar Paw, near Belmopan, Cayo District
8. Ian Anderson's Caves Branch, near Belmopan, Cayo District
9. Pook's Hill, near Belmopan, Cayo District
10. Fallen Stones, near Punta Gorda, Toledo District

place at the south end of Corozal Town on the bay, with swimming pool, has two-bedroom suites, fully furnished, with kitchens.

Hok'ol K'in, Corozal Town, tel. 501/4-23329, email maya@btl.net. (Budget): Run by an ex-Peace Corps worker and her Belizean business partner, Hok'ol K'in ("coming of the rising sun" in Yucatec Maya) has attractive rooms with bay views and breezes, plus some of the best-value tours in the country.

RESTAURANTS:
Café Kela, First Ave., Corozal Town, tel. 501/4-22833. (Budget): A five-table bistro with incredibly cheap and delicious French and Belizean food. The best restaurant in Northern Belize.

ACTIVITIES:
Maya sites (Lamanai, Cerros, Cuello, La Milpa), Baboon Sanctuary, Crooked Tree, Sarteneja, fishing, nature hikes.

Dangriga/Hopkins Area

Dangriga and Hopkins are Garifuna settlements. They may remind you of coastal villages in Senegal. Hopkins has one of the two best beaches on the mainland, the other being on the Placencia peninsula. Besides the three options listed below, three new resorts opened in late 2000/early 2001 in Hopkins: Kanantik, an all-inclusive with rates of about US$300 per person per day; Hamanasi, a dive-oriented resort; and Pleasure Cove, an adults-only European-style small lodge.

LODGING:

Hamanasi Resort, tel. 501/5-12073, email info@hamanasi.com. (Expensive): New, full-service resort on beach near Sittee Point. Friendly management, attractive beachfront rooms and suites, pool, good dive operation.

Tipple Tree Beya Inn, tel. 501/5-12006, email tipple@btl.net. (Budget): Modest spot on the beach in Hopkins. Self-catering cabin and beach camping available.

RESTAURANTS:

Beaches and Dreams, tel. 501/5-37078. (Moderate–Budget): Try the Cajun chicken or any of the seafood specials at this pub-style restaurant and inn on the beach, just south of Jaguar Reef Lodge.

ACTIVITIES:

Fishing, diving, Cockscomb Preserve, Maya sites (Mayflower)

Placencia

Placencia used to be described as a little bit of the South Pacific in Central America. With a real estate and tourism boom underway, it's looking more like a resort area. But even with its own cybercafé and a growing number of good restaurants, it's still laid-back. The largest grocery, Wallen's, is about the size of your living room—it was a big deal when it finally got

church near Gallon Jug

Lan Sluder

air-conditioning in late 1999—and few of the roads or streets have names. Placencia village is Creole; Seine Bight is Garifuna.

LODGING:

Inn at Robert's Grove, Seine Bight, tel. 501/6-23565, www.robertsgrove .com. (Expensive): This 24-room resort owned by a couple from New York has raised the bar on luxury in Placencia, with air-conditioning, pool, and even tennis courts. Good restaurant.

Kitty's, tel. 501/6-23227, www.kittysplace.com. (Expensive–Moderate): Near-legendary small resort has a great barefoot Belizean feel, on one of the peninsula's best beaches. The cabañas (Expensive) are just about perfect.

Barnacle Bill's, Maya Beach, tel. 501/6-37010, www.gotobelize.com/ barnacle. (Moderate): If you're the independent type, go for one of these two cottages on the beach, new in 2000.

Tradewinds, tel. 501/6-23122. (Budget): Collection of pastel cottages on the water at the south end of Placencia Village. Self-catering cottages are a good buy at US$55 in season and around US$35 off-season.

RESTAURANTS:

Franco's at Luba Hati, Seine Bight, tel. 501/6-23402. (Expensive): Franco Gentile, from Italy by way of Manhattan, has lavished money and affection on his resort's Mediterranean restaurant, the most sophisticated eatery in southern Belize. Unfortunately, as of publication Franco has his restaurant and hotel up for sale.

Omar's, no phone (Budget): The best cheap place to eat, on the sidewalk in Placencia village.

ACTIVITIES:

Diving, snorkeling, fishing, day trips (Monkey River, cayes)

Punta Gorda

Punta Gorda, the largest town in Toledo District, has an outpost feel. It's wet, getting 150 inches or more of rain annually.

LODGING:

Fallen Stones Lodge, tel. 501/7-22167, www.fallenstones.co.uk. (Moderate): Enjoy great views of the Maya Mountains and into Guatemala from this hilltop lodge 20 miles north of Punta Gorda, near the Lubaantun ruins. It's also a working butterfly farm, and you can see up to 3,000 blue morphos in one room.

Seafront Inn, Front Street, tel. 501/7-22300, email seafront@btl.net.

(Moderate): This is the best hotel in PG, with comfy rooms in a four-story house and annex across the road from the water. Keep an eye out, and you might see a pod of porpoises swimming by.

St. Charles Inn, 23 King St., tel. 501/7-22149. (Budget): Clean, safe, comfortable rooms near the center of town.

RESTAURANTS:

Punta Caliente, 108 José Marina Nuñez St., tel. 501/7-22561. (Budget): Garifuna grannies cook up delicious seafood and other dishes.

ACTIVITIES:

Maya sites (Lubaantun, Nim Il Punit), fishing, boat charters, day trips to cayes, Maya villages, caving, Fallen Stones Butterfly Ranch.

Ambergris Caye

Ambergris Caye is the most popular tourism and expat destination in Belize. It has the feel of a Caribbean resort island—with the clock set back to the 1970s, though unfortunately the prices are not 1970s-vintage.

LODGING:

Victoria House, tel. 501/2-62067, www.victoria-house.com. (Expensive): A variety of accommodations from thatch casitas to deluxe villas, in a barefoot deluxe setting about two miles south of San Pedro Town. Pool, good restaurant.

Banana Beach, tel. 501/2-63890, www.bananabeach.com. (Expensive–Moderate): One-bedroom condos, friendly staff, on one of the island's best beaches, about 1.75 miles south of town. Pool. Excellent value.

The Palms, tel. 501/2-63322, email palms@btl.net. (Expensive): One- and two-bedroom nicely furnished condos. Great location at the south edge of town. Pool. Within walking distance of many restaurants, bars, and shops.

SunBreeze, tel. 501/2-62191, email sunbreeze@btl.net. (Moderate): Motel-like rooms, but management is tops and the location at the south end of town can't be beat. Nice shady pool.

Ruby's, tel. 501/2-62063, email rubys@btl.net. (Budget): The tightwad's favorite, with clean rooms from $25. Good, inexpensive restaurant too.

RESTAURANTS:

Capricorn, tel. 501/2-62063, email rubys@btl.net. (Expensive): The best restaurant on the island. It's on North Ambergris, requiring a water-taxi ride, but the food and setting are worth the trip.

Best Places To See Belize's Wild Side

Belize has more than 550 species of birds, 600 species of butterflies, 700 species of trees, 4,000 species of native flowering plants, and hundreds of species of fish, mammals, and reptiles. The Belize Zoo, on the Western Highway about 30 miles from Belize City, is the easiest place to see many of Belize's wildest creatures.

Jabiru Storks: (the largest bird in the Western Hemisphere, standing 5 feet tall with a wing span of up to 10 feet) Crooked Tree Preserve and Northern Lagoon, Belize District, January to April

Whale Sharks: (the world's largest fish) Off Placencia, Stann Creek District, in April and May

West Indian Manatees: Lagoons and shallow seas, all along the coast, especially in Southern Lagoon near Gales Point, Belize District, and in Placencia Lagoon, Stann Creek District, but they can show up anywhere. In mid-2000, for example, a large family of manatees could be seen just off the seawall on Barracks Road in Belize City.

Crocodiles: Belize's two species of crocs, Morelet's and the larger American crocodiles, are called alligators in Belize. New River Lagoon, Orange Walk District

Jaguars: Cockscomb Preserve, Stann Creek District, and Chan Chich Lodge, Orange Walk District

Scarlet Macaws: Red Bank Village area, Stann Creek District

Black Howler Monkeys: (called baboons in Belize) Baboon Sanctuary, near Bermudian Landing, Belize District; also at Lamanai ruins in Orange Walk District, along the Belize River valley in Cayo District, and near Monkey River, Stann Creek District

Gentle Nurse Sharks and Stingrays: Shark-Ray Alley, Hol Chan Marine Reserve, near Ambergris Caye

El Patio, Coconut Dr., tel. 501/2-63063 (Moderate): Next to the Rock's II grocery, you can dine and stock your condo kitchen at the same stop. Mexican guitarists serenade during dinner.

The Reef, Pescador Dr., tel. 501/2-63216. (Budget): Where the locals eat, with big portions of fish and rice and beans, at modest prices.

ACTIVITIES:

Snorkeling, diving, fishing, boat charters, golf on Caye Chapel, day trips to mainland and to other cayes.

Caye Caulker

Caye Caulker is a backpacker's version of Ambergris Caye. It's smaller, cheaper, and even more laid-back.

LODGING:

Iguana Reef, tel. 501/2-22213, www.iguanareefinn.com. (Moderate): This is the Ritz-Carlton of Caye Caulker, with spacious, attractive suites near the back side of the island.

Treetops, tel. 501/2-22008, email treetops@btl.net. (Budget): Spic-n' span guesthouse, run by an English-German couple.

Seaside Cabanas, tel. 501/2-22498. (Moderate–Budget): New cabana colony on water near main pier. Friendly management, dive and tour shop.

RESTAURANTS:

Sandbox, Front St., tel. 501/2-22200. (Moderate): Easily the best restaurant on the island, the Sandbox serves huge portions.

ACTIVITIES:

Diving, snorkeling, day trips to mainland and other cayes.

Other Cayes

Belize has some 400 offshore islands, most of them just specks of sand or coral. The few accommodations for visitors are generally expensive, and many of them require a stay of a week.

LODGING:

Pelican Beach Cottages, Southwater Caye, tel. 501/5-22044, www.pelican-beachbelize.com. (Expensive–Moderate): Associated with Pelican Beach Hotel in Dangriga, these cottages (one is a former nunnery) aren't fancy—the electricity is solar and the potties are composting—but you can snorkel off the beach and enjoy a near-perfect island experience.

Lighthouse Reef Resort, Northern Caye, 800/423-3114 or 941/439-2118 in the United States, www.scuba-dive-belize.com. (Expensive): If all you want to do is dive, eat, sleep, and dive, this is ideal. The colonial-style villas are lovely, and the surrounding sea is incredible. Weekly packages include transfer by air to the airstrip here.

St. George's Lodge, St. George's Caye, tel. 501/2-12121, www.teleport.com/~belize. (Expensive): A favorite choice of divers, and only 20 minutes by boat from Belize City.

ACTIVITIES:

Diving, snorkeling, fishing, boating, kayaking.

PART II
Belizean Culture

4 ¿Se Habla Español? Or Creole?

Sarteneja
community pre-school
ministry of education

You don't need to learn a new language to live in Belize. English is the official language of the country, and all legal documents and public records are in English, along with most newspapers and broadcast programs. In contrast to other popular retirement and relocation destinations in the region, such as Costa Rica, Honduras, and Mexico, that's one of the great benefits of Belize. Even if you already know some Spanish or are willing to spend time learning it, it can take years for an adult to become truly proficient. After all, it's one thing to know how to ask for directions to the bathroom, and it's entirely another to discourse in Spanish on the intricacies of golf or on the jargonized details of your profession.

> *Many Belizeans are trilingual—speaking English, Spanish, and Creole.*

Spanish

But if you *habla Español* or have always wanted to, never fear. Spanish is widely spoken in Belize, and in some areas of northern and western Belize, it is the first language. In Mestizo-dominated tourist areas such as Ambergris Caye, locals speak English in public but Spanish at home or among friends. One study a few years ago found that Spanish was the first language of about 40 percent of Belizeans and, with the influx of immigrants from neighboring Latin countries, that percentage has grown. The current prime minister of Belize, Said Musa, has said be believes all Belizeans should know Spanish as well as English.

Your best bet for learning Spanish while in Belize is to enroll in a continuing education or evening course at one of the community colleges or universities in Belize. In most cases tuition is a bargain at about US$10 per credit hour.

Among colleges and universities in Belize offering Spanish-language instruction:

Corozal Community College, San Andres Road, Corozal Town,
    tel. 501-4-23280
Muffles College, Otro Benque, Orange Walk Town, tel. 501-3-22033
University of Belize, Belize City Campus, University Drive, Belize City,
    tel. 501-2-32732
University of Belize, Punta Gorda Campus, José/ Maria Nuñez Street,
    Punta Gorda, tel. 501-7-22720
University of the West Indies School of Continuing Studies, Princess
    Margaret Drive, Belize City, tel. 501-2-35320

Creole

Creole is the country's *lingua franca*, spoken by people of every background and social class. In colonial Belize, as in Jamaica and elsewhere in the Caribbean and also in antebellum America, a new vernacular developed in the intersection of languages spoken by West African slaves and the English, Spanish, and other languages spoken by slave masters and colonizers. Then, as now, Belize Creole uses many common English words, but the syntax and much of the grammar derive from African languages. When you hear Creole spoken, you can grasp quite a few of the words, but the way the words are put together make it almost impossible for an outsider to understand.

A few words in Creole, spoken at the right moment, go a long way.

After emancipation in America, the former slaves lost much of their Creole patois, except in remote coastal islands of Georgia and South Carolina where dialects such as Sea Island Gullah and Geechee are still used today. Creole, however, stayed alive in Belize and some other parts of the British Empire in the Caribbean after emancipation. The best estimates are that more than 50,000 Belizeans speak Creole as a first language and another 90,000 or more speak it as a

CREOLE WORDS, PHRASES, AND PROVERBS

You don't need to speak Creole to get along in Belize, but knowing at least a few words helps you fit in. Here are a few helpful words, phrases, and proverbs in Creole.

backra: White person, as whites in tropical climates get raw backs from sunburn

da: is, am, are

deh: there

di: the; also indicates verb tense, as in *yu muma di luk fi yu* (your mother is looking for you)

fowl caca white an tink e lay egg: A chicken mistakes her white droppings for an egg, said of a politician or other self-important person

So yu si, yu get save troo Gaad jeneros gif wen yu bileev. Dis noh hapm sake a eny a fi yu werk, aal a dis da wahn gif frahn Gaad: A translation from the Bible—"For by grace are you saved through faith; and that not of yourselves: It is the gift of God" (Ephesians 2:8).

unu: y'all, second person plural, as in *weh mek unu lef me alone?* (why don't y'all leave me alone?)

wen puss no deh, rat take place: when the cats are away, the rats play

yerisso: gossip, from "Ah yer so" (so I hear)

As a primarily oral language, written versions of Creole vary. To hear part of the Bible, children's stories, and other examples of spoken Creole, visit the Belize Kriol website at www.kriol.org.

second or third language. Sir Colville Young, Governor-General of Belize by appointment of the Queen of England, is the author of several texts on Creole, including *Creole Proverbs of Belize.* (See "Creole Words, Phrases, and Proverbs" sidebar for samples of Belize Creole.)

Sometimes Creole also is a kind of litmus test for determining how much of a Belizean you really are. A few words in Creole, spoken at the right moment, go a long way. Certainly learning some Creole and Spanish is helpful, especially when dealing with domestic or other workers. With a little effort, you can pick up enough of these languages to impress your visiting monolingual friends from the United States. Spanish courses are taught at community colleges in Belize, and the cost of tuition is nominal.

Many Belizeans are bi- or trilingual, fluent in English, Spanish, and Creole. Several Maya dialects also are spoken in Belize, along with the Garifuna language, and, in Mennonite areas, a version of Low German.

Creole (or Kriol) is not taught as an academic subject in Belize. However, if you're interested in learning more about the language, you can contact the National Kriol Council of Belize. The Council has no office or telephone number, but information is available by email: silvana@btl.net.

Maya and Other Cultures

The Maya, including the million or so who lived in what is now Belize during prime time for the Maya empire, must have had many geniuses in mathematics, architecture, engineering, astronomy (or at least astrology), religion, and the military arts, although we know very little about individual Maya. Of the thousands of books the Maya must have created, only four have survived into modern times, the so-called *Dresden, Madrid, Paris,* and *Grolier Codeces.* These works, of which the *Dresden Codex* is the finest example, were written on long strips of bark, then folded and covered with a protective material. Along with these four remaining books, many Maya inscriptions remain on stone *stelae* and on buildings. It took archaeologists many decades, but finally the Maya glyphs writing system was decoded, and now most Maya writings can be deciphered.

According to Michael D. Coe, a curator of the Peabody Museum at Yale and author of *The Maya,* "During a span of six centuries, from about A.D. 250 to 900, the Maya. . . reached intellectual and artistic heights which no others in the New World, and few in the Old, could match at that time."

One of the great intellectual achievements of the Maya, insofar as we can determine from their written records, was a complex astrology and numerology, where movements of planets and stars, and their supposed impact on human affairs, were measured by a sophisticated calendar. The Maya, like the Aztecs elsewhere in Mesoamerica, thought along the lines of a series of cyclical creations and destructions, occurring over long periods of time. According to some interpretations of Maya cosmology, the present universe was created in 3114 B.C. at the beginning of 13th era, an approximately 5,200-year period called a *baktun,* and that death and destruction will overtake the degenerate peoples of this world on the last day of the 13th baktun, or on December 23, 2012. Make your reservations now, as this could be even bigger than the advent of the New Millennium.

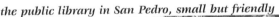

the public library in San Pedro, small but friendly

Lan Sluder

Other cultures brought their own oral and written traditions to Belize. Originally from St. Vincent in the Windward Islands, the Garifuna came to Belize in the early 19th century via Honduras. Today they are concentrated in a few towns and villages in southern Belize. They have their own oral language—a written version is being developed—religion, and culture.

The Garifuna language derives from several African, European and South American Indian languages including Arawak, Yoruba, Swahili, Bantu, Spanish, and English. Good morning in Garifuna is pronounced roughly "bway-tee bee-nah-fi" and good afternoon is "bway-tee gun yong." One of the more unusual aspects of the Garifuna language is that some words are used only by females and others only by males, though many words may be used by both. In a conversation between a man and a woman in Garifuna, the man could use "male words" and the woman "female words" to describe the same thing.

> *Good morning in Garifuna is pronounced roughly "bway-tee bee-nah-fi" and good afternoon is "bway-tee gun yong."*

Latin culture and traditions are increasingly important in Belize. Beginning with the Caste Wars immigration in the 19th century and contemporary waves of legal and illegal immigration from other countries in Central America, Latin culture, language, attitudes, and food have gradually become more important in Belize. Today Belize looks both to the Caribbean and to Latin America for role models in literature and culture, as well as in trade and politics.

The Island Academy, a private school in San Pedro

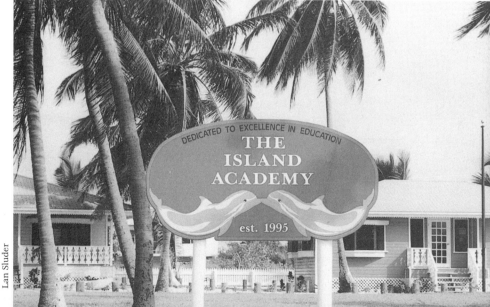

Lan Sluder

Modern Literature

Several of the most celebrated books about Belize are by authors who only visited the country, including John L. Stephens. Stephens' two-volume *Incidents of Travel in Central America, Chiapas, and Yucatan* is a 19th-century classic and still a readable introduction to Maya sites in the region. Ronald Wright's *Time Among the Maya: Travels in Belize, Guatemala, and Mexico* is a more contemporary look at the modern Maya.

Belize has a small but interesting place in world fiction. Zee Edgell's noteworthy novel, *Beka Lamb,* published in England, is all about Belize in the 1950s. Cubola Productions, a small publishing house in Benque Viejo del Carmen in western Belize, has published a number of modern Belize writers. Among those published by Cubola are Zoila Ellis, a Garifuna, who wrote *On Heroes, Lizards and Passion,* a collection of short fiction. *On Words,* one in a series of texts put out by Cubola in the 1990s directed to the student market, collected the works of 35 Belizean poets including Raymond Barrow, Ronald Clark, Leo Bradley, Corinth Lewis, Richard Bradley, and Yasser Musa. *Belize, The Novel* is a Michener-style saga of Belize by former resident Carlos Ledson Miller.(See "Belize Beach Reading").

Emory King, an American shipwrecked in Belize in the 1950s, is the author of a multi-volume history of Belize and is film commissioner for the Belize government

Lan Sluder

The redoubtable Emory King, who was shipwrecked in Belize in 1954 and never left, has written a number of self-published guides and entertaining histories of Belize. His *Great Story of Belize* is a planned four-volume history, of which two volumes have been published already.

On the non-fiction side, Byron Foster, an English-born academic, wrote a number of books on Belize history and archaeology, including *Warlords and Maize Men,* a survey of Maya archeological sites in Belize, and *Heart Drum,* a study of Garifuna traditions. Dr. Foster unfortunately was murdered in 1997 on his farm in Cayo. More recently,

BELIZE BEACH READING

Belize, A Novel by Carlos Ledson Miller (Xlibris Corp., 1999). 402 pages.

Grab the Coppertone, the DEET spray, and a tot of rum and tonic, and settle in for few hours of sunshine and sin. This could be the ultimate Belize beach book. Author Carlos Miller lived for a while in Belize and obviously knows his way around its backwaters and boudoirs.

The novel kicks off in colonial British Honduras on the eve of Hurricane Hattie pounding Belize in 1961. After that explosive start, it tracks the fortunes of Ramón Kelley, an expat mahogany logger and Belize City businessman, and his two sons, Ray and Clive. Ray's mother is an All-American Mom from Louisiana, and Clive's mother is a brown-skinned Creole *gyal.*

Belize then takes the reader on a journey through Belize's independence and growing pains and through the aging Ramón's romances, Clive's adolescent tribulations, and Ray's reluctant love affair with Belize. Along the way, we're exposed to George Price and PUP politics, a wise Garifuna banker, and evil drug lords. The settings in Belize, gritty and authentic, include San Ignacio, Ambergris Caye, Dangriga, Belize City, and Corozal Town. The growth of tourism in Belize plays a role in the plot twists. A jungle lodge in the novel, Xtabay, bears some resemblance to Barry Bowen's Chan Chich Lodge in Gallon Jug.

Miller has one of his characters, a disheveled lawyer, doing business over drinks in the old Fort George Hotel, say to a teetaling Ramón Kelley: "Few men can take this place sober, Ramón."

Richard Timothy Conroy wrote a fascinating memoir of his life as a U.S. diplomat in British Honduras (as Belize was formerly called) in the 1950s and early 1960s—*Our Man in Belize.*

Many first-rate guides to flora and fauna in Belize are in print. Oriented to the amateur, *The Ecotravellers' Wildlife Guide, Belize and Northern Guatemala* by Les Beletsky is a lavishly color-illustrated guide to the most commonly spotted mammals, birds, amphibians, reptiles, fish, and corals. Jonathan Campbell's *Amphibians and Reptiles of Northern Guatemala, the Yucatán, and Belize* is the best guide to herpetofauna of the region. *Jaguar* by Alan Rabinowitz is a popularized recounting of the effort to establish the Cockscomb Jaguar Preserve in Stann Creek District.

5 Belize's People and Culture

Belize is a true multicultural society, where people of many different races and backgrounds live and work side by side. People of color are in the majority and control most political and social resources along with a good deal of the economy. Racial bigots and those who have hang-ups about getting along with people different from themselves shouldn't even consider Belize as a place to live.

Belize's People

Four major groups—Mestizo, Creole, Maya, and Garifuna—make up more than 90 percent of the population, but Belizean life is richly spiced with residents of many other ethnic, geographic, and racial backgrounds, including East Indians, Chinese from Taiwan, Lebanese and Palestinians from the Middle East, and gringos from the United States, Canada, South Africa, Britain, and elsewhere.

Mestizos are people of mixed European and Maya heritage, typically speaking Spanish as a first language and having social values more closely associated with Latin America than with the Caribbean. Mestizos, who make up nearly 45 percent of the population, are concentrated in northern and western Belize, with sizable populations on Ambergris Caye and Caye Caulker. There is often a distinction made between Mestizos who came to

Belize from Mexico's Yucatán during the Caste Wars of the mid-19th century and who are now well-integrated into Belizean life, and more recent immigrants from Central America, who in many cases live on the margins, taking transient jobs in agriculture and living in shanty villages. Mestizos are the fastest-growing segment of the population.

> *As a Creole saying goes,*
> Al a we mek Belize—*all of us make up Belize.*

Creoles are usually, but not always, persons of African heritage. Their ancestors came as slaves to the then–British Honduras, generally by way of English settlements in the Caribbean. Once they were the majority in Belize. Today they make up less than 30 percent of the Belize population. Typically they speak Creole and English and often have a set of social values derived from England and the Caribbean. Creoles are concentrated in Belize City and Belize District, although there are predominantly Creole villages elsewhere, including Monkey River and Placencia villages in Stann Creek District.

At one time Belize was home to more than a million **Maya** Indians. Today about 25,000 live in Belize, about 11 percent of the population. The Maya are mostly of three different groups: Yucatec Maya in Corozal and Orange Walk districts, Mopan Maya in Toledo and Cayo districts, and Kek'chi Maya in about 30 villages in Toledo District.

Garifuna, also known as Garinagu or Black Caribs, are of mixed African and Carib Indian heritage and comprise about 7 or 8 percent of Belize's population. The Garifuna (pronounced Gah-RIF-oo-na) people have a fascinating history. Before the time of Columbus, Indians from the South American mainland came by boat to the island of St. Vincent in the southeast Caribbean. They conquered, and then intermarried with, the Arawak Indians, adopting much of the Indian language. They went by the name Kwaib, from which the names Carib and Garifuna, meaning cassava-eaters, probably evolved. Then, in the 17th century, slaves from Nigeria were shipwrecked off St. Vincent. They too mixed with the Caribs or Garifuna. Europeans called them Black Caribs. For years, Britain tried to subdue them, but the Garifuna, with the support of the French, fought back until the late 1700s, when the French and Garifuna finally surrendered to the British. In 1797, several thousand surviving Garifuna were taken by ship to Roatán in Honduras. Many Garifuna moved from Roatán up the coast of Central America to Belize, where they worked in logging. Some settled in what is now Dangriga. Punta Gorda, Hopkins, Seine Bight, and Barranco also have sizable Garifuna populations. The largest migration to Belize took place in 1823, and today that event is commemorated on November 19 as Garifuna Settlement Day. The Garifuna settlements you may see in Belize appear poor, but below the surface poverty lies a rich culture. The Garifuna in Belize are working hard to continue their language and culture. They have a complex system of religious beliefs, combining African and South American elements as well as Catholicism.

Dugu or "Feasting of the Dead" is one of the ancestral rites practiced by Garifuna. The *Dugu* religious ceremony, which usually lasts several days, is an appeal to a family's ancestors to provide help or advice to the living family. The highlight of the *Dugu* ritual, which usually is attended by a large number of extended family members and requires extensive planning, is a series of four kinds of dancing and two days of continuous drumming. The drumming and dancing are said to set the mood for a dialogue with family's ancestoral spirits.

Garifuna are known as good linguists. Many have become teachers, and quite a number have traveled the world in the merchant marine or on cruise ships.

The "other" group, representing around 6 percent of the population, includes several thousand **Mennonites** who came to Belize from Canada and Mexico in the 1950s. Divided into conservative and progressive groups, they farm large acreages in Belize. Conservatives live mostly in Shipyard, Barton Creek, and Little Belize; avoid the use of modern farm equipment; and speak a German dialect among themselves. Progressives, who own tractors and drive brawny pickup trucks, live mostly in Blue Creek, Progresso, and Spanish Lookout. **Lebanese** and **Palestinians**, most of which emigrated to Belize in the early 20th century, are a small but important segment, running stores and businesses. Belize also has sizable communities of **East Indians**, who live mainly around Belize City and in Toledo, and

Two Garifuna kids in Punta Gorda

Lan Sluder

Chinese, mostly from Taiwan, living in Belize City and in towns throughout Belize. The Taiwan government, fighting its own turf battles with mainland China in the United Nations, has befriended Belize, offering loans and cash grants. Taiwanese business people have invested in Belize real estate and own many of the stores in Belize City, San Ignacio, and elsewhere.

In Belize, **Anglos**, or gringos as they sometimes are called without any intended slur, are mostly expatriate retirees, farmers, ranchers, or tourism operators from the United States, the United Kingdom, and Canada. By one estimate, 80 percent of Belize's hotels are owned by foreigners. Expat communities are concentrated in San Pedro, Placencia, Cayo, Belize City, and Corozal Town.

The Belizean gumbo is even more complex than it sounds, because over the years Belizeans have mixed and intermarried. Walk down a street in Belize City and you may run into a light-skinned Creole with straight black hair and blue eyes talking, in a blur of Spanish, English, and Creole, to a young girl who looks as British as Liza Doolittle except that her skin is a deep bronze and her hair is done up in Jamaican-style braids. Even within the same family, you often see considerable variations in physical characteristics and skin color.

Said Musa, the current prime minister of Belize and head of the presently dominant People's United Party, is of mixed Palestinian and Belizean heritage. The United Democratic Party opposition leader, Dean Barrow, is a dark-skinned Creole. Other political leaders come from nearly every ethnic and racial segment of Belizean society.

Race relations are not perfect in Belize, and Belizeans are as quick to stereotype their neighbors as anyone else. Mestizos claim that Creoles are lazy. Creoles worry that "the Spanish"—by which they mean Mestizos or Latins from other countries—are taking over the country and turning it into a miniature Guatemala or Mexico. Or they rail at Chinese merchants who they say

A Maya girl

Belize Tourist Board

dominate commerce in much of the country. Some expatriates slam the "port city crowd," saying that the country is run by a small minority of Belize City Creole bureaucrats and politicians. Maya and Garifuna intellectuals argue that their cultures are being destroyed by the actions of larger groups in Belizean society.

However, at the end of the day, Belizeans simply aren't as hung up as Americans or the British on racial and ethnic definitions. Overt racism or racial tension is rare. Belize does not suffer from the deep fear and distrust between and among races that, at times, seems to overwhelm America. "Belize is multiethnic. People who don't feel comfortable with different appearances or customs won't feel comfortable here," says John Lankford, a New Orleanian who moved to San Pedro on Ambergris Caye in 1993. He adds, "People who can't abide the occasional categorical snub won't feel comfortable here, either: Belizeans give and take a considerable degree of ethnic reference, even slur and badinage, without resorting to litigation or combat."

As a Creole saying goes, *Al a we mek Belize*—all of us make up Belize.

Belize's Culture

Belize is usually considered to have a Caribbean-style culture, one closer in substance if not in miles to Jamaica than to Mexico. In Belize, however, all generalizations are suspect, as the country is made up of so many different groups with so many different traditions.

It is true, however, that despite the growing influence of the Spanish language and Latin culture, Creole culture and language continue to play a vital role in modern Belize. For much of the 20th century, the Creole culture was dominant in Belize, and political power rested with the elite, usually Jesuit-educated Creoles of Belize City. These self-mockingly named "royal Creoles"—usually lighter skinned Creoles with generations of history in Belize—still are a powerful force in politics and the professions. "Roots Belizeans" generally are Creoles from the lower or middle stratum of society. Tens of thousands of Creoles have emigrated to the United States. Los Angeles, Chicago, New York, and New Orleans now all have sizable Belizean communities.

A Country of the Young

Regardless of background or language, Belize is a country of the young. Almost two-thirds of Belizeans are age 20 or younger. This demographic fact is an important reason why crime is on the rise in Belize, since

Do's and Don'ts of Life in Belize

Kernels of hard-earned wisdom about daily life in Belize:

"Most gringos do not initially understand that Belize has a relationship-based culture. For instance, being respectful of an employee will get you 100 percent farther than offering a raise in pay."
— Diane Campbell, real estate developer on Ambergris Caye, originally from California

"The less you expect from life here, the more often you are pleasantly surprised. I love the exotic climate, the birds, the flowers, the rain, the wonderful ladies who work for me with smiles on their faces all the time."
— Pamella Picon, resort owner in Cayo district, originally from Colorado

"It's a mistake to be too generous. Generosity can backfire and become an obligation if not dealt out sparingly. Never pay in advance for goods and services. Always hold out at least 20 percent until you are satisfied."
— John Burks, head of the realty department at Regent Realty, Belize City, an American who first came to Belize in 1972 as a cattle rancher

"Do not show political affiliation at all. Belize politics is for Belizeans, so never be caught in the position of espousing any political party outright, since the winds of political change occur about every five years."
— Hugh Parkey, an American dive shop operator who has lived in Belize for 15 years

teenagers and young adults nearly everywhere have higher rates of crime than older groups. It affects Belize's economy, since youngsters who don't work don't pay taxes and contribute little to the social weal. It also impacts society at large, where young single mothers struggle to raise children.

Role of Women in Belizean Culture

Though they often are loath to admit it, Belizeans frequently have dysfunctional family relationships. Many children are born out of wedlock, and kids in a family may come from several different parents. The United Nations Committee on the Elimination of Discrimination Against Women in its 1996 report on Belize noted that "Common-law marriages are prevalent as are the 'visiting' relationships found in other parts of the Caribbean. The majority of children are born out of wedlock (59 per cent in 1990), which does not necessarily mean being born into an unstable union."

Belize doesn't have the same *machismo* tradition of its Latin neighbors, although a man paying attention to a married or "spoken for" woman may find himself in serious trouble with the husband or boyfriend.

Especially in Creole and Garifuna families, women traditionally have played important roles, economically and otherwise. Belizean women routinely work outside the home and run a number of successful family businesses in the country. Many women are active in politics and in social and civic organizations. However, completely equal rights for women are far from a reality in Belize, and many rights of women taken for granted now in Europe or the United States may not be present under Belize law or common practice.

"In my opinion, women in Belize are still second-class citizens," says Karen Cochran, a South Dakota native who owns a house in Independence village in Stann Creek District. She continues: " I caution women coming to Belize to make sure if property purchases or car or boat registrations are involved that the husband makes it very clear that he wants the name of his wife to be on the title of anything of value. If not, the woman will find herself automatically excluded. To most Belizeans, women have no rights to the property, and in case of the husband's death it bypasses the wife and goes to the kids."

Religion: A Catholic Country

Its British heritage notwithstanding, Belize is a Roman Catholic country, with about two-thirds of the population professing to be at least nominally Catholic. Proseletyzing religious groups, including the Mormons and Jehovah's Witnesses, along with a number of Protestant evangelical groups and some fundamentalist sects, have made inroads in Belize in recent years. Missionaries are active in Belize. It is said that hotels in Punta Gorda and

Maya Centre on the Southern Highway at the entrance to the Cockscomb Jaguar Preserve

Lan Sluder

Corozal Town, already suffering low occupancies, would go broke completely if it weren't for the business of missionaries, who often arrange for long group stays at the local hotels. At present there are no Jewish synagogues anywhere in Belize.

Generally tolerant, with a live-and-let-live attitude, Belizeans have welcomed expats from Europe and the United States and Canada. Immigrants, often illegal, from El Salvador, Honduras, Nicaragua, and Guatemala, have been less well received, as have some Chinese. As in many countries, there is an undercurrent of resentment of "wealthy" foreigners who buy up prime beachfront property and farmland.

Where You Fit in Belizean Society

By comparison with most of its neighbors in Central America, Belize is almost middle-class, with a well-educated and literate population, good standards of health and hygiene, and family incomes several times higher than in neighboring Guatemala or nearby Honduras.

As in all societies, there is a social and political pecking order in Belize. Creoles, especially old-family Creoles trained in the country's elite Catholic schools and in England, are at the top, and this group still dominates politics and the professions in Belize City and in Belmopan. The Maya generally are at the bottom of the ladder, with the Garifuna about on the same rung. Mestizos are becoming a potent political and economic force, especially in the far north and west.

Anglos, including expat retirees, are not so much at the bottom or top as off to the side, as with rare exceptions they do not vote or have good political connections. This can be a rude shock for white North Americans who are used to running things "back home." Belize politicians usually listen politely to complaints or suggestions from gringos, but somehow no action is ever taken.

Getting Along Day by Day

Dress in Belize is informal. Men rarely wear coats and ties. Even the prime minister and other top government officials conduct the business of office wearing just a *guayaberra* shirt (a loose-fitting shirt, not tucked into pants, usually with pleats and an embroidered front. It is commonly worn in Mexico as well as Belize and some other Latin American countries) or long-sleeved white shirt. Women in business wear cotton dresses or simple skirts and blouses. On the cayes, T-shirts and shorts rule, for both sexes.

REALITY CHECK

Yes, the weather is warm and the Caribbean is blue. But Belize has its downsides too. Here's a reality check:

"There is a negative about Belize we didn't find out until we had spent more time there, and finally knew people well enough that they would tell us the truth. There is an animosity, distrust, dislike, call it what you will, of the locals for expats that is exacerbated by the Belize government. For example, if I want to build a pier in front of my business/house and a Belizean wants to build one in front of his, the Belizean will get permission within two weeks while I may get an OK in two years, if I'm lucky. There is an attitude of 'We like your money, but we don't much care for you.' "
—Catherine McCabe, a Californian who decided to build a house on Roatán, Honduras, rather than in Belize

"Crime is definitely a big problem. The cheaper hotels in San Pedro are always having thieves break into their rooms. You can't leave anything of value in your golf cart, or guaranteed it will be gone when you get back."
—Kathy Wangsgard, San Pedro

Rules of etiquette and social interaction in Belize are at least superficially the same as in the United States or Canada, and the influence of stateside television via cable or satellite has if anything increased the similarity. However, behind the surface likeness are some important cultural differences. Family connections in Belize are very important, and Belizeans often have a complex web of family relationships—cousins, in-laws, and other relatives. Belizeans tend not to be confrontational; they may say "sure, man" when they really have no intention of doing what you ask. Belizeans of most backgrounds tend to be open and outgoing, and this is something that any visitor to Belize will notice immediately. People will come up to you on the street, or sit next to you on the bus, and immediately start a friendly, even intimate, conversation. They're not trying to sell you something or hustle you in any way, they just want to get to know you. You'll be invited to visit in people's homes, and before long you are considered a friend of the family. Beware, though, of being too much of the family's benefactor. As a "rich" foreigner, regardless of your income, you'll be expected to buy Fantas or Belikins all around, to provide rides to the doctor, or to make small loans, which rarely are repaid.

One expatriate couple handles the "will-you-loan-me-some-money?" problem this way: For someone who is not a friend who comes looking for a loan, they give ten Belize bucks. "Then they owe you money and usually will not come back for more," according to this couple. "If they do, remind them that they owe you money."

Another option, which works best for men who are approached by a Belizean male asking for a loan, is to tell the borrower that your wife handles the money. Most Belizean men are reluctant to go to a woman for money.

Showing respect and maintaining personal dignity are very important. Never, ever, run down an employee in front of others. It is such a loss of face that the dressed down person may wait and find an opportunity get back at you, possibly even with a physical attack in the dark of night. We know of at least one case where an American hotel staffer, following a problem with employees at the hotel, was set upon on her way home from the hotel and severely beaten. No one was ever charged with the attack, but some suspected that a disgruntled worker was responsible.

In the same vein, don't run down one Belizean to other Belizeans. You never know who is related to whom. Also, because politics are so intensely personal in Belize and almost every Belizean is either blue (the colors of PUP) or red (UDP), it's wise for the expatriate resident to avoid taking sides or expressing a political opinion.

The manly firm handshake, so popular with Type A American business-men, is rarely used in Belize. In this respect, Belizeans are more like their Latin neighbors. A Belizean-style handshake involves a gentle meeting of the hands and a soft, almost feminine, shake.

While brothels operate openly in Belize and marital infidelity is hardly uncommon, by and large Belizeans have a conservative public attitude toward sex. Blame it on the British influence. Don't look for nude beaches in Belize, because there are none, and it is only the occasional Italian or French tourist who goes topless at beach resorts.

Festival dress

Homosexuality is technically still illegal in Belize, albeit no one has been prosecuted for it in recent times. Openly gay or lesbian bars or clubs don't exist, and the country's only openly gay hotel, on Ambergris Caye, has closed. (The cause of the closing apparently had nothing to with the resort's sexual orientation, however.)

The attitude of Belizeans toward time is more like that of Mexicans than of Americans or Canadians. *Mañana* sometimes is the busiest day of the week. The worker you arranged to come and chop

Fran Dwight

your yard at eight on Friday morning may decide to go fishing. He'll stop by Monday morning, saying nothing of the failed appointment. Shop clerks will open an hour later than the sign on the door claims, and lunch hours are flexible. The farther you get from Belize City, the less time-consciousness you find. According to Emory King, the American who was shipwrecked in Belize in the 1950s and never left, there are three time zones in Belize: In Belize City, if you are within an hour of your appointment you are on time; in Belmopan if you are within two hours of your appointment you are on time; elsewhere in the country if you get there the same day you are on time. In remote villages, many Belizeans have never held a full-time job and may have never worked for pay. They may not own a watch or clock. These good folks simply aren't used to the strict and punctual routines we in industrialized countries have had drilled into us all of our lives.

One way in which Belizeans do differ greatly from their Latin neighbors is in their attitudes toward bribes. The system of petty bribes common in many Latin countries is absent in Belize. Customs officials and low-level government workers in Belize want respect, not *mordida*. Corruption is hardly unknown in Belize, but it exists at higher levels than in Mexico or Honduras. The system in Belize is more like the "old boy" network that still exists in places like Japan, Nigeria, and New Orleans, whereby those who get government or other contracts are expected to share with family and business associates. Doing so is not considered unethical, and in fact not to do so would be a breach of ethics. Painless loans and fat contracts to well-connected political chums are a routine part of Belizean party politics, just as they traditionally have been in Louisiana. It's a share-the-wealth system, and everyone, at least at a certain level of society, gets a turn eventually. But don't even think about slipping the police constable or customs officer at the airport a twenty.

Belizeans do like to party. Thursday, not Friday, often is considered the beginning of the weekend. Drinking—favorites are rum and the local beer, Belikin—is a national pastime. It's all part of the more laid-back, easygoing lifestyle in Belize. Puritans will hate it, but many uptight North Americans come to love the don't worry, be happy attitude.

Music, Art, and Traditional Crafts

Punta rock, a modern version of traditional Garifuna music, is Belize's best-known contribution to music. Andy Palacio, born in the southern coastal town of Barranco, is considered the king of punta rock. However, Belize music goes in every direction, from Creole *brukdown* and *cunga* to *Mestizo marimba*, not to mention Caribbean-style ska, reggae and calypso. Imported and homegrown rap also is popular in Belize. It's impossible to explain many of these styles of music, especially as interpreted by local players—you simply have to experience them, preferably over a cold Belikin. Well-known Belize musical artists, besides Palacio, include Creole classic groups such as the Original Turtle Shell Band, Mr. Peter's Boom and Chime and Bredda David, but young hipsters will quickly smell out the best new talents. Stonetree Records, a division of Cubola Productions in Benque Viejo del Carmen, is a top Belize record studio.

THE ARTS

Established artists such as Walter Castillo, originally from Nicaragua, who now has a shop on Caye Caulker, and Benjamin Nicholas, a Garifuna with a studio in Dangriga, command high prices for original work, but Belize also has a growing number of young, highly creative artists working in various media. The Image Factory, a gallery at 91 North Front Street in Belize City, is a good place to see their work and, sometimes, to meet the artists themselves.

While Belize does not have the crafts tradition of neighboring Guatemala and Mexico, it has a number of talented wood carvers who turn out well-made kitchen bowls and sea and wildlife art from *zericote* and other local woods. One of the best places to see and buy authentic Belizean crafts at fair prices is the National Handicraft Center in the Fort George area of Belize City. Mennonites have developed a small Belize industry in building inexpensive furniture, and Mennonites often show up at local markets to sell their chairs and other items. Boat building, from traditional wood or modern materials such as fiberglass, is an important skill in Belize. There are well-known boat builders in Belize City, Sarteneja and elsewhere.

An American expatriate, Carolyn Carr, who with her husband, John, runs Banana Bank Lodge near Belmopan, is one of Belize's most popular painters. Her realistic paintings of Belize street scenes and

A Mestizo boy

Marty Casado

wild creatures (sometimes both in the same scene) have been widely exhibited, and she has a studio at the lodge. One of her best-known works is titled *Jimmy Hines,* which shows the old market in Belize City where fishermen are cleaning lobster, snapper and jimmy hines, the local name for a type of sea bass or grouper. A few years back, one of her paintings appeared on the cover of the Belize telephone directory.

Belize in the Flicks

For movie buffs, two movies with extensive footage of Belize are *The Dogs of War* (1981) and *Mosquito Coast* (1986). In *The Dogs of War,* starring Christopher Walken and Tom Berenger, Belize City stands in for a fictitious African country in the throes of political change. *The Mosquito Coast* is based on the Paul Theroux novel about a would-be escape from modern society. Its star, Harrison Ford, got to know Belize well during the filming. A brooding TV version of Joseph Conrad's novella *Heart of Darkness* was shot in Belize in 1994. It starred John Malkovich. *After the Storm,* based on a Hemingway short story and shot in San Pedro, Placencia, and Belize City in 2000, is the latest movie filmed in the country. A "reality-based" TV show, *Temptation Island,* was shot on Ambergris Caye in the fall of 2000. The show's production crew were caught by Hurricane Keith but escaped without injury. Emory King, an American who was shipwrecked on Belize in the 1950s and decided to stay, is Belize's official commissioner of film. His job is to entice movie and television producers to use Belize as a locale for their film or video productions.

(*For more books and videos about Belize, see the chapter "Useful Resources" in the appendix.*)

6 A Brief History of Belize

Much of the history of Belize is the history of the Maya. Hunter-gatherers from Asia, the ancestors of the Indians of the Americas, first came to what is now Belize and the rest of Mesoamerica around 25,000 years ago. Maya Indians began farming in Belize three to four thousand years ago, or earlier. By 2500–1000 B.C. the Maya were building sophisticated structures at Santa Rita, Cuello, and elsewhere in northern Belize.

The Maya

During the Classic period (about A.D. 250–950), there were perhaps a million Maya in what is now Belize, four times the population today. Achievements of the Maya in architecture, engineering, mathematics, and astronomy during their Golden Age far exceeded that of Europe of the same period. They undertook extensive road building projects and created elaborate cities in the jungle, quarrying and moving huge blocks of stone. Two temples in western Belize, one at Caracol and another at Xunantunich, remain to this day the tallest man-made

> *Belize is a nation in the making, but it's also a land with a four-thousand-year history of achievement.*

Key Dates in Belize's History

2,500 B.C. First important Maya centers in Belize established at Santa Rita and elsewhere.

A.D. 300–900 Classic Maya period, when what is now Belize was the heart of the Maya empire with a population of one million.

1500s First Europeans—Spaniards—arrive in Belize; Maya resist.

1600s English buccaneers use Belize coast as base to attack Spanish ships; later settle in Belize River Valley and begin logging.

1798 Baymen defeat Spanish at Battle of St. George's Caye on September 10, Belize's national day.

1823 Garifuna from Honduras settle in southern Belize.

1838 Slaves emancipated.

1848 Caste Wars begin in Yucatán, driving Mexican Mestizos into northern Belize.

1862 Britain declares British Honduras a colony and a member of British Commonwealth.

1931 Worst hurricane in Belize history strikes on September 10, killing 2,500.

1949 Protests against devaluation of British Honduras dollar lead to formation of People's United Party headed by George Price, sowing seeds of independence.

1954 All literate Belizean adults get right to vote.

1958 As many as 5,000 Mennonites from Canada and Mexico begin settling and farming in northern and central Belize; some later relocate to South America.

1961 Hurricane Hattie nearly levels Belize City on the night before Halloween, killing 300.

1964 Constitutional self-government begins January 1. Price and his People's United Party (PUP) dominate politics in Belize for much of the rest of the century.

1973 Name officially changed to Belize; capital moved to Belmopan from Belize City.

1981 On September 21, Belize becomes fully independent member of British Commonwealth.

1984 Opposition United Democratic Party (UDP) under Manuel Esquivel wins election and comes to national power for first time. UDP and PUP, both centrist, alternate winning elections for most of rest of century.

1985 Tourism development begins in earnest on cayes and mainland.

1998 PUP, riding wave of dissatisfaction with economy and taxes, sweeps national elections; Said Musa becomes prime minister.

2000 Hurricane Keith slams Ambergris Caye, Caye Caulker, and central coast; damage estimated at US$275 million, but there are few deaths and country recovers quickly.

structures in Belize, rising 15 stories from the jungle floor. The Maya understood the mathematical concept of zero, unknown even to the wise philosophers of ancient Greece and Rome. Their number system was based on 20, rather than 10, and through complex calculations they were able to predict eclipses and other astronomical events with astonishing accuracy. The "long count" calendar invented by the Maya allowed them to conceive of enormous spans of time and to make predictions thousands of years in the future.

During the Maya reign, Altun Ha, Lamanai, Cerros, Lubaantun, and Nim Il Punit were among the important trading centers or sizable cities in the region. In its heyday, the city-state of Caracol alone probably had a population of about 200,000, nearly as many people as live in all of Belize in present times. In the sixth century A.D., Lord Water, ruler of Caracol, conquered the warlords of mighty Tikal in Guatemala.

Achievements of the Maya in architecture, engineering, mathematics, and astronomy during their Golden Age far exceeded that of Europe of the same period

By A.D. 1000, for reasons that are still debated, the Maya "empire" went into decline. Some archaeologists think that, rather than a single factor, a combination of several factors, including possibly climatic changes, social disruptions, and waning agricultural output contributed to the decline, which took place at different times in different areas. Some sites such as Lamanai were occupied into colonial times, even after the arrival of the Spanish and the British. Belize today has about two dozen major Maya sites in various stages of excavation and restoration. Hundreds of other sites remain to be excavated.

The Europeans Arrive

The first Europeans arrived—they were shipwrecked—in 1511. In 1525, the *conquistador* Hernán Cortes passed through the southwest corner of present-day Belize. The Spanish established missions in northern Belize beginning in the late 1500s.

Over the next century, conflicts developed between British settlers, known as the Baymen, and the Spanish, culminating in the Battle of St. George's Caye in 1798. About 350 British pirates and their slaves—with one sailing sloop, a few fishing boats, and seven rafts—defeated a larger Spanish force of 500 men in a fleet of 30 vessels. St. George's Caye Day is now a major national holiday in Belize, celebrated throughout the country each year on September 10.

In the early 19th century, Belize, like the southern United States, had an economy dependent on slave labor. Slavery in Belize was associated with the cutting of timber, first logwood and then mahogany. Several thousand slaves, mostly from Benin, the Congo, and Angola, were brought to Belize through West Indian markets.

The origin of modern Belize's population mix continued to develop in the 19th century with the arrival of Garifuna from Honduras in 1823, the emancipation of African slaves in 1838—freed slaves remained in Belize, mainly around Belize City—and the Yucatán Caste Wars in the mid-19th century, when Mestizos from Mexico, fleeing Indian attacks, escaped to Belize.

> *In 1862, Belize, then known as British Honduras, became a part of the British Empire.*

In 1862, Belize, then known as British Honduras, became a part of the British Empire. It was at that time, and remained, one of the Empire's backwaters, valued mainly for its mahogany and, later, its chicle and sugar. A debate between Britain and Guatemala over ownership of Belize began early in the 19th century and has continued until recent times, although officially Guatemala has renounced its territorial claims to Belize. Britain pulled most of its troops out of Belize in 1994, but the British still do jungle training in Belize and their Harrier jump jets remain on call in case Guatemala decides—an unlikely event—to reassert its claim over what jingoist Guatemalan politicians refer to as their 13th province.

During the colonial period, land ownership in Belize became highly concentrated in a few hands, mostly English and Scottish investors.

An old bridge near the Hummingbird Highway, a relic of a banana railroad built in British colonial days, stands abandoned.

Lan Sluder

Indeed, one company, the British Honduras Company (later known as Belize Estate and Produce Company) was a London firm that owned one-half of all the private land in Belize. Belize Estate and Produce dominated the Belize economy and politics for more than a century, well into the 20th century.

Modern Belize

In modern times, the history of Belize has been dominated by several key themes. One is the struggle to escape from colonialism and build, with very limited resources, a new nation. Another is the effort to maintain an English-speaking culture in a predominantly Hispanic region. Still another is the effort to meet the needs of it citizens of many different races and backgrounds.

Belize gained internal self-government in 1964 and became independent in 1981. George Cadle Price, an ascetic, Jesuit-educated Creole and cofounder of the People's United Party, became the first prime minister. Price is considered the "George Washington of Belize," While he no longer leads the PUP, Price is still in the government, currently holding the title of senior minister.

Over the last two to three decades, waves of immigrants from neighboring Latin countries, combined with the emmigration of tens of thousands of Belizeans, mostly Creoles, to the United States, changed the nature of

A cabaña with a bay thatch roof at Chan Chich Lodge, which is built directly on top of a Maya ruin.

Sheila Lambert

Belize's population and politics. This change has given more importance to Spanish as a language and Mestizos as a political force. Major hurricanes, one in 1931 and one in 1961, also influenced the course of development in Belize. After Hurricane Hattie in '61, Belize's capital was moved from Belize City on the coast to the new town of Belmopan, located 50 miles inland.

Beginning in the late 1970s, expatriates from Britain and the United States, along with a few Belizeans, began developing Belize's fledgling tourism industry. While tourism has increased, growing from only a few thousand visitors a year in the 1970s to more than 175,000 today, Belize has never been, and likely never will be, a mass tourism destination. For a while, the most popular T-shirts sold to tourists sported the line "Where the hell is Belize, anyway?"

More recently, an increasing number of adventuresome investors and retirees have begun looking at Belize, drawn by plentiful low-cost farm-land and relatively inexpensive beachfront real estate. Unlike some other former British colonies, Belize never had a large European settler commu-nity. Visitors to Belize today often are surprised that the country has so few resident Brits, numbering at most a few hundred. Americans far out-number the British in Belize, and American influence, from television shows to NBA basketball, is paramount. The United States has provided all types of aid to Belize, from hurricane relief to a large cadre of Peace Corps volunteers. At one time, in the 1980s, the Peace Corps had more than 200 volunteers in Belize, the organization's highest volunteer-to-country-population ratio in the world; the number of volunteers in Belize has since declined.

Mayan ruins atop a hill

Belize Tourist Board

An Economical Perspective

Belize's economy, always subject to cyclical booms and busts, has had its ups and downs in recent years. With a gross domestic product of only about US$750 million, a small domestic market, a limited ability to raise money from internal taxation, and shrinking demand for key products such as sugar and bananas, Belize's governments have borrowed heavily from the World Bank and other international lenders, including the government of Taiwan. They also have depended on regressive import duties and consumption taxes to raise funds.

Belize's National Holidays

The following are public holidays in Belize:

New Year's Day—January 1
Baron Bliss Day—March 9
Good Friday
Holy Saturday
Easter Sunday
Easter Monday
Labour Day—May 1
Commonwealth Day—May 24
St. George's Caye Day—September 10
Independence Day—September 21
Columbus Day—October 12
Garifuna Settlement Day—November 19
Christmas Day—December 25
Boxing Day—December 26

The Belize economy grew rapidly in the late 1980s and early 1990s, expanding at a rate of 9 percent a year, according to World Bank estimates. In the mid-1990s, the economy slowed dramatically, with growth at no more than 3 percent a year. With a growing population, per capita incomes stagnated and unemployment rose. Many of Belize's most-skilled workers have moved to the United States, yet unemployment in Belize remains high, averaging 12 to 14 percent in recent years.

The PUP government, which swept back to office in 1998, eliminated an unpopular 15 percent value-added tax, cut income taxes, and introduced a series of economic reforms designed to get the economy growing again. Some of the PUP plans may be working. Tourism, fueled by a strong North American economy and a new television travel marketing campaign in selected U.S. cities, is enjoying a boom. The year 2000 was the best year for tourism in Belize's history, despite a downward blip due to Hurricane Keith. Many new lodges and hotels, a championship golf course, and a large casino have opened. Real estate sales and construction of retirement and vacation homes are driving the local economy in several areas of Belize.

Despite having faced many social and economic problems, Belizeans by and large appear optimistic about the future. Roads are being paved, new houses and schools are being built, and the exciting work of building a country continues. The average Belizean today enjoys better opportunities

THE FRUSTRATIONS OF LIFE IN BELIZE

What drives expats crazy about life in Belize? Here's a sampler of comments from Americans and Canadians who have made the move to Belize.

"The first thing I tell people is everything will take longer and cost more money than you originally planned."

—Ben Routi, owner, Nautical Inn, Placencia, originally from Arizona

"Many Belizeans are not what I would call productive. This includes both government and private enterprise. For example, getting car tags. The tag office in Dangriga is open till 5 p.m. Show up at 3:45 and they say 'Oh, we stop issuing tags at 3:30,' so you have to ask yourself 'then why in the heck do you say you are open to 5?' Last time we went at 8 a.m. when they were open, got the truck inspected, and then they said, 'The man with the money is not here yet so we can't take your payment. Be here shortly.' At 8:30 he finally shows up for work. I mean this stuff drives you crazy."

—Karen Cochran, Florida resident with second home in Independence, Belize

"In Belize, there are not many options for phone service, electrical service, water service, banks pretty much are all the same, just different uniforms on the employees, so be prepared to accept whatever comes your way in terms of service. Believe me, it is getting better, but slowly. With such a small population base it is not viable to have lots of providers of services. Those service providers that do a great job are so busy it is hard to be placed in their rotation. Computer repair, car repair, air-conditioning, refrigeration, printing, office supply, dry cleaners, the list can go on of services that are truly limited in Belize."

—Hugh Parkey, dive shop owner in Belize City, an American who has lived in Belize for 15 years

"[Some Belizeans] seem to have the here-comes-another-rich-American attitude. We, along with many of our friends, have had several caretakers for our houses, and we all seem to have had the same problems with them. They take what isn't theirs without hesitation. We've also had problems with a local we hired as our mechanic. We paid him US$2,000 for his labor and shipped parts to him worth in excess of US$1,500. He now has a new engine in his golf cart and we have a broken-down one."

—Kathy Wangsgard, Utah resident with second home on Ambergris Caye, Belize

"My BIG complaint here is the telephone company, Belize Telecommunications. The service is very unreliable. I use the Internet a lot, not only for my website but also to keep in touch with family and friends. Out of 30 days that I pay for, I might get 20 days that I actually have service. Ten days out of the month, I'm raising holy hell in the BTL office. And the rates are just plain ridiculous!"

—Tammy Martinez, Ambergris Caye resident who moved here from Florida

for a good education and a decent job than ever before. Besides, whatever happens, the sun is still warm, the sea is still beautiful, and rice and beans remain cheap.

PART III

Daily Life

7 Keeping in Touch

When it came to communications, Belize used to be a black hole. There were no television stations, no daily newspapers, radio was mostly Spanish language stations from Mexico or Guatemala, and many villages had no telephones. The "coconut telegraph"—word of mouth—was the state of the art in communications.

Today Belize still has no daily newspaper, and the coconut telegraph is still remarkably effective in circulating the latest news and gossip, but almost everything else has changed. The country has two local television stations, and cable or satellite TV from the United States is beamed into even remote villages. Belize radio stations blare rap, reggae, *punta* (a modern version of traditional Garifuna music, popularized by such musicians as Andy Palacio), *soca* (short for soul calypso, soca is a 1970s evolution of Caribbean calypso music that is played for dancing rather than listening), and other music day and night. Weekly tabloid newspapers compete for circulation with lurid headlines and crime news. Cell phones and pagers are everywhere. And Belize is wired: Most businesses and many individuals are hooked to the Internet. Cybercafés have opened in most towns and resort areas.

Whether all this is good for Belize and how modern communications may be changing daily life for the worse are subjects that are often debated in Belize. Like it or not, little Belize is in the middle of the global information revolution.

Telephones

Belize has one of the best telephone systems in the region, with a combination of fiber-optic cable and microwave. There are more than 33,000 telephone lines in Belize, about one for every seven people. You can dial to or from even remote areas of Belize and usually get a clear, clean line. That's the good news. The bad news is that telephone service in Belize is expensive. Belize is about where the United States was in the early 1980s, before the breakup of AT&T. Belize Telecommunications, Ltd. (BTL), a private company, has a legal monopoly on all types of telecommunications services in Belize, including the Internet. With only a few limited exceptions, it's against Belizean law for anyone but BTL to provide any kind of telecommunications services. The company has even tried to block the use of Internet-based long-distance programs, claiming these money-saving systems violate BTL's charter. BTL keeps rates high, and it's a very profitable company. The company's license to be the sole telecommunications provider expires in 2002. What will happen then is anyone's guess. A well-connected Belizean entrepreneur, Glenn Godfrey, is working to provide wireless telecommications in Belize.

Like it or not, little Belize is in the middle of the global information revolution.

Basic local service is actually fairly inexpensive. Installation of a residential phone costs US$45. It may take several weeks, but it's not necessary, as it is in some other developing countries in the region, to bribe telephone installers to get your service. In a few cases, that might help move you up to the top of the list, but if you're patient you'll get your phone installed without paying off anybody. Basic monthly residential service is only US$5 with about 100 local calls included. After that, calls are US$0.075 cents each in most areas. Most of the latest add-ons are available for an extra charge, including voice mail, call waiting, and call forwarding.

Long distance is where BTL rakes in the dough. Long-distance calls within Belize currently range from US$0.125 to $0.275 cents a minute. International calls to most of North and South America from Belize are around US$1.38 a minute during the day and US$1 a minute after 10 P.M. and on weekends. Even at that reduced rate a one-hour call to friends or family in the United States will set you back US$60.

To call the United States or Canada from Belize, dial 001, plus the country code, area code and number. To call Belize from the United States or Canada, dial 011-501, the Belize area code (drop the 0 from the Belize area code when dialing from outside Belize) and then the five-digit Belize telephone number. For example, you'd dial 011-501-5-55555.

Public phones are common in towns and in Belize City. Deposit BZ$0.25

for a local call, BZ$1 for an in-country long-distance call. Prepaid phone cards are available from—natch—BTL, in amounts of US$5 to $25. Remote villages have a community phone.

Cellular service is available within about a 15-mile radius of Belize City, Corozal, Orange Walk, San Pedro, Caye Caulker, Belmopan, San Ignacio, Benque Viejo, Dangriga, Independence, Placencia, and Punta Gorda. In rural areas and some villages, BTL provides what is called "fixed cellular." This is a wireless cellular service fixed inside a home or business. It's fine for voice communication but isn't fast enough for Web browsing on the Internet, although email works OK.

A single telephone book of about 300 pages covers all of Belize. Published for BTL by Verizon, it comes out annually, usually in February, and is available from BTL. For information on any telecommunications service, contact BTL's sales and consumer services office at 1 Church Street, Belize City, tel. 501/2-77085, fax 2-77600. In Belize, call toll-free 0-800/225-5285. BTL's website is at www.btl.net.

Internet

Internet access in Belize, also controlled by BTL, is good, but it's several times more expensive than in the United States. Email only or full Internet accounts are available. Dial-up service is available all over Belize, via a toll-free number. Connection speed is moderate, usually 28 to 52 Kbps. At present, cable modems and DSL are not available in Belize. Full Internet service is US$20 a month, which provides 10 hours of access. After that, access is US$2 an hour. Most businesses, hotels, and many expats in Belize have Internet access. Internet access is also available at BTL offices and at cyber-cafés in San Pedro, Placencia, San Ignacio, Punta Gorda and elsewhere.

Mail

The postal system in Belize is generally reliable and fairly efficient. Don't send wads of cash by mail, but otherwise you can usually depend on letters and packages getting where they're supposed to go. Airmail to and from Belize City to the United States or Canada typically takes about a week. However, service to outlying towns and villages is slow. Some villages have only weekly mail service. Mail between remote areas and the United States or Canada may take two to three weeks, or longer. A first-class air letter from Belize to the United States or Canada costs US$.30.

FedEx and DHL Worldwide Express offer shipping services to and from Belize City and larger towns in Belize. For information, contact the

The Best of Belize on the Internet

Belize is wired. Almost anything you want to know about Belize is available somewhere on the Internet. Here are a few of the best websites about Belize:

www.ambergriscaye.com: This site, run by Oregon resident Marty Casado, who loves to visit Belize, focuses on Ambergris Caye, but it has tons of information about other areas of the country as well. The message board here is an active one. Marty's www.belizenews.com brings together the Web editions of most of Belize's leading newspapers, magazines, and broadcast outlets in one handy location.

www.belizenet.com: Tony Rath, an American by birth who now lives in Dangriga and who is one of Belize's top nature photographers, has put together a superb collection of websites about Belize. Tony's company, Belize by Naturalight, also designs and hosts many websites for Belize businesses and organizations, including the Belize Tourist Board. The message board on belize.net is one of the best.

www.travelbelize.org: This is the official website of the Belize Tourist Board, a pubic/private group with ties to the Ministry of Tourism. It has a wealth of information about hotels and sightseeing.

www.belizeretirement.org: This is the Belize Tourist Board's site for the Qualified Retired Persons Incentive Act program, a program designed to attract retirees from the United States, Canada, and elsewhere to live as official residents of Belize (see chapter 11, Making the Move, for details on this program).

www.placencia.com: Coordinated by the Belize Tourism Industry Association (BTIA), a private group representing hotels and other tourism operators, this site has links to most businesses on the Placencia peninsula.

www.belizex.com: Another BTIA-coordinated site, this one focuses on Cayo District but also has information on other parts of Belize.

www.corozal.com: Operated by two community colleges in Corozal, this is a friendly and helpful site about Corozal and northern Belize.

www.belize.gov.bz: The official website of the Government of Belize.

www.belizeans.com: "All ad we da Belizeans," Creole for "We are all Belizeans," is the motto of this site, which is focused on Belizeans at home and abroad.

companies' customer service offices in the U.S., or contact FedEx, 32 Albert Street, Belize City, tel. 501/2-73529 or DHL, 38 New Road, Belize City, tel. 501/2-34350.

Television

Two main television stations broadcast in Belize: Channel 5 and Channel 7. Channel 5, Belize's first licensed television broadcaster, has the better local news and information programming. Its evening news, a transcript of which is available online on the station's website at www.channel5belize.com, is

Belize's single best source of reliable, professional news. The station, which began as a video production company, also maintains the world's largest video archives about Belize. Mexican and Guatemalan TV stations can also be picked up in Belize.

Cable TV, usually with 30 or more U.S. and Mexican channels, is available in Belize City, and in most towns and some villages. Rates are around US$15 to $20 a month for basic cable, including channels such as HBO that would be premium channels in the United States. In the past, some Belize cable operators pirated cable signals and put them on their systems without paying anything for them. However, with the passage in 2000 of a new Belize copyright law, this practice is changing, and cable rates may be increased.

The situation with satellite TV in Belize is currently in a state of flux. DirecTV, one of the large satellite systems, offers service in Mexico and Guatemala but not in Belize. Most people with cable in Belize still use the older-style, and expensive, 66-inch receiver disks rather than the newer, inexpensive 18-inch disks. SkyTV, using the smaller disks, is available from Mexico. Check with one of the satellite installers in Belize City, such as Techtronics (tel. 501/2-76967) or elsewhere to see what is available when you're ready to hook up to a bird in the sky.

Other Media

The media in Belize is free and often freewheeling, if not always fully professional. Reporters and editors sometimes butcher the Queen's English and fail to follow basic journalistic procedures such as getting multiple sources. The best of Belize's weekly newspapers are *The Reporter, San Pedro Sun,* and *Amandala.*

The Reporter is a feisty tabloid heavy on crime news. Annual subscriptions by mail to *The Reporter* (147 Allenby/West Sts., Belize City, tel. 501/2-72503, fax 2-78278, email report@btl.net) are US$33 in Belize and US$70 in the United States. A Web edition is at www.reporterbelize.com.

The *San Pedro Sun* (P.O. Box 35, San Pedro Town, Ambergris Caye, Belize, tel. 501/2-62070, fax 2-62905, email sanpdrosun@btl.net) is a chatty, informal, and sprightly weekly published by an expat couple from Pennsylvania, Dan and Eileen Jamison. They bought the paper from its founders, a couple from California. *The Sun* concentrates almost entirely on news about Ambergris Caye and claims the largest foreign circulation of any paper in Belize. Six-month mail subscriptions are US$20 in Belize and US$40 elsewhere. A Web edition is at www.sanpedrosun.net.

Amandala (3304 Partridge St., Belize City, tel. 501/2-24703, email amandala@btl.net) claims to have the largest circulation of any newspaper in

A Few Headlines from Belize's Colorful Free Press

Belize's weekly tabloid newspapers are full of local color, even if the news is not always 100 percent accurate. As in the United States, Belize news is heavy on crime and politics. But even the trials and tribulations of daily home life make headlines in little Belize. Here's a selection of headlines, all from the year 2000, from *Amandala*, a weekly newspaper in Belize City.

"AMERICAN RETIREE, 51, GIVES UP LIFE
    AFTER WIFE LEAVES!"

"BARRIOS BULLETS, BELIZE BODIES!"

"MANGOS + MINORS = MURDER"

"UNRULY TEENAGERS PACK UP AND
    LEAVE HOME"

"ALLIGATOR TRIES TO SNACK ON NEW
    RIVER SWIMMER"

"BUS-RIDING COP GUNS DOWN EX-COP
    TURNED JACKER"

"RAMPAGING GUAT GUNMEN
    TERRORIZE BORDER SETTLEMENT"

"THE TRAVAILS OF A 15-YEAR-OLD GIRL
    AND HER NUTTY NEIGHBOUR"

"VILLAGER DRANK POISON BECAUSE HE
    'WAS A FAILURE'"

Belize. It serves up independent political commentary and a healthy dose of sports. A Web edition is at www.belizemall.com/amandala.

The *Belize Times* is the official organ of the People's United Party and the current Belize government. There are also a number of other weekly and monthly newspapers around the country.

In addition, there is *Belize First* magazine (Equator, 287 Beaverdam Road, Candler, NC 28715), that focuses on general interest topics on Belize. A web edition is available at www.belizefirst.com.

Many people considering Belize for retirement or relocation hope to find classified ads for home rentals and sales, but few of the Belize newspapers have more than a handful of classifieds. The best classifieds are in the *San Pedro Sun*, but they relate only to Ambergris Caye.

LOVE-FM, which programs mostly easy listening at 95.1 and 98.1 MHz, is the most popular radio station. Several other stations broadcast in Belize, and stations in Guatemala, Honduras, Mexico, and elsewhere can be heard in various parts of the country. The government-run BCB, Broadcasting Corporation of Belize, no longer operates.

8 Money Matters

The first question most people ask about living in Belize is "How much does it cost?" When you pose that question you'll often hear that there are two ways of looking at the cost of living in Belize: either Belize is the most expensive place in Central America or it's the least expensive in the Caribbean. That's true enough, but there's another point to make about living costs in Belize: they vary tremendously depending on what *lifestyle* you choose and *where* in the country you decide to live.

Cost of living

Like most places, Belize has not one but several costs of living. If you want to live in the North American–style, the cost of living is higher than for a similar lifestyle in the United States or Canada. However, if you live closer to the Belizean style—choose a simple frame house built to catch the cooling breezes, eat beans and rice and chicken, drink local rum, and take the bus or ride a bike—you can live for less than in the United States, and even a modest Social Security check will stretch a long way. In between the two lifestyles, you can live well on a moderate income by enjoying some American-style "necessities," such as a car, along with Belizean luxuries, such as full-time domestic help, which usually runs only about US$10 a day.

Costs also vary a great deal depending on where you live in Belize. Generally, real estate and other living costs are highest in Belize City and on Ambergris Caye. Punta Gorda is also expensive because it is in the far south with poor transportation access. (The road to Punta Gorda, the Southern Highway, is as yet only partly paved.) Costs are lowest in rural areas and in smaller towns and villages.

In general, the cost of anything that is labor intensive in Belize is likely to be less expensive than in the United States, Canada, or Western Europe, because wage levels and salaries in Belize are usually one-third or less of what they are in developed countries. Thus, domestic help, medical care, and all types of services generally cost less in Belize. Keep in mind, though, that lower costs for labor may mean lower efficiency. It may take two people in Belize to do the job of one well-trained person elsewhere. Materials that are produced in Belize using Belize labor may also be relatively inexpensive, and that holds for fruits and vegetables grown in Belize, seafood and other Belizean foodstuffs, along with things like Belizean-made furniture. There are exceptions, though, sometimes due to high taxes and import restrictions and also due to natural inefficiencies in the small Belize marketplace. For example, it typically costs more to grow kidney or black beans in Belize than it does to import them from the Guatemala, and beer is artificially expensive in Belize because imports of cheap Mexican beer are prohibited and alcohol is taxed at a fairly high rate. Anything that is imported is likely to cost more in Belize than in its country of origin. That is due both to the shipping costs and to import duties. Thus, most manufactured goods, including home appliances, cars and trucks, clothing, sporting goods, and toys, cost more in Belize, and often up to twice as much as in the country of origin.

Cost of living, like beauty, is often in the eye of the beholder.

Because every situation is different, it's impossible to provide hard and fast figures on what it costs to live in Belize. Remember that the average Belizean family lives on US$5,000 or less annually. However, here are a few guidelines for a couple to live in Belize. For purposes of comparison, it is assumed that housing is rented. (*For more specifics on housing costs, see chapter 12.*)

To live in a large modern, American-style house in a high-cost area such as Belize City or Ambergris Caye, with all the modern conveniences—air-conditioning and electrically powered appliances, a car (except on Ambergris Caye, where most residents travel around by golf carts, bicycle, or on foot), imported personal goods and food items, dining out and entertaining frequently, with occasional visits to the United States for medical care—would cost as much or more as to live in Florida or other retirement areas

PRICE SAMPLER: WHAT THINGS COST IN BELIZE

Here's a sampler of costs for common items in Belize, as of early 2001. All prices in U.S. dollars. As in the United States, prices for many items vary depending on where and when you buy them.

Transportation

Gallon of unleaded gas: $3

Bus fare from Belize City to San Ignacio: $2.50 regular, $3 express

Ferry from Belize City to San Pedro, Ambergris Caye: $12.50

One-way airfare from Belize City Municipal Airport to Placencia: $68

Utilities/Telecommunications

1 kilowatt hour of electricity: $0.21

Installation of residential telephone: $45

Monthly charge for residential telephone: $5 (includes 150 minutes of local calling)

10-minute call from Corozal to Belize City: $2.75

10-minute daytime call to United States: $13.75

Internet access: $20 for 10 hours, plus $2 for each additional hour

Water and sewer service: $10 (varies by area)

Staples in Groceries

Potatoes: $0.50 per pound

Coffee: $6.50 per pound

Milk: $4.25 gallon

Ground beef: $1.50 per pound

Pork chops: $2 per pound

Chicken: $1 per pound

Loaf of white bread: $0.65 (whole wheat $1.35)

Corn tortillas: $0.02 each

Bananas: 20 for $1

Onions: $0.40 per pound

Soft drinks: $0.50 each

Local rum, liter: $6–9

Sugar: $0.20 per pound

of the States: US$3,000 or more per month. Depending on housing costs and other factors it could be much higher.

To live in a nice but unpretentious small home in a town such as San Ignacio or Corozal, with some modern conveniences and a car, moderate spending on entertainment and dining out, medical care provided locally or in Belize or Guatemala, the monthly cost is likely to be in the US$1,000 to $1,500 range. Many frugal expatriates in Belize live nicely for less than this. To live more in the local style, in a modest Belizean-style frame or concrete home, with electricity and running water but without air conditioning or luxury appliances such as a dishwasher, using local transportation, eating Belizean-style food, and getting health care in Belize, the cost per month would be well under US$1,000. Depending how tightly you squeeze a shilling, it could be under US$500.

Cost of living, like beauty, is often in the eye of the beholder. Some expats complain that living in Belize costs much more than they expected. On the other hand, John Lankford, a former New Orleanian now resident in San Pedro, Ambergris Caye, says: "For me, Belize is cheaper. I need neither heating nor air-conditioning with their attendant bills, nor insulation in my house, nor much of a house, nor much in the way of shoes. One casual wardrobe serves all purposes except travel back to the United States. I neither have nor need a car—the Army taught me five-mile walks aren't fatal, and the custom here when I arrived was to walk almost everywhere. Now many choose to have cars or golf carts. I don't. I have a bicycle, but I don't use it. With my plebeian tastes, food is cheaper than in the United States. Virtually anything manufactured, or, say, a meal or drinks bought at the tourist-catering facilities, are going to bear a cost ranging from about the same as in the United States to about triple that. Canned or processed foods tend to be double or triple their U.S. prices. It should be remembered that food prices in the United States are among the lowest in the world, item by item, due to domestic production and incredible economies of scale."

Judy duPlooy, who has operated a lodge in Cayo District since the 1980s, wisely says, "Living well in Belize does not mean living lavishly. It is a place to come and scale down and appreciate life for its own richness."

The Belize dollar is pegged to the U.S. dollar at the rate of two Belize dollars to one U.S. dollar.

Daily living costs in Belize can vary a great deal, and, again, whether you consider them high or low depends on how and where you live.

Belize City has modern supermarkets. The two best are *Save U* and the Northern Highway location of *Brodies*, both in the northern "suburbs." District towns including San Ignacio and San Pedro have smaller but still well-stocked groceries. Most towns have weekly markets (usually Saturday morning) where fresh fruit and vegetables are sold at low prices. In coastal areas and on the cayes, fresh seafood is sold off the dock or at a local seafood co-op.

Many grocery items in Belize are imported from the United States, Mexico, or England and are more expensive than back home. Examples: 15 oz. box of Kelloggs Raisin Bran, US$5.13; 3 oz. box of Jello brand gelatin, US$.80 ; can of Campbell's Chicken Soup, US$1.75; single 12 oz. can of Budweiser beer, US$2.65; bottle of Gallo Turning Leaf Cabernet, US$12.50. But locally produced products are fairly inexpensive: red beans US$0.40 a pound; dozen eggs (only brown eggs are legal in Belize, due to import prohibitions against foreign white eggs) US$1.25 a dozen; T-bone steak, US$2.50 a pound; ground beef, US$1.50 a pound; liter of premium One Barrel local rum, US$7.30; corn, US$0.10 an ear; pork chops, US$2 a pound; banana, US$0.05 cents; potatoes, $0.50 cents a pound; milk, US$4.25 a gallon.

Restaurant dining costs vary but generally are about the same as in a small city in the United States. At the top end, at the most expensive restaurants in Belize City and on Ambergris Caye, figure US$30 to $40 a person for a three-course dinner with drinks and tip. But at a restaurant catering to locals in Corozal Town, Caye Caulker, or San Ignacio, you can have a filling meal of stew chicken with rice and beans for US$4, a spicy Mexican meal for US$3, or fresh local fish with salad and sides for US$6 or less. Good local beer (Belikin) is US$1.50 to $2.50 in most restaurants, and local rum drinks are seldom more than $2. Wine is expensive. A 10 percent tip in most restaurants is sufficient.

Electrical power, at 110 volts AC/60 cycles, is the same in Belize as in the United States or Canada, so your home appliances and computer will work fine. Electricity is about twice as expensive as in the United States, at about US$0.21 per kilowatt hour. Telephone service is controlled by **Belize Telecommunications, Ltd. (BTL)**. This could change in 2002, when the BTL's monopoly franchise is set to end. Local service costs about the same as in the United States, or a little less, unless you make a lot of calls, but long distance is much more expensive, with long-distance calls during the day to the United States costing US$1.375 per MINUTE. Internet service, also controlled by BTL, is US$20 for the first 10 hours, and US$2 per hour for additional hours.

Water and sewerage costs vary, being generally lowest in Belize City and highest on the cayes. Water in Belize City costs US$4.40 per 1,000 gallons. As of this writing, the **Water and Sewerage Authority (WASA)** in Belize is being privatized, so costs may change. In rural areas and villages, homes usually get water from wells or cisterns, and sewage is taken care of with septic tanks.

ONE FAMILY'S BUDGET IN BELIZE

Here's an actual monthly budget for a retired couple, Rick and Charlotte Zahniser, who moved to Corozal Town in northern Belize from Colorado in 1999. In 2000 they obtained their permanent residency status. They live in town in a small concrete house, which they rent. They have a car, entertain a lot, and are taking a Spanish course at a local community college. Note that this budget does not include items such as medical care or medical insurance (Chetumal, Mexico, next door, has inexpensive, good-quality medical services), travel, or some other items other retirees might want in their budgets.

Monthly Budget (in U.S. dollars)

Rent	$87.50
Electricity	40.00
Water	10.00
Bottled water	25.00
Butane for cooking	20.00
Telephone, long distance and Internet service	120.00
Cable TV	15.00
Food	120.00
Cigarettes	20.00
Beverages, ice, and entertainment	120.00
Auto expenses	140.00
Clothing	20.00
Personal services	63.00
Lawn care/gardening	37.50
School tuition	28.00
Total:	$866.00

Currency

The Belize dollar is unofficially pegged to the U.S. dollar at the rate of two Belize to one greenback, although money changers at border areas sometimes will give a little more than that, occasionally as much as 2.15 to 1. If exchanging through a bank, you'll normally get a little less than 2 to 1, typically around 1.96 to 1.98 to 1. U.S. dollars are accepted everywhere in Belize, so if you have American money there's no need to exchange anything; in stores you may get change in Belize dollars. Canadian dollars and other currencies are rarely accepted in Belize, except at banks where the exchange rate may be poor. It's best to convert other currencies to U.S. dollars before you arrive in Belize.

Credit cards—mainly Visa, MasterCard, and American Express—are widely accepted in Belize, except at small shops and restaurants. Sometimes if you pay with plastic rather than cash, you'll be hit with a surcharge, usually 3 to 5 percent but occasionally as high as 10 percent.

Banking

Belize has two domestic banks, **Belize Bank** and **Atlantic Bank.** Each is about the size of a small community bank or savings and loan in the United States, with assets of under US$200 million. Belize Bank (main office: 60 Market Square, Belize City, tel. 501/2-77132, fax 2-72712, email bzbnk@btl.net) has 11 offices around the country, including three in Belize City, one at the International Airport, and others in Belmopan, Big Creek, Corozal, San Ignacio, San Pedro, Orange Walk, Punta Gorda, and Dangriga. Atlantic Bank (main office: Atlantic Building, Freetown Road, Belize City, tel. 501/2-34123, fax 2-33907, email atlantic@btl.net), majority-owned by a

Honduras holding company, has eight offices including two in Belize City, one at the international airport, and others in San Ignacio, San Pedro, Corozal, Placencia, and Caye Caulker.

There also are two large international banks with branches in Belize: **Barclays**, a large English bank, and **ScotiaBank**, based in Canada. Barclays (main office: 21 Albert Street, Belize City, tel. 501/2-32425, fax 2-78572) has two offices in Belize City along with branches in Belmopan and Dangriga. ScotiaBank (main office: Albert Street, Belize City, tel. 501/2-77027, fax 2-77416, email scobel@btl.net) has two offices in Belize City, with branches in Dangriga, Orange Walk, Corozal, and San Ignacio.

Banks in Belize provide the usual modern services including a variety of loans, credit cards, and checking and savings plans. In Belize City, a few bank branches have drive-up windows. Banking hours vary but generally are 8 A.M. until 1 P.M. Monday–Friday, with additional afternoon hours, usually 2–4:30 P.M. on Friday. Most Belize banks require a reference from your former bank before they will open a local account for you.

Many bank branches in Belize have ATMs, but don't count on being able to access your U.S. accounts through Belize ATMs. A few, including those at Barclays, accept foreign-issued ATM cards, but most, including those at Atlantic Bank and Belize Bank, which have the largest number of ATM machines in Belize, as of this writing do not accept ATM cards issued outside of Belize. This

> *"Living in Belize does not mean living lavishly. It is a place to come and scale down and appreciate life for its own richness."*

could change soon, however, as the banks modernize. Almost all banks will issue a cash advance on your Visa or MasterCard, but there's a fee of about US$3 to $15 for each advance, plus whatever your bank charges.

While U.S. dollar accounts theoretically are available, they are not easy for the average person to open in a Belize bank, and nearly all accounts are Belize-dollar accounts. The Belize dollar is not a "hard currency," and outside Belize it is difficult if not impossible to convert it to other currencies. Devaluations of the Belize dollar are occasionally rumored. From time to time, the Belize Central Bank also runs short of U.S. dollars and businesses in Belize have to scramble to find enough greenbacks to take care of their international business transactions. Therefore, most expats find it wise to limit their exposure to Belize currency. Nearly all expats and business owners maintain their principal banking relationship with a bank outside Belize, typically in the United States. Funds are then transferred as needed to a local bank in Belize, by check, wire, or cash from an ATM or credit card advance. Western Union has offices in Belize City and in most towns and is frequently used by those wishing to wire U.S.-currency-denominated funds to Belize.

If you do deposit money in a certificate of deposit or other savings instrument at a bank in Belize, you can, at current rates, expect to earn about 6 to 10 percent interest.

Belize also has a thriving offshore banking business. In fact, for an annual license fee of as little as US$15,000 to $20,000 and with capital of just US$200,000 to $500,000, depending on whether it is a restricted or unrestricted banking license, you can open your own offshore bank chartered in Belize. Offshore banks based in Belize cannot, however, accept deposits from, make loans to, or otherwise conduct banking business with residents of Belize.

Loans

Bank loans are available to permanent residents or business owners in Belize, but rates are high. They've been in the 12 to 18 percent range in recent years. Those who do borrow complain that some Belize banks pile on hidden fees and requirements, such as requiring a sizable account balance and expensive credit life insurance or adding a commission. Most expats who need them try to get loans outside Belize or, in the case of loans for purchasing property in Belize, try to arrange owner financing. About the best owner-financing deals available for property in Belize are 10-10-10, that is, 10 percent down, pay-out over 10 years, at 10 percent interest.

Taxes

Here are the main kinds of taxes you'll be hit with in Belize:

A **national sales tax** of 8 percent covers most goods and services. Basic foodstuffs such as rice, beans, flour, bread, fresh meat, corn and sugar are excluded, as are many medicines. This sales tax replaced the unpopular 15 percent value-added tax (VAT) in 1999.

A **hotel tax** of 7 percent is charged on hotel room rates.

The government of Belize gets about one-half of its revenue from import duties. This is one reason why many imported items, from automobiles to home appliances, are more expensive in Belize than in the United States or Canada. (See sidebar in chapter 11, Making the Move, for examples of current import duties.)

Belize has a **progressive personal income tax**, with top personal rate of 25 percent. As workers who earn US$10,000 or less pay no income tax at all, the vast majority of Belizeans are not subject to income taxes. Of course, this leaves Belize tax workers with a lot of time to look at the returns of those who DO owe taxes. If you have a sizable income in Belize, you can expect to be audited.

As an expat resident of Belize, you will be subject to Belize income tax only on income you earn in Belize, not on income, earned or unearned, from elsewhere. American citizens living in Belize may face income taxes in the United States based on their total income, including income in Belize. If you are an American citizen who lives in Belize and runs a business or works for pay, you may owe U.S. income taxes on any income or business profit over US$74,000 (the exemption rises to US$80,000 by 2008 and thereafter is indexed to inflation), plus self-employment taxes (Social Security and Medicare). The American tax system is of course incredibly complex; if in doubt, best consult your tax advisor. That holds for citizens of other countries with highly evolved tax systems too.

In 1999, the Belize corporate income tax was replaced with a confusing combination of **corporate income tax and gross revenues business tax.** In brief, businesses are taxed at a rate of 25 percent on their taxable profits. In addition, a business tax of 0.75 percent to 25 percent is levied on gross or top-line revenues. The business tax is credited toward the total corporate income tax due. If the corporate income tax due is less than the business tax, the difference between the business tax and the corporate tax due is payable. Thus, a company that is losing money hand over fist can still be liable for sizable business tax. Business tax rates vary by industry and type of business. Here are some of the rates on gross income: professions and trades, 4 percent; media, 0.75 percent; telecommunications, 19 percent; most retail and service businesses: 1.25 percent. Business with annual revenues under US$27,000 are exempt from the business tax, though not from the corporate income tax. Yes, it's confusing, and business owners in Belize are advised to consult an accountant or attorney in Belize.

Property taxes in Belize are low. Outside of town limits the annual property tax is 1 percent of the assessed value of the land, with no tax on

the house or other improvements. Within city limits, taxes vary from area to area but are in the range of 3 to 8 percent of the land value (not the developed value.) Tax bills even for luxury properties are seldom more than a few hundred dollars, and most expats have tax bills of under US$100.

Land transfer taxes, usually paid by the purchaser, for noncitizens are a one-time charge of 10 percent of the sales price, consisting of a 5 percent stamp duty and 5 percent alien land holding tax.

At present Belize has no **capital gains** or **inheritance tax**. A capital gains tax has been under consideration by the government.

Entertainment

Most entertainment in Belize is of the do-it-yourself variety—outdoor walks, picnics, tubing on a river, fishing off a pier, or visiting with friends. Belize has no symphony orchestra, no opera, no amusement parks, no video game rooms, only one movie theater (a small one in the Princess Hotel, admission about US$4). The country has no big-league sports teams, but there are semi-pro basketball and football (soccer) leagues, with teams representing most towns Admission rates vary but are rarely more than a couple of U.S. dollars. Cable television is available in most towns and villages, at rates a little less than in the U.S., around US$15 to $20 a month. Among some expats, drinking is the major form of entertainment. A local rum drink or a Belikin beer in a nice bar is usually US$2 to $3, and a fifth of rum at a grocery store is US$7 or $8. Meals in restaurants run from US$3 or so for beans and rice with stew chicken in a neighborhood eatery to $35 or more for lobster or steak in expensive restaurant in a resort area.

9 *Staying Healthy*

Health care in Belize presents a mixed picture. On the one hand, health and hygiene standards in Belize are considerably higher than in most other countries in Central America; on the other, as a developing country Belize's medical resources are in no way comparable to those offered in the United States, Canada, and Western Europe. If you are older and especially if you face chronic health problems, you will have to look closely at the health-care trade-offs—a healthier way of living, lower medical costs and more personalized care in Belize versus the high-tech, low touch, high cost of health care and health insurance back home.

Health and Living Conditions

Bad water and poor sanitation are major causes of illness in much of the third world. In Belize, happily these are less of a problem than in Belize's larger neighbors such as Mexico and Guatemala. One hundred percent of residents in Belize City and in nearly all towns have access to safe and adequate water supplies, "pipe water" as it's called in Belize—and close to 70 percent of rural residents do, according to the Pan American Health Care Organization. Belize City, major towns—except Dangriga, which has had continuing problems with its water supplies—and quite a few villages, including those on the Placencia peninsula, have safe, treated

95

water systems. Thanks to the plentiful rain in Belize—from 50 to 200 inches or more per year—drinking water literally falls from the sky, so even if you decide to live in an area without a community water system, you can collect drinking water in a cistern. Concrete or plastic cisterns, with accompanying pipes and drains to gather rain from your roof, are sold in building supply stores or can be constructed by local workers, if your home does not already have one. To be safe, this "sky juice" should be treated by filtering or with a disinfectant such as chlorine bleach. Overall, about 85 percent of Belizeans have access to potable water. In short, in most areas of Belize, including nearly all areas of interest to expats, you can drink the water and not worry about getting sick.

> *In short, in most areas of Belize, including nearly all areas of interest to expatriates, you can drink the water and not worry about getting sick.*

Rural Areas Lack Sewage Systems

Sewage disposal is less adequate. The Water and Sewerage Authority (WASA), which was privatized in the spring of 2001, with majority ownership by a European consortium called CASCAL, operates sewerage systems in Belize City, Belmopan, San Pedro on Ambergris Caye, and a few other areas. There is still a lack of facilities in rural areas, and even in urban areas more than one-third of houses do not have adequate sanitation, according to Belize government figures. In rural parts of Belize, refuse disposal is not organized at the community level; households are responsible for the disposal of their own solid wastes. While many homes have reasonably effective septic systems, or at least well-maintained pit latrines, in poorer areas Belizeans dump their household wastes into rivers or the Caribbean Sea.

Life Expectancy Similar to the United States

Life expectancy at birth in Belize is about 72 years, similar to that in the United States. Heart disease is the leading cause of death from illness for both males and females, but Belizeans, as are Americans, are paying more attention to the causes of heart disease, such as smoking, lack of exercise, and a diet high in fats. Because of this, the incidences of death from heart disease are declining.

Smoking

There are no reliable statistics on how many Belizeans smoke. Certainly, the antismoking crusade hasn't progressed as far as it has in the United States. Few businesses, public buildings, or restaurants are smoke free, and many Belizeans feel it is their right to light up anytime and anywhere. My own very unscientific survey of foreigners resident in Belize suggests that a large number, maybe as many as one-half, smoke. Perhaps some of these came to Belize just to be able to smoke without being harassed by the lifestyle police? However, with local brands of cigarettes costing US$15 a carton and imported brands US$20 to $25 or more, the vast majority of Belizeans can't afford the habit.

Immunizations

Belize has an ambitious if underfunded program to immunize children. Between 1993 and 1998 measles were eliminated, and the measles, mumps, and rubella (MMR) vaccine was widely introduced in Belize. Vaccination rates for common childhood diseases now are well over 80 percent. The infant mortality rate in Belize is now about 20 per 1,000 live births, a rate that compares well with those in Central America but is still considerably higher than among most countries in the Caribbean Basin.

Drivers, Beware!

The overall leading cause of death in Belize is not illness, but traffic accidents. Rarely a weekend goes by without news reports of a deadly car crash. About one-fourth of all deaths in Belize are now due to traffic accidents. The high rate of traffic deaths is remarkable given that the vast majority of Belizeans don't have cars. Often the cause of accidents is alcohol-related. Belizeans unfortunately are all too prone to drink and drive. Speed limits, such as there are in Belize—and most roads have no posted speed limit—don't mean much because Belize has very few traffic enforcement officers. The use of seat belts is now required in Belize, but this rule too is rarely enforced. Finally, many Belizeans simply aren't good drivers. Driver's education programs are virtually unknown. You can usually get a Belize driver's license simply by showing up at your local Transport Department office with the necessary forms, including a certificate from a doctor that you are in good health and two passport-size photos, and paying US$10. Driving test? What's that?

AIDS an Increasing Problem in Belize

AIDS has become a serious epidemic in Belize, say local health officials. Although government figures are lower, AIDS workers estimate that as many as 7,000 people in Belize are HIV positive. Given Belize's small population of 240,000, this estimate means that one in 34 Belizeans is HIV positive, thought to be the highest infection rate in Central America.

Worldwide, about one in 120 persons is believed to be HIV positive. In Belize, nearly three-fourths of HIV infection is spread by heterosexual contact. The highest number of reported AIDS cases are in Belize and Stann Creek districts. All blood for transfusion in Belize is screened for HIV, with the cost absorbed by the government.

What about Malaria?

Some expatriates, mostly those whose knowledge of Belize is limited to the kinds of booze sold in the bars on Ambergris Caye, will tell you that you need not worry about malaria or other tropical diseases in Belize. Don't believe them. Every year, thousands of cases of malaria are reported in Belize. In fact, on a per capita basis Belize has one of the highest incidences of malaria in the world, and the highest in Central America, with 300 cases per 10,000 population. On the positive side, thanks to a widespread program of spraying for mosquitoes, the incidence of malaria in Belize has been declining from its peak of more than 10,000 reported cases in 1994. Another good thing is that more than 95 percent of the malaria cases in Belize are the *Plasmodium vivax* strain, which is less dangerous than *Plasmodium falciparum* and which can be prevented with the use of chloroquine, a time-tested and fairly inexpensive drug. Most of the cases of malaria in Belize are in remote areas of Toledo, Stann Creek, and Cayo districts. Children and young men, often immigrants from Guatemala or elsewhere in Central America, are most at risk.

Other Diseases

Dengue fever is transmitted by another type of mosquito. It causes flu-like symptoms that are unpleasant but which in most cases are not life threatening. Dengue has been reported in Belize, mainly in the northern districts, but it is not common. There is at present no preventative medication for dengue, but its symptoms can be treated effectively with Tylenol or its generic equivalent. Avoid taking aspirin if you think you have dengue, as aspirin can exacerbate internal bleeding sometimes associated with dengue.

Both cholera and typhoid fever are occasionally present in Belize, but only a handful of cases have been reported in recent years.

If you decide to live in Belize City, Belmopan, Corozal, Placencia, around San Ignacio, or on one of the cayes, you face little more risk from exotic diseases than you would living in Florida. In remote areas, where mosquito-vectored diseases are more common, you should have good screens on your windows and consider sleeping under a mosquito net. Avoid wearing dark clothes, which tend to attract mosquitoes, and use bug juice with DEET if you must be outside when mosquitoes are hunting.

For the latest information, check with the Centers for Disease Control and Prevention in Atlanta (www.cdc.org, 800/311-3435 or 404/639-3311).

Healthier Lifestyle Comes Naturally

A truly positive side to the typical Belize lifestyle, especially outside urban areas, is that compared to the usual way of living in developed countries you tend to walk and exercise more, get more fresh air, and eat simpler, healthier meals of complex carbohydrates and fresh fruits. One Canadian, a chef in Placencia, says after a year in Belize he went for a health checkup. He found his blood pressure was down 15 points and his weight down 15 pounds. "But what do you expect?" he asks, smiling. "I live on the beach, walk 25 feet to work, and eat almost nothing but fresh fish and fruit."

The Essene Way on Ambergris Caye, a resort and religious retreat

Lan Sluder

Belize's Health Care System

Belize has a mixed public and private health-care system. The vast majority of Belizeans get medical care through a system of government-run hospitals and clinics. There are eight public hospitals in Belize. Besides **Karl Heusner Memorial Hospital** in Belize City (tel. 501/2-32548), which functions as a national referral center, there are **district public hospitals** in Belmopan (tel. 501/8-22264), San Ignacio (tel. 501/9-22066), Dangriga (tel. 501/5-220780), Punta Gorda (tel. 501/7-22026), Orange Walk Town (tel. 501/3-22072), and Corozal Town (tel. 501/4-22076). In addition, Rockview Hospital (tel. 501/2-44016) in Belize City is a psychiatric center. The quality of these hospitals varies considerably. Karl Heusner—named after a prominent Belize City physician—opened in 1997 and has much modern equipment, such as a CAT scan, though some Belizeans and expats complain that even this hospital is chronically short of supplies even including toilet paper. The **Southern Regional Hospital** in Dangriga, which opened in 2000, is another modern facility, with much of the same medical technologies and equipment as you'd find in a community hospital in an American town. For example, the hospital's printed materials and website boast that its surgical operating rooms have "Narkomed anesthesia and Bovie electrosurgical units with laryngoscope sets, ECG monitoring spacelabs, Vilatert monitoring systems, resuscitators and 'Shampaine' surgical tables." However, other hospitals leave a lot to be desired. The one in Orange Walk, for example, looks more like a refugee camp than a hospital, with low concrete block buildings and limited equipment.

In addition to these public hospitals, Belize has two private hospitals— **La Loma Luz** in Santa Elena near San Ignacio (tel. 501/9-22087) and **Belize Medical Associates Hospital**, a 20-bed hospital in Belize City (tel. 501/2-30302).

Sample Costs for Medical and Dental Care in Chetumal

Chetumal, Mexico, is just a hop, skip, and a jump from Belize, especially if you live in the northern part of the country. Mexican health care is considered—by Belizeans and expats alike—as generally better than Belizean care, and less expensive too. (All prices are given in U.S. dollars)

Teeth cleaning: $25

Filling: $20
Root canal and crown: $250
Physical: $50–$100
EKG: $45
X-Ray: $20
Private room in a hospital: $60–$125 per day
Minor surgery including surgeon's fee and hospital stay: US$600–$800

A new hospital is being built on Ambergris Caye, thanks to the efforts of the San Pedro Lions Club. The new hospital is expected to be completed by 2002.

Besides these hospitals, Belize has a network of around 75 public health clinics and rural health posts that provide primary medical and dental care in many towns and villages around the country. Most of these suffer from inadequate staffing, too many patients for their available resources, and lack of equipment and medicine. Doctors may diagnose health problems accurately, but they may not be able to provide the proper medications to cure them.

Government figures show Belize has about five physicians per 10,000 population, about one-fourth the 21-per-10,000 rate in the United States. Altogether there are perhaps 500 trained medical personnel in Belize. They are not distributed evenly around the country, however. More than one-half are in the Belize City area, which has only about one-third of the population.

Medical care professionals in Belize earn very modest incomes compared with those in the United States. Physicians employed by the government start at US$10,000 a year, though they may supplement their income in private practice. Nurses start at US$6,000.

Most physicians and dentists in Belize are trained in the United States, Guatemala, Mexico, or Great Britain. There are two so-called offshore medical schools in Belize—Belize Medical College in Belize City and St. Matthews on Ambergris Caye—but these take students who were unable to get into traditional medical schools, and their graduates are unlikely to practice in Belize. A nursing school, affiliated with the University of Belize, trains nurses for work in Belize.

Belize medical professionals, like Belizean society, come in every shape and flavor. "My dentist is Garifuna, my ear doc is

A water jug—from an old bleach bottle

Lan Sluder

Mayan, my eye doc Mestizo and my OB-GYN is Spanish," says Katie Volk, a former New Yorker who now lives in Belize City.

In the late 1990s, health care in Belize got a boost, thanks to the arrival of a group of several dozen medical volunteers from Cuba. These doctors and nurses were assigned to clinics in areas of Belize that, until then, did not have full-time medical personnel available to the local people. These hard-working Cubans, who exist on stipends of only a few dollars a month, have won many new friends for Fidel in Belize, regardless of what Belizeans may think of his politics. Medical and dental volunteer teams from the United States and Canada also regularly visit Belize to provide short-term care.

The use of herbal remedies also is common in Belize. Bush doctors or snake doctors often have an extensive knowledge of plants with healing properties. Don Elijio Panti, who died in 1996 at over 100 years of age, was one of the best known of the herbal healers. He was a Guatemalan by birth but a long-time resident of Cayo in western Belize. His work was popularized by Rosita Arvigo (with Nadine Epstein and Marilyn Yaquinto) in the 1993 book, *Sastun: My Apprenticeship with a Maya Healer.* Dr. Arvigo today operates an herbal healing facility and spa along with the Rainforest Medicine Trail near San Ignacio.

What you won't find in Belize is top-notch emergency care. There are no high-tech trauma centers in Belize. While there are ambulances and even an emergency air transport service operated by Wings of Hope, a U.S.-based charitable organization with an operations center in Belize City, Belize's poor roads and spread out population mean it could take hours to get you to a hospital.

Cost of Medical Care

Even if medical care isn't always up to snuff in Belize, at least it is cheap. In fact, the vast majority of health care is provided at no charge. Belizeans who can't afford to pay are treated in about the same way as those with more means. Only a tiny percentage of Belizeans have medical insurance. Nowhere in the public health system in Belize will anyone be turned away for lack of cash or insurance.

Public hospitals and clinics may bill nominal amounts for tests and procedures—for example, a woman's clinic in northern Belize charges US$3 to $15 for a Pap smear, cervical exam, and breast exam, and under US$15 for an ultrasound—or they may ask for a donation. In some waiting rooms you will see a box where you can leave a donation. But even visitors are routinely treated for free. A friend of mine, a guidebook writer, was injured in a boating accident off Dangriga. In great pain, he was taken to the hospital in Dangriga where he was diagnosed as having broken ribs.

BAD TOOTH IN BELIZE

It was Friday night. I was sipping a Belikin at Cheer's just up the road from the Belize Zoo when I felt it. Zowee! It was a pain in my tooth, one that I'd chipped a few days earlier. This was no garden-variety 50-year-old-teeth type of hurt. It was deep down, festering, I'm-sorry-I-didn't-floss bad tooth pain.

I pretended the pain wasn't there. I sipped another Belikin. But the pain persisted. Over the weekend, it got progressively worse. By Sunday night, I was gulping aspirin by the fistfuls and soaking my tooth in vodka. The only good thing was that my entire jaw was beginning to go numb. But the tooth itself, a pesky lower molar, still felt like Jimmie Hendrix was playing riffs on it with an ice pick.

After getting some advice about dentists from friends in San Ignacio, I called Dr. Osbert Usher's office in Belize City on Monday morning. His receptionist gave me several choices of appointments, all that same afternoon. I drove to the Usher Dental Clinic, across from the Venus Bus station on Magazine Road.

Dr. Usher's office looked about like any other dentist's office in the United States. It was packed with patients: two nuns, several Creole kids, a very large Mestizo woman dressed to the nines, a Mennonite woman in a conservative calico dress, a British businessman. I answered a couple of questions from the receptionist, none of them about money, waited 10 minutes and was ushered into one of the patient rooms and seated in a standard dentist chair. Dr. Usher's dental diploma, from a university in Guatemala City, was on the wall. Dr. Usher, a trim man in his 30s, wasted no time taking X rays or getting my dental history. He just looked at the tooth, probed it, felt my cheek, and said, "That's a bad one."

But, he said, it was no problem. He'd take care of it. He'd save the tooth. Soon he was sticking me with Novocain, wielding a drill (the old kind with a comforting low-speed sound), and filling my mouth with cotton. This was dental care the way it used to be—no happy-face newsletters to generate referrals, no mood music on the stereo, no assistants lined up to do charts, no expensive film, no second opinions. In 45 minutes the root canal was done, and I was on my way, with the pain a fading memory and another appointment set for later in the week for a follow-up to check on the infection. Appointments, I noticed, were available on Saturdays and on evenings during the week. Dr. Usher gave me a prescription for antibiotics and painkillers, which I filled at Community Drugstore for less than US$6. On my second visit, Dr. Usher finished prepping the tooth for a crown; I was on my way back to the States and would have the final work done at my regular dentist in North Carolina. I asked what I owed. Dr. Usher declined any payment, saying that since I had been nice enough to send him some copies of my magazine for his waiting room, he wouldn't let me pay. I insisted on paying something, and finally he agreed to take US$50 for the two appointments. For completing the job, my dentist in North Carolina charged me something in the three figures.

If you need a dentist in Belize, may I recommend Dr. Osbert Usher? He's at 16 Magazine Road in Belize City, tel. 501/2-73415.

He was then transported by air to Belize City where he was hospitalized for several days. His total bill, including X rays, hospital stay, transport, and medications: Zero.

If you can accept long waits and less than state-of-the-art medical technology, you won't have to spend all of your pension to afford care. "Medical, dental, and eye care is a fraction of the cost of the United States. I have my teeth checked and cleaned for US$40, pay US$10 to $20 for an office visit to my physician, and medications are cheap," says one Californian who now lives in Belize full-time.

Even if you opt for private care, office visits to a physician generally are just US$5 to $20. A root canal with crown might cost US$250 to $500, although some Belize dentists charge more. Hospitalization runs under US$100 per day even at private hospitals. Prescription drug costs vary but generally are inexpensive compared to costs in the United States. In 2000, I paid just US$5 for a course of antibiotics. Pharmacies are in Belize City and in all towns. By the way, prescription drugs in Belize are usually dispensed in plastic bags or envelopes rather than in bottles.

While it is difficult to compare costs between Belize and the United States since the quality of care is different and the amount of medical tests done in Belize pales beside those routinely ordered in America, it's probably fair to say that even in the private sector overall costs for health care in Belize are one-fourth to one-third that in the United States.

Be aware that as of this writing the government of Belize is in the process of reevaluating its total health-care delivery system. Residents are supposed to use their Belize Social Security identity cards when they go for public medical or dental care. It is still too early to say whether this will have an impact on the cost or availability of care for foreigners in Belize. It appears, however, that charges for many medical procedures will increase. For example, the fee for delivery of a baby (including hospitalization),

The Radisson Fort George Hotel—where modern conveniences abound.

Radisson Fort George

which formerly cost US$20 or less in district hospitals, in late 2000 was increased to around US$400.

Of course, Medicare and Medicaid do not pay for medical care outside the United States, except for some limited situations in Canada and Mexico. The U.S. Department of Veterans Affairs will pay for coverage outside the United States only if you are a veteran with a service-related disability. For Americans, this is a major drawback of expat life in Belize, or indeed anywhere else outside the United States and its territories. For visitors and short-term residents, some private insurance policies do cover you regardless of where you become ill or have an accident (see below for one company that specializes in coverage in Latin America and the Caribbean). Also, some credit cards–the American Express Platinum Card is one—pay for medical evacuations back to the cardholder's home country.

Options for Care for Foreign Residents

For routine primary care, most foreign residents in Belize make do with the low-cost public system, or they go to a private physician, dentist, or clinic. Mostly they pay cash. They "self-insure," taking a calculated risk that what they save in medical insurance premiums will more than pay for their actual medical costs in Belize. Health insurance policies for care in Belize are available from insurance firms in Belize, including **Belinsco** (tel. 501/2-77025) and **Belize Insurance Centre Ltd.** (tel. 501/2-77310), but the cost structure of health care in Belize, and the relative lack of specialist care, means that it doesn't necessarily make sense to pay for Belize health insurance.

In specialized care, such as for heart disease or cancer, Belize is far behind the United States and Canada and even its Latin neighbors such as Mexico, Guatemala, and Honduras. "The big minus in Belize is that there is not adequate medical care for chronically ill people who need regular visits to specialists," says Judy duPlooy, who with her husband, Ken, owns a lodge near San Ignacio. "My husband suffers from congestive heart failure and is treated in Guatemala, which has excellent care and is the quickest place to get to in an emergency," she says.

While many expats do go to Guatemala, or to Chetumal or Mérida, Mexico, for specialized treatment, others who can afford it go to Houston, Miami, New Orleans, or elsewhere in the United States. For example, in 2000 when Barry Bowen, the Coca-Cola distributor and Belikin beer brewer in Belize, had an automobile accident on the way to his shrimp farm in Placencia, he was first treated and stabilized at Karl Heusner Hospital in Belize City. Then, he and his family opted to have him flown to Miami where he underwent treatment for his back injury.

A few insurance companies write health-care policies for expatriates, with the premiums covering medical transportation back to the home country along with actual health care. One that specializes in coverage for foreigners living in Latin America and the Caribbean, including Belize, and which has gotten good reviews from those in Belize who have used it, is **Amedex** (7001 Southwest 97th Avenue, Miami, FL 33173, 305/275-1400, email amedex@amedex.com). This company says it has more than one million policyholders in Latin America and the Caribbean, with a 90 percent renewal rate. Policies cover direct payment to any hospital in the world, 24-hour medical assistance and medical evacuation. You cannot reside in the United States for more than six months in a year. Premium costs vary based on age, but an individual $5 million major medical policy with a US$1,000 deductible for a person age 50 would be around US$1,600.

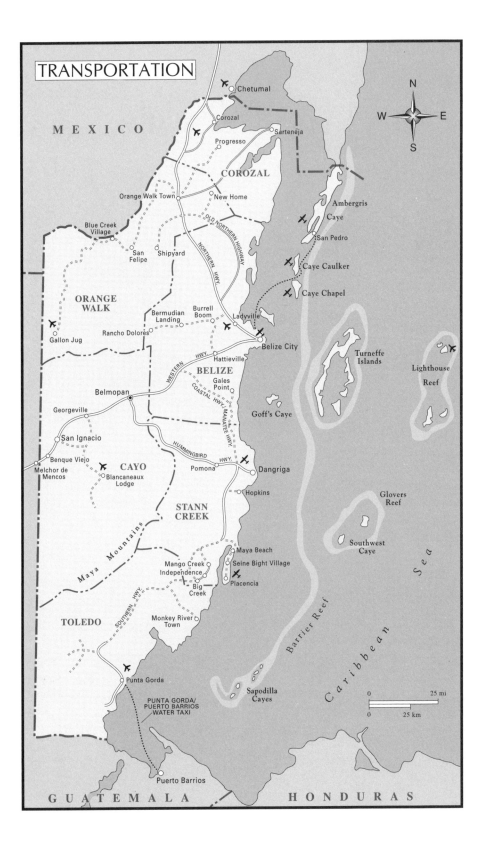

10 *Getting Around*

Belize is less than three hours by air from major gateways in the United States. Even with changes of planes, you can leave most major U.S. cities in the morning and be sipping a cold drink in Belize by the late afternoon. Once in Belize, you can get around very cheaply by bus, and driving is similar to that in the rural United States or Canada. Belize's main roads, once rated among the worst in Central America, have been vastly improved in recent years. Driving is on the right.

Flying to Belize

At present, three international airlines fly to Belize: **American, Continental**, and **TACA**. Continental has two nonstop flights a day from Houston. American has one daily nonstop from Dallas–Fort Worth and one from Miami. TACA's routing to Belize is in flux, but at present it has a nonstop from Houston. Miami flights to Belize City require a change of planes in San Pedro Sula and its other flights stop in San Salvador, where TACA hubs. At present there is no nonstop or direct service, scheduled or charter, from Canada or Europe.

One complaint I hear often is about the high cost of air travel to Belize. From most U.S. cities, you can expect to pay US$500 to $700 round-trip. My advice: Find a good travel agent—agents often help you find a good price

AIRLINES

American: www.aa.com; 800/433-7300; in Belize City, tel. 501/2-32522

Continental: www.continental.com; 800/231-0856; in Belize City, tel. 501/2-78309

TACA: www.grupotaca.com; 800/535-8780; in Belize City, tel. 501/2-72332

on air, even if they know nothing about hotels in Belize—or keep checking the online reservation sites such as Expedia.com or Travelocity.com. Fares change constantly. Priceline.com, www.skyauction.com, and other auction sites on the Web may produce lower prices for you.

Another idea is to fly into Cancun or Cozumel on a cheap scheduled or charter flight and bus it from there. However, a new Mexican tourist entry fee of 160 pesos (about US$17) per person makes flying into Mexico a little less economical. If flying into the island of Cozumel, you'll need to take the ferry (under US$6) to Playa del Carmen on the mainland, then walk to the bus terminal where ADO and other buses run to Chetumal. If arriving at Cancun, when you buy your ticket for transportation out of the airport explain that you want to go to the central bus terminal in Cuidad Cancun; you will be dropped off at the front of the terminal. Mayabus and ADO are among carriers to Chetumal from Cancun. First class express buses make fewer stops. Deluxe and first-class buses have reserved seats, air-conditioning, free videos, and clean bathrooms. Some have attendants who provide drinks. Rates vary with the value of the peso, bus class, and other factors but most are under US$15 from either Playa or Cancun to Chetumal. It takes about five to six hours from Cancun or Playa to Chetumal, depending on the stops and traffic.

At the Chetumal main bus station, you switch to a **Batty** bus. About a dozen Batty buses a day go from Chetumal to Belize City, starting at 4 A.M. and running to 6:30 P.M. The trip to Belize City takes three to four hours and costs US$4.50 for regular buses and US$6 for "premier class," which offers newer air-conditioned buses. **Venus** buses also make the run about five times a day for US$5, but at press time these leave from the Nuevo Mercado or New Market station, not the main station.

Once in Belize, you can get around very cheaply by bus, and driving is similar to that in the rural U.S. or Canada

The Belize buses stop at the border. You get off and clear Mexican immigration (having shown your passport and Mexican Tourist Card). Then you reboard the bus, cross the Rio Hondo, and go through Belize immigration and customs. The whole process usually takes about 30 minutes.

All visitors need a passport to enter Belize. You also are supposed to have an onward or roundtrip ticket and US$50 a day for the period you plan to spend in Belize or other proof such as a credit card that you can support yourself in Belize. However, as a practical matter it is unlikely you will have to show your ticket or proof of solvency. Most items for personal use, including a carton of cigarettes and a liter of alcohol, are permitted entry without duty. Fresh fruits or vegetables may not be brought in, and in this age of Mad Cow and Hoof-and-Mouth diseases, frozen or fresh meat also is usually not allowed. Firearms and spear guns (except the style called Hawaiian sling) are not permitted to be carried into Belize.

If you just want to go from the border to Corozal Town, the cost by bus is US$0.75. Belize does not observe daylight savings time, but Mexico does. Keep track of the time change when crossing the border.

Driving to Belize

A few adventurous folk drive through Mexico to Belize. The trip from Brownsville, Texas, is about 1,225 miles and usually takes about three to four days. Total nonstop driving time is around 28 hours. The fastest route from Brownsville/Matamoros is via Veracruz, Tampico, and Villahermosa. You stay on Mexico National Route 101 for about 118 miles, then Route 180 or, for part of the way, 180D (a toll road) for 742 miles, then Route 186 for 357 miles and then about 5 miles on Route 307 to the Belize border. The toll roads are expensive, but you can make 70 mph on them, much faster than on the regular roads—toll roads vary in cost, but typically the fee is the equivalent of 5 to 10 U.S. cents per mile. Depending on your route through Mexico to Belize, you might pay US$50 in tolls.

You should exchange enough American or Canadian money into Mexican pesos to get you through your trip, since the further you are

BEST BELIZE MAPS

- *Belize Traveller's Map* from ITMB, in Vancouver, Canada, at 350,000:1-scale and lasted updated in 1998, is the best available general map of Belize.
- Emory King's *Driver's Guide to Beautiful Belize,* updated annually, is a mile-by-mile driver's guide with excellent color maps of all main roads, Belize City, and most towns in the Belize.
- *Topographical Map of Belize,* British Ordnance Survey, a two-sheet topographical map at 250,000:1-scale, was last revised in 1990–91 so it's not as up-to-date as it could be, but it looks nice on your wall. The reverse sides have helpful maps of Belize City and all the towns. Also from the Ordnance Survey are area topographical maps. Belize has been divided into 44 sections and mapped at 50,000:1-scale.

  Unfortunately, some of these maps were done years ago and are much out-of-date.

from the border areas the fewer shops, service stations, and hotels in Mexico there are that accept foreign currency. Credit cards are not accepted at most gas stations. Do not drive at night.

Driving through Mexican towns can be confusing, because roads are poorly signed. In general, avoid going through the town centers *(Centro)*, as you can easily get lost and the hotels are more expensive than the hotels at the edges of the town.

To enter Mexico (and later, Belize) by car, you need your original vehicle title, and if your vehicle is not paid for a notarized letter of permission from the lien holder. Besides paying the new Mexico tourist entry fee of 160 pesos, which allows entry for up to six months, you have to provide a credit card in lieu of posting a cash bond to guarantee that you will bring the car back out of Mexico. By car, you are allowed only US$50 per person in merchandise to be carried into Mexico, although as a resident of the United States or Canada you can bring in such items as binoculars, laptop computer, TV, camping equipment, and fishing equipment.

If you are transporting goods of US$1,000 or more and are going through Mexico to Belize, you are supposed to use the services of a customs broker at the U.S.–Mexico border and get transmigratory status, which costs money in fees and, many say, in bribes to Mexican federal officers along the way. It's best just to enter Mexico as a tourist and not go the transmig route, most people say.

Mexican auto insurance is required; it costs from around US$50 for five days. Insurance for a month or two is not much more than for a few days.

A modern Texaco service station, where gas is about US$3 per gallon.

Lan Sluder

Sanborn's (800/222-0158, email info@sanbornsinsurance.com; www.san-bornsinsurance.com) is a good source of information on travel in Mexico and for Mexican auto insurance. A website with all types of helpful information on Mexico is www.mexconnect.com.

For current road conditions in Mexico, call the **Green Angels** (if you speak Spanish), tel. 011-52-5-250-8221 from the United States or 91-5-250-8221 within Mexico. Except on toll roads, driving after dark in Mexico is not advised. You may be stopped frequently for inspections. As of late 2000, gas in Mexico was about US$2.05 for regular unleaded *(magna sin)*, US$2.25 a gallon for premium, and US$1.70 a gallon for diesel.

Don't forget: You should exchange enough U.S. dollars to get you through Mexico, as U.S. dollars are not widely accepted, or are accepted at a low rate of exchange.

On arrival at the Mexico-Belize border, you need your original title (no photocopies) for your vehicle, or, if you do not own it free and clear, a notarized statement from the lien holder that you have permission to take the car out of the United States. You also have to buy Belize auto insurance (there are brokers at the border). Three months of insurance should cost about US$50 to $60, or one month about US$30. Crossing the border you may have to have your car sprayed to kill hitchhiking bugs—the fee is around US$4.50.

If you plan to stay in Belize and keep your vehicle there, you have to pay import duty. The import duty is 45 percent of value, based on the *N.A.D.A. Blue Book* plus evaluation by the customs official, plus 8 percent sales tax and in most cases 15 percent replacement tax. (The replacement tax isn't imposed on vehicles with four cylinders.) Thus, if you're driving a six-cylinder car with a value of $10,000, you'd be hit with an import duty of a whopping US$6,800. If you have permanent resident status you can bring in your vehicle duty free. *(See chapter 11 on moving to Belize.)* If you are just visiting, you should not have to pay the import tax, but the car is entered on your passport so you cannot sell it in Belize. There are customs brokers at the border to assist you with your paperwork. They're worth the small fee—perhaps US$20 to $40—they typically charge. Avoid border crossings on Mondays, the busiest day.

Belize from Top to Bottom by Bus: US$17

Travel by bus in Belize is inexpensive. You can travel the whole length of the country from the Mexican border in the north to Punta Gorda in the far south for about US$17 or go from Belize City to the Guatemala border in the west for US$3. It's also a good way to meet local people and to get a real feel for the country.

Bus travel in Belize falls somewhere between the chicken-bus experience in rural Guatemala or Nicaragua and the deluxe coaches with comfortable reserved seats and videos in Mexico. Buses are usually recycled American school buses or old Greyhound diesel pushers. On the Northern and Western Highway routes, a few buses are modern coaches offering "premier" service at slightly higher rates. Surprisingly, there is no city bus service from point to point within Belize City; you either have to take taxis or walk. The country has a franchised bus system, with the government granting rights for certain companies to operate on specific routes. Belize City is the hub for bus service throughout Belize. Four main bus companies have terminals in the same area of Belize City, west of the city center in an area called Mesopotamia: **Novelo's** (W. Collet Canal, tel. 501/2-77372) goes west to Belmopan and San Ignacio; **Batty's** (15 Mosul St., tel. 501/2-72025), purchased in 2000 by Novelo's but still operating independently, covers most Northern Highway and Western Highway routes; **Z-Line** (Magazine Rd., tel. 501/2-73937) runs to Belmopan, Dangriga, Placencia, and Punta Gorda, among others; and **Venus** (Magazine Rd., tel. 501/2-77390) heads north to Orange Walk and Corozal. A new bus terminal, which will accommodate a number of different bus lines, with shops and a hotel, is planned at the site of the Old Pound Yard.

Crossing the Belize River near Belmopan by a hand-pulled ferry.

Lan Sluder

Here is a survey of current schedules and prices, but note that these do change. Prices vary only a little among bus lines on the same route. For additional information, check the BelizeNet website at www.belizecentral.net/bus_schedule/schedule.html.

Belize City-Belmopan-San Ignacio-Benque Viejo: There are more than 30 departures a day each way, primarily on Batty (which has the morning runs going west and afternoon runs going east) and Novelo's (which has the morning runs going east and the afternoon runs going west). Departures each way start before dawn and continue to the early evening with the trip taking about 2.5 hours. Regular service between Belize

City and San Ignacio is US$2.50, with premier or express service (the buses are usually nicer and stop less frequently) costing US$3.

Belize City-Orange Walk-Corozal-Chetumal: Batty, Urbina's, and Venus together have about two dozen departures from Belize City, with additional service on the Belize City–Orange Walk leg, the first bus leaving at 4 A.M. and the last at 6:30 P.M. Coming south, there are about 17 departures from Chetumal on Batty and Venus, with the first being at 4 A.M and the last at 6:30 P.M. The trip between Belize City and Chetumal costs US$4.50 (US$5 for express and US$6 for premier service) and takes about four hours. Between Belize City and Orange Walk Town the cost is US$1.50 to $2 and the trip takes a little over an hour. Any of the buses can drop you at the entrance to the Crook Tree causeway or other points on the Northern Highway.

Belize City-Dangriga-Punta Gorda: Z-Line buses dominate this route with 10 daily departures from Belize City to Dangriga. To Dangriga, some buses go the coastal route (two hours) and other the Hummingbird (three hours) via Belmopan, but the cost is the same–US$5. About five buses (again, mostly Z-Line) leave daily from Belize City to Punta Gorda, a trip that takes eight hours and costs US$11.

Belmopan-Placencia: Z-Line runs two buses a day from Belmopan to Placencia, each taking two hours and costing US$7. You can also make connections in Dangriga for buses going south to Placencia or to Mango Creek where you can catch a boat to Placencia village.

You can make advance reservations by calling the bus lines, although most people don't make reservations. If boarding at a terminal in Belize

Crossing the suspension bridge near Gallon Jug.

Lan Sluder

City or elsewhere, you pay for your ticket at the window and get a reserved seat. If boarding elsewhere, you pay the driver's assistant.

Domestic Air

Belize has two domestic carriers, **Tropic Air** (tel. 501/2-45671 or 800/422-3435 in the United States, www.ambergriscaye.com/tropicair/index.html or www.tropicair.com) and **Maya Island Air** (tel. 501/2-31140, www.ambergrisCaye.com/islandair/index.html or www.mayaairways.com).

Which is better? It's a toss-up. Tropic is a little bigger, and some claim more professional in its operation, but Maya has twin-engine equipment, and some say it is a little friendlier. Both have good safety records and very similar prices. For most people, the decision comes down to which airline has the more convenient flight. Tropic and Maya both fly to Ambergris and Caye Caulker as well as Dangriga, Placencia, Punta Gorda, Corozal Town, and Flores in Guatemala. Domestic flights from the Municipal Airport, about a mile from the center of Belize City, are about 15 to 45 percent cheaper than from the Philip S.W. Goldson International Airport (which is located about nine miles north of Belize City). In addition to the the Municipal Airport, Belize has smaller domestic airports in Corozal, San Pedro, Caye Caulker, Dangriga, Placencia, and Punta Gorda. For example, a flight to San Pedro on Ambergris Caye costs approximately US$93 round-trip from International, US$52 from Municipal; from international to Placencia, US$140 round-trip, from Municipal, US$118; and from International to

The Municipal Airport in Belize City

Lan Sluder

Punta Gorda, US$177 round-trip, from Municipal, US$152. There is usually no saving on round-trip over two one-way fares, and except for occasional off-season specials, fares are about the same year-round, with no advance-purchase or other discounts.

The airlines fly only during daylight hours, except at peak times when the airlines have permission to continue flying into San Pedro until all waiting passengers are taken care of. Currently both airlines have about five flights a day going south, running every couple of hours from both Belize City airports, stopping at Dangriga, Placencia, and Punta Gorda. Both airlines also have about a dozen flights a day between Belize City and San Pedro; many, but not all, flights to and from International make stops at Municipal.

Driving in Belize

About 350 miles of highway in Belize are paved, primarily the Northern, Western, Hummingbird and Southern Highways and in Belize City and district towns. The roads in Belize continue to get better. There still are sections of washboarded dirt that will shake your fillings out, but more roads are now paved and even the gravel or limestone byways seem to be scraped more frequently. A few roads, such as the newly completed Hummingbird Highway, are very good indeed, among the best in all of Central America and the equal of any rural road in the United States or Canada. Signage, too is improving, being better than in most of Mexico or the rest of Central America. Most critical turns and junctions are marked. Around Belize City, new signage helps visitors navigate to key destinations such as the city center or the international airport. Road signs are in miles, not kilometers. You occasionally see a speed limit sign in Belize, but there is little traffic law enforcement. Speed-breaker bumps are used to slow traffic coming into residential areas.

Despite Belize's British heritage, you drive on the right, as in the United States. Driving rules in Belize are similar to those in the U.S., but enforcement of them is much more lax. Traffic cops are rare and speed limit signs are few. Most people drive as fast as conditions allow, slowing down only for "sleeping policemen" in village—*topes* or big speed bumps designed to reduce your speed or destroy your suspension. Seatbelts are required for all passengers, though again enforcement of this rule is another matter. When turning left on a two-lane road (which is most roads in Belize), pull over to the right, let cars behind you pass and then make your turn when the coast is clear in both directions.

Car theft, and even carjacking, is of some concern in Belize City but unlikely elsewhere. Belizean car theft rings make the headlines from time

NATIONAL PARKS IN BELIZE

About two-thirds of Belize's land area is still forested, and about 40 percent of the country's land is protected in reserves and national parks.

Among the major parks and preserves in Belize are:

Cockscomb Basin Wildlife Preserve, Stann Creek District. The world's first jaguar preserve, this lush jungle reserve of more than 100,000 acres is a must-see for anyone interested in natural Belize. New trails are open to Victoria Peak, one of the highest points in Belize at about 3,700 feet.

Half Moon Caye Natural Monument, Lighthouse Reef. Belize's first nature preserve, Half Moon Caye is a beautiful island on Lighthouse Reef, with 10,000 acres of surrounding reef.

Mountain Pine Ridge Reserve, Cayo District. More than 300 square miles of nearly unpopulated land in western Belize. Controlled logging is allowed.

Rio Bravo Conservation and Management Area, Orange Walk District: More than 200,000 acres of jungle, including mahogany forest, in Orange Walk District, privately managed by Programme for Belize.

Other national parks and preserves include:

Crooked Tree Wildlife Sanctuary, Crooked Tree
Community Baboon Sanctuary, Bermudian Landing
Bacalar Chico National Park and Marine Reserve, Ambergris Caye
Blue Hole National Park, Hummingbird Highway
Five Blues Lakes National Park, Hummingbird Highway
Hol Chan, Ambergris Caye
Shipstern Nature Reserve, Corozal District
Tapir Mountain Nature Reserve, Belmopan Area
Sapodilla Cayes Marine Reserve, off southern Belize (proposed)
Manatee Preserve, Belize District (proposed)
Laughing Bird Caye National Park, off Placencia
Guanacaste National Park, Belmopan
Port Honduras Marine Reserve, off southern Belize
Slate Creek Preserve, Cayo District

to time, but these are mostly involved in bringing in stolen vehicles from the U.S. or elsewhere and selling them in Belize or Guatemala. Never leave valuables in your car in Belize, even if the car is locked.

If you decide to ship your vehicle to Belize, you'll likely want to contact a freight forwarder in the U.S., who will probably work with a customs broker in Belize. Expect to pay about US$700 to $1,000 to ship a car from Florida or Texas to Belize, plus freight insurance (around US$100 depending on the value of the vehicle.) Be sure to remove the license plate before shipping, as plates are sometimes stolen during shipping or after arrival.

Ford, Jeep, Suzuki, Mitsubishi, and other American, Japanese, and European vehicles are sold at new-car dealerships in Belize City. Due to import taxes, and limited competition among dealers, the cost to buy a new or used car in Belize is 50 to 80 percent higher than in the United States. Unleaded gas is around US$3 a gallon, diesel about one-third less. Many expats get by without a car in Belize. Golf carts and bikes are the preferred method of transportation on Ambergris Caye and other islands, and on the mainland bus service is cheap and frequent. Car insurance in Belize is inexpensive, rarely being over US$200 a year. Driver's licenses cost US$10 and must be renewed annually at a Transport Department office.

Car Rentals

Some novice travelers in Belize are reluctant to rent a car. They've heard that car rentals are expensive and roads are terrible. Auto rentals in Belize are more costly than in most of the United States (though generally less than in Europe or Asia), and some roads are bad, especially in rainy weather. Overall, though, on mainland trips you're likely to save money if you have your own wheels, and that's doubly true if you're traveling with several other people. The focus of car rental in Belize is the International Airport, where about 10 rental agencies have booths. Just walk out the main airport exits from the lobby, cross the street, and the car rental offices are a few yards away at the far side of the airport parking lot.

Among recommended auto rental firms are **Budget** (international airport and 771 Bella Vista, Northern Hwy., tel. 501/2-32435, fax 2-30237, or in the United States and Canada 800/527-0700, email jmagroup@btl.net, www.budget-belize.com); **Crystal** (international airport and Mile 1 1/2 Northern Hwy., tel. 501/2-31600, fax 2-31900 or 800/279-7825, email crystal@btl.net, www.crystalbelize.com); **Hertz** (international airport and 11A Cork St. next to the Radisson Fort George, tel. 501/2-35395 or in the United States and Canada 800/654-3131; email safarihz@btl.net; and **Thrifty** (corner Central American Blvd. and Fabers

Golf carts are the most popular form of transportation on Belize's cayes.

Lan Sluder

Rd., tel. 501/2-71271, fax 2-71421 or in the United States and Canada 800/367-2277, email thriftybze@btl.net.)

The operator of the Budget franchise in Belize, JMA Motors, also owns the Suzuki and Mitsubishi new car dealerships, so Budget vehicles tend to be well maintained and have lower miles than most. We've found Budget to be, overall, the best auto rental company in Belize.

SOME TYPICAL PRICES FOR RENTALS:

A Geo Tracker 4x4 convertible, from Crystal, costs about US$78.95 per day or US$449 a week. A Nissan Pathfinder 4x4 SUV, from Crystal, costs about US$98.95 per day or US$599 a week. A Suzuki Jimny 4x4, from Budget, costs about US$75 a day high-season, US$70 off-season, or US$450 a week high-season, US$420 off-season, and a Mitsubishi 12-person van, from Budget, costs about US$100 a day high-season, US$95 off-season, or US$600 a week high-season, US$570 off-season.

Rates are unlimited mileage and do not include 8 percent sales tax or Collision Damage Waiver (CDW) insurance. Cars rented in Belize have liability insurance included in the rate, but not collision, and auto rental firms usually try to sell you CDW, at US$10 to $15 a day, to cover damage to the car from an accident, burglary, broken windshields, or such similar kinds of damage. Even with the CDW insurance, you may be liable for the first US$500 to $1,000 or more of damage. We call this a rip-off. Some credit cards cover CDW in Belize. Call to see if yours

Despite Belize's British heritage, you drive on the right, as in the United States.

does and save yourself up to US$90 or more a week in CDW costs. However, be sure it covers four-wheel drive vehicles or when you are driving off paved roads. Belize does not have an AAA or other auto club, so your club membership will do you no good in Belize.

Taxis

Taxis are available in Belize City, all towns, and in some villages. The cost from the international airport to Belize City is US$17.50 (for the taxi, not per person). Within Belize City, most fares are under US$3. Rates elsewhere vary, though prices are usually higher than they should be. Tipping of taxi drivers is not customary.

BOATS AND WATER TAXIS

Water taxis and small ferries connect Belize City with San Pedro on Ambergris Caye (75 minutes) and with Caye Caulker (45 minutes). The cost is US$12.50 one-way to San Pedro and US$7.50 one-way to Caulker. The most dependable boats are operated by the Caye Caulker Water Taxi Association and leave from the Marine Terminal on N. Front Street, near the swing bridge.

For boats to the southern cayes (typically US$25 to $50 per person and up), inquire in Dangriga, Hopkins, Placencia, and Punta Gorda. A regularly scheduled boat runs from Placencia to Puerto Cortez, Honduras, weekly, and there is water taxi service several times a day between Punta Gorda and Puerto Barrios and Livingston, Guatemala.

Rail

Belize has no railroads. Under British colonial rule, bananas and timber were transported by rail—old railroad bridges still can be seen on the Hummingbird Highway—but these railroads were shut down before World War II and have remained closed.

PART IV

Moving In

11 Making the Move

Before even thinking about moving to Belize, spend some time in the country. That's a point made frequently in this book, and it's advice echoed by nearly everyone who has chosen Belize as a relocation or retirement destination. Don't just daydream about living in Belize. Come experience the country firsthand, so you can make an informed decision.

> *Don't just daydream about living in Belize. Come experience the country firsthand ...*

OK, let's say you've done your due diligence, and you're ready to make the move. How do you go about doing it?

There are four main options for those wishing to retire in Belize or to spend extended periods of time in the country. Each has advantages and disadvantages.

Living in the Country as a Perpetual Tourist (Tourist Card)

This is the easiest, cheapest way to live in the country for awhile, and it requires no long-term commitment. On entry, you get a free visitor permit good for up to 30 days. This permit can be renewed for up to six months at US$12.50 a month. To renew it, you'll need to visit a government immigration office in Belize City or Belmopan, or a police station in

Comparing the Four Options for Staying in Belize

(All figures are in U.S. dollars)

	Tourist Card	Retired Residency	Regular Residency	Economic Citizenship
Age Requirement	None	45 +	None	None
Fee for Individual	$12.50/mo.	$705	$625 (U.S. Citizen)	$8,000 fee $15,000 registration $25,000 contribution
Fee for Couple	$25/mo.	$705	$1,250	$10,000 fee $25,000 registration. $25,000 contribution
Money Required for Deposit in Belize	None	$1,000– $2,000/mo.	None	None, except one-time $25,0000 contribution
Time in Belize Before You Can Apply	None	None	1 year	None
Period Valid	30–180 days	Lifetime	Lifetime	Lifetime
Duty-Free Import of Goods, Car	No	Yes	Yes	Yes
Work for Pay	Only with Work Permit	No	Yes	Yes

district towns. You are supposed to show that you have sufficient resources to maintain yourself in Belize, at least US$50 a day, but this requirement is rarely enforced as long as you look respectable. After six months, you must leave the country and start the process again. If you fail to renew your permit in a timely way, or if you overstay your allotted time, technically you are in violation of Belize law and can be deported. As a practical matter, if you can offer a good reason why you failed to follow the law, you'll probably be let off with a short lecture from the immigration official.

Official Retired Permanent Resident

The Qualified Retired Persons Incentive Act passed by the Belize legislature in 1999 is now in force and being implemented by the Belize Tourism Board (BTB). The program, which resembles the formerly popular but now defunct *pensionado* program in Costa Rica, is designed to attract more retirees to Belize. As of late 2000, according to Gina Escalante of the Belize Tourist Board, more than 200 people have applied for the program, and about 100 have been so far been approved. Interest in the program is high, Escalante says, with thousands of people visiting the program's website monthly and hundreds of them calling or emailing for information.

For those who can show the required monthly income from investments or pensions, this program offers benefits of official residency and tax-free entry of the retiree's household goods and a car, boat, and even an airplane. This program eliminates some of the bureaucratic delays built into other programs. The BTB guarantees action on an application in no more than three months, but we have heard of qualified retirees getting approval for this program in only two to three weeks. Key features of the act include:

- Open to anyone age 45 or older who is a citizen of the United States, the United Kingdom of Great Britain and Northern Ireland, Canada, or Belize; a person who qualifies can include his or her dependents in the program, including children under 18 (up to age 23 if enrolled in college).
- Applications for the program must be made to the Belize Tourism Board and should include the following:

  - Copy of birth certificate for applicant and each dependent.
  - Marriage certificate (if applicant is also applying for a spouse).
  - Notarized copy of complete passport of applicant and all dependents.
  - Copy of police record from last place of residence (completed within one month of application). You should request this from the police department where you last lived. Sometimes there is a small processing charge of US$10 or so.
  - Copy of medical exam including AIDS testing. Inexpensive medical exams are available in Belize or you can have one done by your physician back home.
  - An official statement from a bank or financial institution certifying that the applicant is the recipient of a pension or annuity (including U.S. Social Security) of a minimum of US$1,000 per month or that the applicant's investments will generate a minimum of US$2,000 per month. The two types of income can be

combined—for example US$500 from a pension and US$1000 from investments, but all income must be in the same applicant's name. A husband and wife each with a US$500 pension cannot combine that to qualify as having a US$1,000 monthly pension income. Within a month of approval of residency status, the first deposit of at least US$1,000, if qualifying on the basis of pension, or US$2,000, if qualifying on the basis of investments, must be made. It can be deposited in any bank operating in Belize, either annually in a lump sum or monthly. There is no restriction as to type of account, savings or checking, but it must be a Belize dollar, not U.S. dollar, account. The funds are available for living expenses of the retiree.

- Four front and four side-view photos of applicant and each dependent.

- Funds from pension or investments must be deposited monthly in a bank in Belize.
- Persons applying for residency are subject to a background check by the Belize Ministry of National Security.

Donna and Cy Young moved from Florida to build and operate Jaguar Paw Lodge.

Lan Sluder

- Persons residing in Belize under the program cannot work for pay in Belize.
- Persons retiring in Belize under the program are exempt from the payment of all Belize taxes on all income or receipts from a source outside of Belize whether that income is generated from work performed or from an investment.
- Persons retiring in Belize under the program qualify for duty and tax exemptions not exceeding US $15,000 on new and used personal and household effects. A list of all items with corresponding values that will be imported must be submitted with the application. In addition, a personal vehicle, which must not be more than three

years old, a boat used for recreational purposes and a light aircraft—any of these or all three—can be imported duty free under the law or can be purchased in Belize. Duty-free import of these items can be done in stages but must be completed within one year of moving to Belize.

- Fees for the program total US$705 per application (individual, couple, or family.) These consist of a nonrefundable application fee of US$100 payable to the Belize Tourism Board submitted with the application; a program fee of US$500 payable to the Belize Tourism Board upon acceptance into the program; on first entering the country after approval, a fee of US$100 must be paid to the Immigration Department; a Belize $10 stamp (US$5) must be attached to each application that is submitted to the Belize Tourism Board for processing.

For information on the program, contact:
Belize Tourist Board
Central Bank Building, Level 2
Gabourel Lane
P.O. Box 325
Belize City, Belize
Tel: 501/2-31913 or 800/624-0686
Fax 501/2-31943
Email: gina@travelbelize.org

The BTB has a website covering the program at www.belizeretirement .org. An application form for this program is available online at www .belizeretirement.org/applicationform.htm.

Official Permanent Resident

Requirements and benefits are similar to those of the Retired Persons Incentive Act. For example, as a regular permanent resident you can import household goods and a personal vehicle duty free. The application process and supporting documents needed are virtually the same as for retired residency. Here are the main differences:

- You must live in Belize for one full year before you can apply for regular permanent residency. During this period, you can not leave the country for more than 14 consecutive days.
- As a regular permanent resident, you do not have to deposit any particular sum in a bank in Belize. However, you do have to show financial resources sufficient to obtain residency status.
- You can work for pay in Belize.
- You must live in Belize for one full year before you can apply for regular permanent residency.

ADVICE FROM EMORY KING

Emory King is Belize's best-known expat. An American who was shipwrecked in Belize in 1954, Emory decided to make Belize his permanent home. He became a Belize citizen, a successful businessman, and the author of many books on Belize. Here's his advice for those contemplating retirement in Belize:

I would tell the potential retiree:

1. If you can afford US$2,000 per month to deposit in thebank, then comply with the new retirement program.

2. Come down first and spend a month here at least, visiting each district, talking to people, getting a feel of the place.

3. By that time you will know that Belize is not a cheap place to live. We have plenty of poor people here. We don't need any more. People trying to stretch their Social Security or other meager income should try Mexico or somewhere else. You can't enjoy life on a shoestring in Belize.

4. Understand, there are no laws governing real estate agents. No licenses, no examinations, no bonds. Any jerk who says, "I am a real estate agent" is one. So be very careful about buying land.

5. Avoid anyone who tells you he is friendly with someone in the government who can get you permits, licenses, etc. for the payment of graft.

These last few years the level of dishonesty has risen alarmingly in this country. And, worse, the idea seems to have acceptance in the society. Some say it's perfectly OK to lie, cheat and steal from tourists, foreigners, investors—because they are rich and they only come here to swindle us out of our heritage anyway. So, as they say, when "thief thief from thief, God laugh".

Otherwise, Belize is still the delightful place it always was.

- It is more expensive to apply for regular permanent residency than for retired permanent residency. Individual application fees vary according to your country of origin, ranging from US$125 (citizens of Mexico and Guatemala) to $1,500 (citizens of Mainland China). Citizens of the United States pay US$625, and Commonwealth country residents pay US$500. A couple pays twice the individual rate. Once residency is granted, you pay a fee of US$62.50 for a residency card.
- You apply to the Belize Immigration Department rather than through the Belize Tourist Board. For information and application form, contact:

Immigration and Nationality Service
Ministry of National Security and Immigration
Belmopan, Belize
Tel. 501/8-22423
Fax 501/8-22662

Economic Citizenship Investment Program

This controversial program, also called the buy-a-passport plan, was started by the previous government and continued (at least for now) under the present People's United Party government. It provides for Belizean citizenship, including a Belize passport, by "investing" in Belize. Actually, that just means paying a big chunk of cash to the government of Belize and a smaller chunk to someone with ties to the government.

The program stipulates that in any one year the number of heads of households granted economic citizenship should not exceed 1/4 of 1 percent of the Belize population, or about 600 heads of households. The exact number of economic citizenships granted is not known, but to date it is in the several thousand at least. Many of the "buyers" have been ethnic Chinese from Taiwan and Hong Kong. According to media reports in Belize, many of these economic citizens have never set foot in Belize, nor do they intend to do so. They simply have written a check to the Belize government as insurance against political changes in their homelands.

Belize recognizes dual citizenship so individuals under this program can retain their original citizenship. Economic citizens enjoy all rights, privileges, and diplomatic protection as full citizens of Belize. They are not required to live in Belize or to serve in the military or to pay any taxes except those that a regular citizen would be required to pay, such as income tax if working in Belize for pay. Holders of a Belize passport can travel to more than 85 countries without a visa.

"Immigration consultants"— typically well-connected Belizeans with an eye for a buck—assist in processing the application for economic citizen. Immigration consultants should be licensed and bonded. Several legal and CPA firms also are in the immigration consulting business, including Deloitte, Touche, Tohmatsu Belize (40A

Bob Jones came to Belize as a British soldier—and stayed on.

Lan Sluder

Central American Blvd., Belize City, tel. 501/2-73656, fax 2-75792, email deloitte@btl.net) and KPMG Belize (Jasmine Court, 35A Regent Street, Suite 201, Belize City, tel. 501/2-71755, fax 2-71117, email kpmg-csbl@btl.net) and Barrow and Williams, Attorneys-at-Law, 99 Albert Street, Belize City, tel. 501/2-75280, fax 2-75278, email barwil@btl.net.)

Immigration consultants submit the application to something called the "Belize Economic Citizenship Investment Programme Unit" for review by the "Scrutinizing Committee." If all the papers are in order and, more importantly, if all the cash has been paid, a decision is forthcoming from the "Scrutinizing Committee" in seven days. Successful applicants can be sworn in as Belize citizens either in Belize or overseas at a Belize embassy, consulate, or high commission.

Costs for the program are as follows:

- Fee to an immigration consultant for processing the application, typically US$10,000 for a couple or family and US$8,000 for a single person; this fee is not refundable.

John Carr was an authentic Montana cowboy before moving to Belize in the 70s to run a cattle ranch and, later, a jungle lodge.

Lan Sluder

- US$25,000 registration fee paid to the government of Belize, which covers the applicant, spouse, and dependent children 18 or under. Single applicants pay US$15,000. If the applicant has dependent children over 18 or other dependents also desiring economic citizenship, a fee of US$15,000 is required for each of these. Except for a processing fee, usually US$1,000, the registration fees are refundable if the application is not approved.
- In addition, US$25,000 must be contributed to the government of Belize in the form of a deposit to a Special Fund with the Central Bank of Belize. This deposit is fully refundable if the application is not approved; thereafter, it is not refundable.

Applications for economic citizenship must be submitted through a licensed immigration consultant to the Director, Belize Economic Citizenship Investment Programme (BECIP) Unit, Ministry of Finance, Belmopan, Belize. Applications must include the following supporting documentation for each family member, which must be in English or accompanied by a certified English translation:

- Birth certificate
- Eight passport photos
- Two character references
- Marriage certificate or divorce decree if divorced
- Criminal record certificate
- Certified copy of present passport or identification card
- Medical certificate indicating that applicant is free of AIDS and other communicable diseases
- Application form for Belize passport
- Receipt showing payment of registration fees paid to special fund of the Central Bank of Belize.

In addition to these four programs, **regular citizenship** in Belize is a possibility for those living in Belize over a long period. To acquire citizenship, applicants must have been a resident or have had permanent residency status for a minimum of five years. Applicants for citizenship need to provide essentially the same supporting documentation as those applying for permanent residency.

Each option has pluses and minuses. The main advantages and disadvantages of each option are:

Tourist card

Pros: No commitment, no financial requirement, flexibility, little red tape.

Cons: No tax advantages, no official status, inconvenience of having to renew and leave the country periodically, possibility rules may change, can't work for pay in Belize.

Official retiree permanent residence

Pros: Quick (as little as three weeks) approval, application through Belize Tourist Board rather than Immigration Department, full residency rights (except voting), tax-free entry of household effects, car, boat, and airplane.

Cons: Must deposit US$1,000 to $2,000 a month in a Belize bank, costly application process, can't work for pay in Belize, must be age 45 or over.

Sample of Belize Customs Duties on Imports

Those obtaining official residency in Belize can bring in household goods, a vehicle, and other items duty-free. See details in this chapter.

Automobiles New or Used:
(Customs used U.S. Kelley Blue Book value as basis, plus evaluation by customs officer)
4 Cylinder: 45% duty + 8% sales tax
6 Cylinder: 45% duty + 15% replacement tax + 8% sales tax based on evaluation of vehicle by customs
8 Cylinder: 45% duty + 15% replacement tax + 8% sales tax based on evaluation of vehicle by customs
Golf cart: 25% duty + 8% sales tax

Household Appliances:
Dishwasher: 20% duty + 8 % sales tax
Vacuum Cleaner: 20% duty + 8% sales tax
Stove or Refrigerator: No duty, 8% sales tax
TV: 20% duty + 8% sales tax

Power Tools and Building Supplies:
Drill/Saw/Sander: 20% duty + 8% sales tax
Building Supplies (Various): 15%–20% duty + 8% sales tax

Other:
Computer: No duty, 8% sales tax
Books: No duty, 8% sales tax

Duty information courtesy of Lane Thomas

Official permanent residency

Pros: Full residency rights (except voting), can work, open to anyone regardless of age, tax-free entry of household effects and car.

Cons: Year-long residency before applying, costly application process, more red tape, must pay alien property tax transfer fee (5 percent) if buying property.

Economic citizenship

Pros: Provides most rights of citizenship, including passport, can work, reduces real estate transfer fee.

Cons: Very expensive, some Belizeans oppose this "buy-passport" plan.

Moving to Belize with Children

Belize's education system is a joint effort of the Catholic Church and the Belize government and is based in many ways on the British system. Public schools vary, being generally best in Corozal and Belize City, worst in the far south, where schools often are crowded and lack basic textbooks and other supplies. In villages and rural areas schools are usually small concrete buildings with open windows and a pump for water. Some expatriates choose to do home schooling.

Since primary education is compulsory in Belize, parents who are home schooling are supposed to teach their children the basic curriculum offered at Belizean schools. After that, to enter high school and college in Belize, students who are home-schooled have to pass the same tests as those who attend regular schools. The secondary education school system in Belize covers six years divided into two cycles, lasting for four and two years. Normally on conclusion of the lower cycle, pupils may take the examinations for the Ordinary 'O' levels of the British Boards, or alternatively the Caribbean Examinations Council Certificate. Successful scores on this test allow students to move on to the last two years of secondary school. After the further two years, they may take the Advanced 'A' examinations of the British Boards. Those with questions about home schooling or other educational matters can contact the Ministry of Education & Sports in Belmopan, tel. 501/8-22380 or e-mail educate@btl.net.

Private schools are available in a few areas. The Island Academy on Ambergris Caye, as an example, charges US$250 per month per student. Primary education is free and compulsory through age 14. However, as many as two in five Belizean children do not complete primary school. Only about 60 percent of teachers are professionally trained. Secondary education, consisting of a four-year high school, is competitive, requiring passage of a comprehensive exam. The student's percentile ranking on the admissions test in part determines which school the student can attend. Charges for books and fees at secondary schools are beyond the reach of many Belizean families. About three-fourths of primary school students do go on to secondary schools, though not all graduate.

The "sixth form" in Belize, again patterned after the British system, is a two-year, post-high-school program at such schools as St. John's in Belize City or Muffles in Orange Walk Town. Only in the last few years has a four-year degree program been available in Belize. The University of Belize, established in 2000 as an umbrella system for a number of Belize colleges, offers baccalaureate degrees in nursing, engineering, business, and other subjects on campuses in Belmopan, Belize City, and elsewhere. Many Belizeans go to college in the United States, Guatemala, or England. Unfortunately, few of these students return to work in Belize.

Community college and four-year college tuition rates are extremely affordable in Belize. Tuition is rarely more than US$250 per semester. At the University of Belize, tuition is US$10 per credit hour for associate degree students and US$45 for four-year-degree students.

Bringing Pets to Belize

Pets can be brought into Belize without being quarantined. Owners must get a certificate from a veterinarian following examination not more than

48 hours prior to shipment stating that the animal is free from infectious diseases and has been vaccinated for rabies not less than one month and no more than six months prior to departure. For information, contact Dr. Michael Deshield (Animal Medical Centre, Castle and Lancaster Streets, Belize City, tel. 501/2-33781, email deshield@btl.net).

Not all pets adapt well to Belize's subtropical climate. Mange and venereal disease are endemic. Belizeans generally do not have the same view of pets as do Americans—they rarely allow dogs in the house, for example. Dogs are used more as watchdogs than as companions.

Shipping and Forwarding

Shipping companies and freight companies in Texas and Florida routinely handle shipments of vehicles and household goods to Belize, either by truck from Texas or by ship from ports in Texas, Florida, and elsewhere. Among the shipping and freight companies recommended by expatriates (but check them out yourself before committing to them) are:

MARITIME SHIPPING
Tropical Shipping, 14 Fort St. (P.O. Box 281), Belize City, tel. 501/2-78855, fax 2-77100, or in U.S. 800/367-6200, email eurocaribe@btl.net

Hyde Shipping, 115 Albert St., Belize City, tel. 501/2-77396, fax 2-77681, or in the U.S. 800/323-3906, email stanlong@btl.net

OVERLAND SHIPPING
Sterling Freight, P.O. Box 42809-400, Houston, TX 77242, tel. in Belize 501/9-24242

Daniel Bellini, 11203 Sageville Lane, Houston, TX 77089, tel. 281/922-1248

Customs brokers in Belize can be helpful in smoothing the way and in getting materials quickly released from customs. Here are some brokers and freight-forwarding agents. Check their references.

Billy Valdes, Custom House Brokers, 160 N. Front St. (P.O. Box 4), Belize City, tel. 501/2-77436, fax 2-33979

Herbert Bradley, Custom House Broker, 117 Albert St., Belize City, tel. 501/2-70702, fax 2-70727

Kuylen's Custom Brokerage, Santa Elena Border, Corozal, tel./fax 501/4-37069, email cusbroker@btl.net

Lane Thomas, Belize Business Development/XpressLane, Alijua Suites, San Pedro, Ambergris Caye, tel. 501/2-63083, fax 2-63084, email lane@btl.net, www.AmbergrisCaye.com/xpress/

12 A Roof Over Your Head

Of the many appealing things about Belize, probably none is more important to prospective relocatees than the relatively low cost of housing. To be sure, in a few prime areas you can spend hundreds of thousands of dollars on North American-style luxury homes, but you can also buy raw land at prices not seen in the United States since the 1960s and in some areas find a simple but pleasant rental house near the sea for under US$100 a month.

Add to that the ease of purchase or rental—there are few restrictions on the purchase or use of real estate by foreigners, and legal documents are in English and follow English common law traditions—and it's even more apparent why Belize can be a terrific alternative to other retirement or relocation areas.

What's Different, What's Not?

Most of the same rules of thumb that apply when looking for a home, land, or apartment in the United States or Canada also apply in Belize:

- **Location, location, and location are the three most important factors in determining price.** Demand drives price. For example, many people dream of living on the beach, so beachfront property in

Belize is in great demand, and prices are high compared with similar property inland or even one lot back from the beach.

- **Prices vary greatly depending on your negotiation skills.** If you're a good horse trader, you'll likely get a better deal in Belize than the guy who isn't. Keep in mind that in most parts of Belize there is far more available real estate than buyers with cold cash, so don't jump at the first deal that comes your way. Remember, too, that in real estate you almost always make your money when you buy, not when you sell.

- **The more you know, the better price you'll get.** A common saying among expats in Belize is that the second house you buy or rent is twice as large as the first and costs one-half as much. Spend as much time in Belize as you can before you put any money in real estate.

- *Caveat emptor.* Buyer beware applies as much in Belize as anywhere else. Real estate agents in Belize aren't licensed. That beachfront lot that looks wonderful in the dry season may be under two feet of water in the rainy season, and there are no laws in Belize that provide for you to get your money back if the real estate agent didn't provide full disclosure. In addition, as soon as the word gets out that you're in the market for a place to live, everybody and his brother will tell you about this little piece of property owned by a cousin of theirs. It may be a great deal, but look before you leap.

But a couple of things also are quite different about real estate in Belize:

- **In Belize, there almost always is one price for Belizeans and another price for foreigners.** The difference may only be a few dollars, but often the Belizean price may be one-half or less of the "rich foreigner" price. In some cases the differential may be five or ten times or more. From the expat's point of view, this is unfair. From the Belizean point of view, this is perfectly kosher and reflects the reality that Americans (or Canadians or Europeans) make far more money for the same work as Belizeans and can well afford to pay more. One way around this problem is to get a trusted Belizean friend to find out the "local price" for you. Once the owner has quoted the Belize price, he or she won't raise it, even if it's discovered that you're a foreigner. Another is spend enough time in the country to get a feel for the

> *Spend as much time in Belize as you can before you put any money in real estate.*

WHAT EXPATS SAY THEY WISH THEY'D BROUGHT TO BELIZE

- Anything of a technical or specialized nature that you'll want for your work or hobbies, such as fishing gear.

- Small hand tools, power tools, gardening equipment including shovel and hoe.

- Exotic electronic or digital equipment such as large-screen TVs, digital cameras, and video equipment—there are no BestBuy or Circuit City stores in Belize. There's not even a Wal-Mart.

- Sewing machine—good ones are hard to find in Belize.

- Your favorite books—while books are heavy and expensive to ship, there are only a couple of bookstores in Belize and these have limited selections.

- High-quality queen or king size mattress with cotton sheets—good mattresses are nearly impossible to buy in Belize and oversize sheets are unavailable.

- Containers of all types—Rubbermaid-type boxes, large zip-lock bags.

- If you are moving to Belize as an official resident and can import these items duty-free, bring an energy-efficient fridge and washing machine—these are available in Belize, but cost much more than in the United States. Most other household appliances and furniture are available in Belize at reasonable cost, or as in the case of a vacuum cleaner or clothes dryer you likely won't need them in Belize.

difference between the Belizean price and the non-Belizean price, so that at least you can bargain with your eyes open.

- **The Belize market is very small and inefficient.** The real estate market anywhere is inherently not very efficient, since sales involve one-of-a-kind properties sold at high prices to a relatively small pool of potential buyers. In Belize, the marketplace is even more inefficient. There is little real estate classified advertising, and most properties are sold or rented by word of mouth. Except for one or two informal associations of real estate companies, there are no multiple listing services, and many properties are for sale by owner. Thus, it's not easy to find out exactly what is on the market or what the prices are. The pool of financially capable real estate buyers in Belize is small, leaving many sellers dependent on foreign buyers. There are few qualified real estate agents, appraisers, and surveyors. Mortgage financing is not easily available for foreign buyers, further reducing the size of the buying pool and requiring cash sales or owner financing. All this means that prices for similar properties can be all over the board. Also, the time to sell a property may be measured in years rather months—which is something to think about as you buy real estate that you may someday want to sell.

Shopping for Housing

If you are interested in buying or renting property in Belize, how do you go about finding properties for sale or rent?

Except for occasional ads in the *San Pedro Sun* on Ambergris Caye and in Belize City newspapers, few properties are advertised for sale. Real estate agencies do maintain listing brochures, and you can contact them to request a copy. Increasingly, brokers use the Internet as their primary way of presenting listings and of getting prospective buyers. This is as true in Belize as it is in California. See the real estate agent listings below for addresses of real estate websites in Belize. Even with the Internet, however, you'll miss three-fourths of available properties. To find out what's really for sale, you'll have to spend time on the ground in Belize. Most properties are for sale by owner, rather than being listed with a broker. In many cases, you will see no sign or other indication that a property is for sale. Just start asking around, and before long you'll have more deals being offered you than you can even begin to consider.

This goes double for rentals. It is rare to see a house advertised for rent in a newspaper, and brokers handle only the most expensive rentals. About the only way to find a house or apartment to rent is to spend some time in the area where you wish to rent. Drive around and look for vacant homes, or ask foreign residents or Belizeans for tips on what's available.

Real Estate Brokers

In Belize, anyone can be a real estate broker. No license needed. No schooling, no bonding, no continuing education. All you need is enough money to print business cards, and, presto, you're a broker. Selling real estate is a popular first job for expats in Belize, and some do it on the side without a work permit. Quite a few hoteliers, dive shop operators, and taxi drivers peddle real estate to tourists on the side. One of the best-known real estate guys in Placencia, when he's not sailing his boat around the Caribbean, is also the proprietor and barkeep of one of the most popular bars on the peninsula.

Not surprisingly, the quality of agents varies. Some are professional and honest. A few are out for a fast buck. The ones we've listed here and in the Prime Location chapters are among the best we've heard about, but even so your mileage may vary.

Real estate commissions in Belize are similar to those in the United States. Agents typically charge the seller 7 percent commission on residential property, and around 10 percent on raw land. Because many properties are in remote areas, brokers often charge prospective buyers expenses for travel and transportation incurred in connection with showing properties.

Farms for Sale

Not a green thumb? Here are some typical farm and acreage properties in Belize. These properties were available in early 2001. Figures shown are asking prices.

44 acres, Hummingbird Highway, good access, utilities, US$44,000

195 acres, Hummingbird Highway, 37 acres of citrus fruits, two streams, five-bedroom house, on power grid, US$300,000

50 acres, including 10 acres in coconuts and fruit trees, on the Northern Lagoon in the Gales Point area, with small house, US$116,000

67-acre citrus farm, Caves Branch, Cayo District, planted with 6,500 orange trees, 1,000 grapefruit trees, 800 limes, and more, includes tractor and farm equipment, US$80,000

376 acres, Northern Highway, Belize District, 100 acres of cleared land, orchid house, fern and flower production, good access, US$220,000

17,000 acres of uncleared jungle in the Roaring River/Caves Branch area near Belmopan, US$3,400,000

21-acre citrus farm on Hummingbird Highway, including 10 acres in oranges and 5 in grapefruit, US$50,000

Selected Agents

Here some real estate agents who have been given good marks by expats in Belize. Also, see individual Prime Living chapters and the appendix.

Bill Wildman, Belize Land Consultants, P.O. Box 35, Corozal, tel. 501/4-38005, fax 4-38006, email blzland@btl.net, www.consejoshores.com. Bill, a Canadian land surveyor and wife, Jenny, originally from England, developed Consejo Shores near Corozal Town and also have more than 30 years of real estate experience in Placencia and elsewhere in Belize.

Belize Real Estate (W. Ford Young Real Estate, Belize City, and Langdon Supply, Ambergris Caye), 160 N. Front Street (P.O. Box 354), Belize City, tel. 501/2-72065, fax 2-31023, email bzreal@btl.net, www.belizerealestate.com. Properties throughout Belize.

John C. Burks, Regent Realty, 81 N. Front St., Belize City, tel. 501/2-73744, fax 2-72022, email regent@btl.net, www.regentrealtybelize.com. John, an American who first came to Belize in 1972 to raise cattle, has listings all over Belize and represents The Plantation, a real-estate development on the Placencia peninsula.

Madeleine and John Estephan, Emerald Futures Real Estate, 13 Cork Street, #3 (P.O. Box 1442), Belize City, tel. 501/2-36559, fax 2-36559, email realgem@btl.net, www.emeraldfutures.com. Emerald Futures has properties in most areas of the mainland. The Estephans were born and raised in Belize.

Amanda Symes, Sunrise Realty, P.O. Box 80, San Pedro, Ambergris Caye, tel. 501/2-63737, fax 2-63379, email sunrise@btl.net, or go to the website at www.sunrisebelize.com. Focuses on properties on Ambergris Caye.

Diane Campbell, San Pedro, Ambergris Caye, tel. 501/2-65203, email camp@btl.net. Diane is a former Californian who with her husband has built a number of homes on Ambergris Caye, including the Los Encantos development.

Restrictions on Ownership

Belize imposes few restrictions on ownership of land by nonnationals. Unlike Mexico, which prohibits the direct ownership of land by foreigners on or near the coast, in Belize foreigners can buy and hold beachfront real estate in exactly the same way as Belizeans.

The only limitations on ownership by foreign nationals are these:

- An alien license from the government formerly was required for the purchase of properties of 10 acres or more anywhere and for properties of half an acre or more within city limits, on the cayes, or in a few other restricted areas. However, in March 2001 this requirement was repealed. Further changes may be ahead; stay tuned.
- Government approval from the Ministry of Natural Resources is required, before the purchase of any island, regardless of size.

A Geodesic dome house with a thatch roof

Lan Sluder

Real Estate Prices

Property prices vary greatly in Belize from one area to another. They generally are highest in Belize City, on Ambergris Caye, and in Placencia, and lowest in remote rural areas. In large tracts, raw land is available in Belize for under US$100 an acre, but for this price access may be poor and surveying costs may exceed the cost of the land itself. Good agricultural land might range from US$250 to $2,000 an acre, depending on quality and access. Home prices range from under US$15,000 for a simple Belizean-style home in a small village to US$500,000 for a luxury home on the beach in San Pedro. Finished, newer homes typically sell for from US$30 to $80 per square foot, though of course the location of the lot or land also is a major factor.

The condominium type of ownership is new to Belize, and most condos are on Ambergris Caye. Prices start at under US$100,000 for a one-bedroom unit. Belize has a few timeshares, also mostly on Ambergris Caye. These are generally not a good investment.

Property in Belize has appreciated over the past two decades, but by exactly how much is more difficult to say. Real estate agents say that some beachfront property in Placencia and elsewhere that was selling for under US$100 a front foot in 1980 is now going for US$1,000 or more a foot. Real estate agents naturally talk up the appreciation potential, but keep in mind that the Belize economy is closely tied to the economy in the United States. Should America's economic machine go into a tailspin, expect to see little if any growth in real estate values in Belize.

Even with appreciation, real estate prices in Belize are still inexpensive by the standards of the United States or most of Western Europe. That's especially true of beachfront prices. Waterfront lot prices on the Eastern seaboard of the United States, or in Florida, rarely are less than $200,000, and in places like Hilton Head, S.C., or Ft. Lauderdale, Fla., can easily reach several million dollars, whereas beachfront building lots on Belize's Caribbean are still available for US$50,000 to $100,000.

Here's a sampler of what you can expect to get for your money in Belize:

UNDER US$10,000
10 acres of farmland in Cayo or other rural area
Sea-view (not seafront) lot in Corozal
Sea-view lot on Long Caye

UNDER US$25,000
Canal/lagoon lot in Placencia
Sea-view lot on Ambergris Caye
Small Belizean-style two-bedroom home in village or rural area

20-acre farm with small basic dwelling in rural area
6-acre "farmette" with utilities near Consejo Shores and Corozal Bay

UNDER $50,000
Beachfront lot on Ambergris Caye
Beachfront lot in Placencia, Hopkins, or Corozal
Pleasant small concrete home in Corozal or Cayo
Mennonite "prefab" small house on canal/lagoon lot in Placencia

UNDER US$100,000
50-acre farm with dwelling and outbuildings in northern Belize, Cayo, or
      Toledo
Modern 1,000 square-foot home on waterfront in Corozal or Hopkins area
One-bedroom condo on Ambergris Caye

UNDER $200,000
Two-bedroom condo on water on Ambergris Caye
Deluxe 1,800 square-foot home on nice lot in San Ignacio, Placencia, or
      Corozal
150-acre farm with nice home, outbuildings and equipment in rural area

UNDER $500,000
Luxury 5,000 square-foot home on small estate in Cayo
Luxury 3,000 square-foot home on the beach on Ambergris Caye
1,000-acre farm with nice home, outbuildings, and equipment in rural area

---

Fees and Costs of Purchase

Besides the cost of the property, you are likely to incur charges associated
with the purchase that total 12 to 15 percent of the purchase price. These
include the following:

- **Land title transfer fee**, sometimes called stamp tax: everyone in
  Belize pays 5 percent transfer tax; noncitizens pay an additional 5 per-
  cent tax, for a total of 10 percent. At press time, the Belize Tourist
  Board was working to have this additional 5 percent tax repealed for
  those in Belize as permanent residents under the Qualified Retired
  Persons Incentive Act.

- **Attorney's fee:** For around 2 percent of the purchase price, the attorney will draw up transfer documents and search the title.

ISLANDS FOR SALE

Ever wanted to own your own tropical island? In early 2001, these cayes (pronounced "keys") were for sale in the Caribbean Sea off Belize:

Round Caye, located 16 1/2 miles northeast of Placencia, 4.2 acres, US$300,000

200-acre island northeast of Belize City, said to be the largest undeveloped island available in Belize, US$1,500,000 with $300,000 down and balance over 10 years at 10 percent.

Long Coco Caye, located 10 miles east of Placencia, 46 acres with natural harbor and surrounded by coral reefs, US$1,250,000

10-acre island with 2,800 feet of beach, near Placencia, US$700,000 with $200,000 down and balance over 10 years at 12 percent, or $650,000 cash

- **Property taxes:** These are levied in advance and will be about 1 percent of the market value of the unimproved land outside city limits. Taxes within city limits but vary from around 3 to 8 percent of the value of the land (not the buildings and other improvements).

Registration and Title

There are three different real property title systems in Belize:

1. **Conveyance system**, which involves the transfer of land by conveyance and registration. In order to assure that the seller actually owns the land, a title search must be made in the Lands Unit in Belmopan (formerly Registry Office in Belize City) to unearth the chain of title and to uncover any encumbrances such as uncanceled mortgages. This search is normally done by an attorney. The owner holds a deed, but the proof is in the registry search. Unfortunately, it is sometimes difficult or impossible to trace old conveyances with any degree of certainty of results, due to the terrible condition of the index books.

2. **Torrens system**, which involves a First Certificate of Title (FCT) followed by Transfer Certificates of Title (TCT). Unlike the "real" Torrens system in use in parts of the United States and elsewhere, the Belize system is not backed up by a fund that guarantees title. Under this system, the undischarged (uncanceled) "charges" or encumbrances and the transfers from the title are shown on the relevant certificate, so no further search is normally needed before the new Transfer Certificate of Title is issued, following the application for transfer.

3. **Registered Land Act system**, in which application for transfer is made, and a new Land Certificate is issued to the grantee. Under this system, an application is made for title transfer and a new Certificate of Title is issued to the grantee. Any existing "charges" will be shown on the Land Register for that parcel of land. The owner holds a Certificate of Title, and this, together with the relevant Land Register entries is the proof of ownership.

Which system you use depends on where your property is located. With only a few exceptions, you won't have a choice. If, for example, your property is located in an area of Belize where the Registered Land Act system is in place, such as around Belmopan or in a planned subdivision, your property will be registered under that system. Land in Belize is being put into this system area by area until eventually the entire country will be included in it.

Title insurance may be available. Regent Insurance (tel. 501/2-73744 in Belize City) offers title insurance through Stewart Title, a U.S. company. Typically title insurance costs 1 percent of the purchase price.

Need for a Lawyer

You don't hear many lawyer jokes in Belize. In Belize, attorneys remain trusted advisors. They're usually well connected, well paid pillars of the community who wield real power. A roster of attorneys in Belize will reveal the surnames of families with histories in Belize going well back into colonial times along with those of today's political leaders including Barrow, Young, Shoman, Musa, Courtenay, and Godfrey. In any real estate transaction, you should have your own Belize attorney. Typically the fee will be around 2 percent of the purchase price.

Financing

Land in Belize is usually purchased on terms under an Agreement for Sale or Contract for Deed whereby the seller keeps title to the property until it has been paid for in full. Terms vary but can range from 10 percent down with 10 years to pay at 10 percent simple interest per annum—about the best deal you can hope for—to 50 percent down and three years to pay at 12 to 14 percent.

Residential property may also have owner financing, although commonly the lowest price will be for an all-cash deal. It is difficult for a nonresident to get a mortgage loan from a bank in Belize for buying or building, so you should be prepared to pay cash or to get financing through a loan from a non-Belize financial institution on your assets back home.

For citizens and official permanent residents of Belize only, the Development Finance Corporation (DFC), a financial institution owned by the government of Belize, makes loans of US$3,000 to $75,000 for building or buying housing for up to 25 years at interest rates of 8 1/2 to 13 percent. The DFC also has developed housing subdivisions near Belmopan, on the Northern Highway in Belize District, and in Corozal Town. These subdivisions have new homes such as a 680 square footer for US$33,000 and a home of about 1,000 square feet for US$41,000. Financing is at 12 percent for up to 25 years.

Rentals

Rental levels in Belize also vary widely, being highest on Ambergris Caye and in Belize City. In upscale areas of Belize City such as West Landivar and Caribbean Shores, you can expect to pay around US$0.80 to $1.50 per square foot per month, or about US$800 to $1,500 a month for a 1,000 square-foot two-bedroom apartment. On Ambergris Caye, a modern one-bedroom apartment goes for US$400 to $750 and a two-bedroom US$650 to $1,500. Elsewhere, rentals are much lower. In rural areas and low-cost towns such as Corozal, you can find a small house in a safe area for under US$250 a month. We know of several expats in Corozal who rent for under

a colonial home in Belize City

Lan Sluder

US$100 a month, and while their homes are not fancy, they are comfortable. These houses are typically of concrete block construction with a couple of small bedrooms, bath, a living room, and a kitchen with stove and refrigerator.

> *About the only way to find a house or apartment to rent is to spend some time in the area where you wish to rent.*

In all areas, North American–style housing with air conditioning, modern appliances, and security will be many times more expensive than a traditional Belize rental, a simple concrete or wood house, with only basic amenities and probably no appliances except for a butane stove and a small fridge.

Short-Term Rentals

If you're coming to Belize on a scouting expedition, consider a short-term rental. Staying in a house or apartment rather than in a hotel can help you decide if Belize is really for you. Unfortunately, there are not a lot of short-term vacation rentals in Belize. Most of them are concentrated on Ambergris Caye, but there are a few in other areas including Placencia and Corozal.

Here are some sources of short-term rentals:

AMBERGRIS CAYE
Caye Management (Barrier Reef Drive, San Pedro, tel. 501/2-63077, fax 2-62831, email cayeman@btl.net, www.cayemanagement.com) has the best selection of rental houses and condos on the island. Weekly rentals are mostly US$700 to $2,000. Six-month rentals start at around US$600 to $800 a month. Also consider short-term condo rentals. One good option is **Banana Beach** (P.O. Box 94, San Pedro, tel. 501/2-63890, fax 2-6389, email bananas@btl.net, www.bananabeach.com) for around US$1,200 a month.

PLACENCIA
Kitty's Place (P.O. Box 528, Belize City, tel. 501/6-23227, fax 6-23226, email info@kittysplace.com, www. kittysplace.com) manages a number of rental houses in and near Placencia village, starting at around US$300 a week or US$1,000 a month. **Barnacle Bill's** (23 Maya Beach, Placencia, Stann Creek, tel. 501/6-37010, email taylors@btl.net, www.gotobelize.com/barnacle/) has two nice one-bedroom cottages on the beach at Maya Beach, for under US$500 a week. **Serenade** (tel. 501/6-23420, email leenyhus@hotmail.com), a small, newly built two-bedroom house in Placencia village goes for under US$250 a week.

COROZAL TOWN

Corozal Bay Inn (P.O. Box 184, Corozal Bay Road, Corozal Town, tel. 501/
4-22691, email relax@corozalbayinn.com, www.corozalbayinn.com) has
attractive two-bedroom suites with kitchenettes for around US$300 a week.
Bed and Bananas is a lovely two-bedroom house in Consejo Shores owned
by a German couple. It rents for US$650 a month plus utilities. Reserva-
tions are available through a website, www.consejoshores.com/
bedandbananas/.

Building a Home

As a general rule, you will get more for your housing dollar in Belize by
building rather than buying a completed home. If you can put up with the
hassle of construction, you can build a house with details such as built-in furniture, exotic tropical hardwood floors, and custom-made mahogany cabinets
that in the United States would be found only in the most upscale homes.

In Belize as elsewhere construction costs vary depending on such factors
the cost of transportation of materials to the building site, the terrain, and
quality of work. As rules of thumb, in Belize construction costs are highest
on the coast and cayes, because of the need to use hurricane-resistant construction. In the case of the cayes, it costs extra to transport building materials by boat. Building costs also are higher in southern than in northern
Belize. Inexpensive building materials are more readily available in northern Belize since they can be imported from Chetumal, Mexico.

Termites and time take their toll on houses in Belize.

Lan Sluder

Labor in Belize is much less expensive than in the United States, with carpenters getting around US$25 a day or less. While labor may be cheap, jobs usually take longer in Belize. Workers may be skilled at construction techniques common in Belize but may lack knowledge about building in the American style. Outside of urban areas, it is difficult to find qualified craftspeople such as electricians and plumbers. Building materials vary but are mostly no cheaper than in the United States, except for locally produced items such as tropical hardwoods, which run about US$1,000 for 1,000 board feet. Cement is more expensive than in the United States, as are most bathroom and kitchen fixtures, which have to imported. Flooring materials such as *saltillo* tiles from Guatemala and Mexico are moderately priced and of high quality.

Overall, building costs in Belize range from around US$25 to $100 a square foot, not including the cost of land. At the bottom end, that would be a simple Belizean-style block house or frame construction, and at the top it would be high-quality concrete construction with hardwood floors and trim and with many custom details such as handmade doors and windows. Most commonly, you'd expect to pay about US$50 to $60 a square foot, so a 1,500 square foot home would cost US$75,000 to $90,000 to build. That's about one-half of typical costs for construction in the United States.

Of course, if you have a nose for thrift you can build for much less than that. We know one man from Louisiana who built a small house on a lagoon north of Corozal for about US$4,000. He collected building materials such as old planks and boards that were floating in the lagoon, scrounged others from old houses, and did most of the actual construction work himself.

Mennonite builders sell prefabricated frame buildings, which they will install on your site. This is an inexpensive and quick way to get a home up in Belize. See the appendix for a list of builders and contractors, including Mennonites.

In areas at risk of hurricanes and tropical storms, you'll have to put in deep pilings and raise the first floor above ground level to avoid water damage. Reinforced concrete is the preferred construction. Hurricane straps and rafter ties are inexpensive protection against having the roof blown away.

In the past, the only building codes in Belize have been those imposed by local municipalities. Many rural areas had no codes at all. In 1999, work began on developing a national building code calling for nationwide standards of construction. This new code is expected to be implemented soon.

Free Land?

From time to time we get questions about the possibility of homesteading or otherwise getting free land in Belize. Yes, there is such a program in place, but here are the catches: First, you must be a Belizean citizen or have lived in the country as an official resident for at least three years. Second, land is only available in certain areas. Mainly it is small tracts or building lots. This is not the homesteading hundreds of acres of prime farmland that you read about in the your American history book. Third, you have to lease the land from the government, clear it, and actually construct a home. At that point, for a nominal amount you can buy the property from the government, and you will get title. Given all the time and red tape involved, and the low cost of land in Belize, it's hardly worth it to get a small piece of land worth a few hundred to a few thousand dollars. Frankly, if the only reason you moved to Belize is to take advantage of such a scheme, it's unlikely you'll have the financial resources to make it in Belize long enough to qualify for the program.

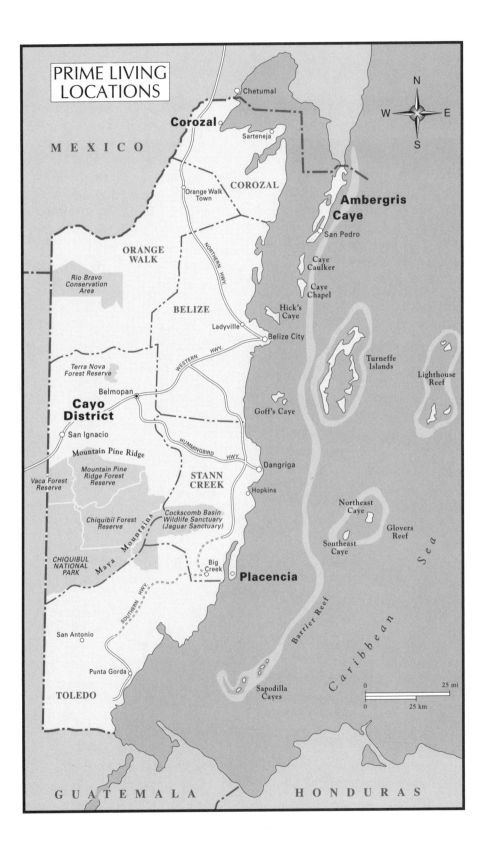

PRIME LIVING LOCATIONS

MEXICO

Chetumal

Corozal

Sarteneja

COROZAL

Orange Walk
Town

NORTHERN HWY.

**ORANGE
WALK**

Rio Bravo
Conservation
Area

BELIZE

Ladyville

Belize City

WESTERN HWY.

Terra Nova
Forest Reserve

Belmopan

**Cayo
District**

San Ignacio

Mountain Pine Ridge

HUMMINGBIRD HWY.

Mountain Pine
Ridge Forest
Reserve

Vaca Forest
Reserve

**STANN
CREEK**

Dangriga

Hopkins

Chiquibil Forest
Reserve

Cockscomb Basin
Wildlife Sanctuary
(Jaguar Sanctuary)

**CHIQUIBUL
NATIONAL
PARK**

Maya Mountains

Big
Creek

Placencia

SOUTHERN HWY.

San Antonio

Punta Gorda

TOLEDO

**Ambergris
Caye**

San Pedro

Caye
Caulker

Caye
Chapel

Hick's
Caye

Goff's Caye

Turneffe
Islands

Lighthouse
Reef

Northeast
Caye

Glovers
Reef

Southeast
Caye

Barrier Reef

Sapodilla
Cayes

Caribbean Sea

GUATEMALA

HONDURAS

N
W E
S

0   25 mi
0   25 km

13 Prime Living Locations

The following chapters discuss the characteristics and appeal of the different regions considered to be prime living locations in Belize. By no means are these the only desirable regions, but they are places where a number of expatriates have decided to live.

Ambergris Caye, Placencia, Corozal, and Cayo attract the vast majority of foreigners. In addition to these areas, Belize has a number of other areas, such as Punta Gorda, Belize City, Sarteneja, Hopkins, and Caye Caulker, that may appeal to retirees, investors, or second-home buyers. The final chapter highlights these locations, organized geographically from north to south, with caye options at the end.

Ambergris Caye, pronounced Am-BURR-jess Key or sometimes Am-BURR-griss, was rated one of the 15 best places outside the United States for retirement by AARP's *Modern Maturity* magazine in 2001. It is the largest and most populous of Belize's islands, welcoming visitors with its friendly, laid-back lifestyle, sandy streets, and climate similar to that of Southern Florida. It is also home to the largest concentration of foreign expatriates in Belize, with estimates of up to 1,000 on the island, and more arriving daily. Most people have moved here to be close to the Caribbean and the Belize Barrier Reef, hence daily life pretty much revolves around activities in, and on, the water. The island is usually among the first stops for those thinking about relocating to Belize, even if they end up choosing another area.

Placencia, located in Stann Creek District, is a gem that offers you a little bit of the South Pacific. It's also excellent for sports fishing. Located on the southern coast of the mainland, the peninsula, only a few hundred feet wide at some points, lies between the Caribbean Sea to the east and the Placencia Lagoon to the west. Most people live either in Seine Bight or Placencia village, the two main towns on the peninsula. With cheaper housing and fewer tourists than Ambergris Caye, Placencia's combination of easygoing resort atmosphere, myriad water activities, and plenty of beachfront has attracted a growing number of real estate buyers.

> *Belize is simply beautiful. It is a place of incredible natural beauty, of mint green or turquoise seas, and emerald green forests ...*

Corozal, which is somewhat off the beaten tourist track, is one of the best-kept secrets of Belize. Less populated than Ambergris Caye, Corozal has only a handful of small hotels and restaurants, but offers more affordable housing and great fishing. Corozol Town itself, nestled in Corozal Bay with a population of about 12,000, is laid out on a small grid with its most appealing section—colorful houses and a market—built along the bayfront. Cool ocean breezes make it one of the most pleasant spots in all of Belize, and should rank near the top of your must-see list if you're thinking of retiring, relocating, or investing in the country. Next door is Chetumal, capital of the Mexican state of Quintana Roo, that offers good, low-cost medical care and inexpensive shopping.

Cayo appeals to those looking for a rural area not by the sea. Located in

The entrance to Belize's first "gated community", developed by the British American Cattle Company.

Lan Sluder

western Belize and bordering Guatemala, Cayo has rolling hills, low mountains, and few mosquitoes or sand flies. It also has a more extreme climate, boasting the hottest and coldest weather in Belize. While Cayo has some lush broadleaf jungle, it also has piney woods and red clay that may remind you of northern Alabama. Here you'll find Belmopan, Belize's capital, a sleepy small town of about 16,000 people. From Belmopan you can easily access Belize's scenic Hummingbird Highway, which takes you through the Maya Mountains. Some foreign retirees who have chosed to live in the Cayo District have purchased small farms and ranchettes, where they've built homes with gardens and groves.

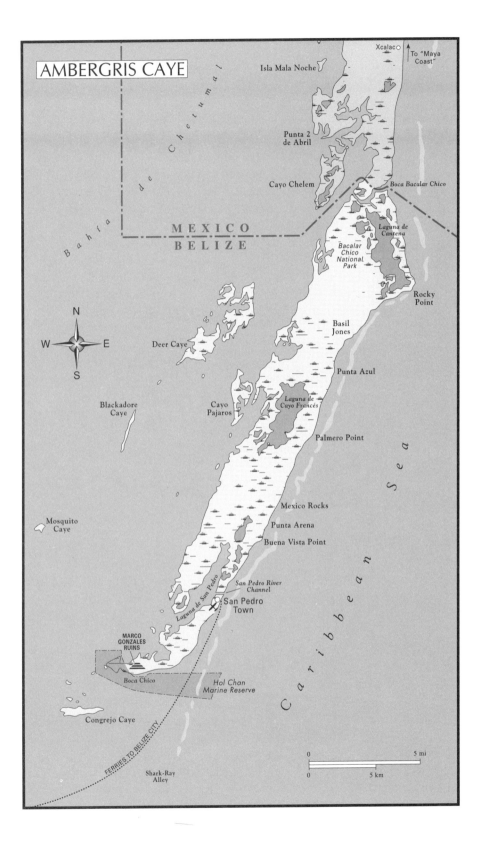

14 Ambergris Caye

Even if you're a world traveler with a bazillion frequent flyer miles, chances are you'll be impressed by your first visit to the islands of Belize. Set in some of the clearest waters you can imagine, with underwater visibility up to 200 feet or more, scores of travel-poster islands dot the Caribbean along Belize's 180-mile-long barrier reef. The reef is an undersea rainforest of incredible diversity, with wildly colored corals and tropical fish, swooping manta rays, and watchful barracudas. Some islands are just spits of coral and sand, here today and possibly gone tomorrow, following a tropical storm. Others are mangrove islands. Three—Turneffe, Lighthouse, and Glover's—are Pacific-style atolls, with some of the best diving in the entire Caribbean.

Ambergris Caye is the largest and most populous of Belize's islands with a population of around 9,000, according to preliminary figures from Belize's 2000 census. About 24 miles long and four miles wide at its widest point, it gets more tourists and has more tourism development than any other part of the country. It's also home to the largest concentration of foreign expats, with estimates of up to 1,000 on the island, and more arriving daily. Don't worry, though, everything is relative, and this is Belize. While Ambergris Caye—locally pronounced Am-BURR-jess Key or sometimes Am-BURR-griss—is no longer the sleepy island of a couple thousand people it was 25 years ago, even today the tallest building is just three stories, no higher than a coconut palm. Except for some cobblestone paving near the airstrip, the streets are all sand. More cars and trucks have been brought to the caye, but golf carts, bikes, and what the Chinese call the Number 11 bus—your legs—are still the main ways to get around.

Expatriates are attracted to Ambergris Caye for its friendly, laid-back lifestyle, combined with a resort atmosphere with plenty of good restaurants, bars and shops, and, of course, lots of activities on the Caribbean, from snorkeling and diving to windsurfing, sailing, and sports fishing. The island is usually among the first stops for those thinking about relocating to Belize, even if they end up choosing another area. Real estate and other costs here are among the highest in Belize, but the level of services also is higher than in many other parts of the country. Residents say that, real estate costs aside, they can live on the island for considerably less than what it costs them to live in the United States. While it's not for everyone, it offers the closest thing to "American-style" living that you'll find in Belize.

> *The island is usually among the first stops for those thinking about relocating to Belize, even if they end up choosing another area.*

The island is shaped something like a banana, hanging down from Mexico's Yucatán peninsula. Indeed, except for a narrow channel at its northern edge, dug by the ancient Maya, Ambergris would be an extension of the peninsula instead of an island. Much of the development has taken place in and around the island's only town, San Pedro, located about three-fourths of the way down the island from its northern tip. Once a fishing village, San Pedro now focuses on tourism, but in a low-key, laid-back way. Most of the resorts on the island are owned by American and Canadian investors, though the vast majority of shops, restaurants, and dive shops are run by Belizeans.

In the fall of 2000, Ambergris Caye, along with neighboring Caye Caulker, was hit hard by Hurricane Keith, the first major hurricane to strike Belize since Hurricane Hattie in 1961. Winds of up to 125 miles per hour pounded the island for much of two days. At least three San Pedro residents, including two American expatriates, died in the storm. Scores of houses, mainly in poorer areas on the backside of the island, were destroyed. Dozens of foreign property owners had water and wind damage to their vacation or retirement homes, and a number of the island's resort hotels were closed for a period of several months for repairs. However, by early 2001, the island had returned more or less to normal. Hotels were brimming with guests, restaurants and shops were open, and local residents had rebuilt their homes and businesses, in many cases improving them thanks to insurance payments.

A Tour of the Island

Let's take a quick tour of the island and San Pedro Town. Along the way, we'll meet some of the interesting folks who live here.

If you're a veteran Caribbean island hopper, you'll recognize San Pedro Town immediately. In many ways, it's the Caribbean of 30 years ago, before the boom in international travel, a throw-back to the days before giant cruise ships turned Caribbean islands into concrete minimalls hustling duty-free liquor and discount jewelry.

In San Pedro there are just three north-south streets, each of hard-packed sand. Wood houses and small shops, painted in bright tropical colors, stand close together. Newer buildings are of reinforced concrete, optimistically girded for the next hurricane.

In an unexpected nod to public relations, a few years ago the local town council changed the names of the town's main streets. Front Street became Barrier Reef Drive; Middle Street was renamed Pescador Drive, and Back Street, Angel Coral Street. Locals, of course, still use the old names.

Many of the town's hotels, restaurants, and tourist shops are on Front, er, Barrier Reef Drive. Just beyond the little primary school at the south end of town is the bite-sized San Pedro Library. Here you don't need a library card to check out books, and even tourists can borrow a book or two for free. Next door is Rubie's, locally owned and the best cheap place to stay on the island, with budget rooms for under US$25 and new air-conditioned rooms on the water for around US$50.

At the Sea Gal Boutique in the Holiday Hotel, gift-shop owner Celi Jean Greif Varela is putting out new inventory bought in Guatemala, Mexico, and Miami. She's the daughter of John Greif, Sr., an American pilot in World War II who came to the island in the 1960s and started the predecessor to what is now Tropic Air, one of Belize's two commuter airlines, and Celi Nuñez McCorkle, who started the Holiday Hotel. The Holiday was one of the first hotels to open on the island, in 1965, when a room and three meals were just US$10 a day. A little farther up the street, you can't miss the hulking concrete Spindrift Hotel, home of the famous "chicken drop" where on Wednesday nights tipsy tourists bet on which square a chicken will poop. The winner gets US$100 and has to clean up the droppings. Sounds like fun, huh?

Beyond Central Park—the name is grander than the park, a little square of sand and cement where kids play basketball and street vendors sell delicious tacos and barbecue for almost nothing—there's Big Daddy's disco, the island's busiest bar and a spot where harder-drinking expats are always to be found. One of the island's characters, "Sexie Eddie" as he calls himself, is talking with a couple of young tourists. Known as a "big sweetheart" by most locals, Eddie tells the youngsters to stay in school and get a college education. "Pisano," another of the town's well-known street characters, claims he was once the island's richest man, but the white-haired gentlemen now naps on the steps of local hotels.

The Catholic church, near the park with a statue of the town's patron saint, St. Peter, out front, is cool and welcoming. Masses are in Spanish and English. Farther up on the left is the Ambergris Caye Museum, cozy but full of interesting stuff from the attics of island grannies. There are two banks, about ten gift shops, and all along the street are small cafés, where residents and visitors alike stop in for a chat or a cold drink. There's even a popular cybercafé where you can check your email. Up the street a block or two, in a blue-painted frame house, lives Ramon Badillo, a sun-tanned and outgoing Mestizo who with his family runs boat trips and guided tours. He says he's "70 years old Belize, 35 U.S.," in a joking reference to the standard exchange rate for Belizean currency.

To the east, beyond the line of low buildings on Barrier Reef Drive, accessible through many alleys, is the Caribbean Sea in all its green and turquoise glory. A narrow strip of beach and seawall between the buildings and the sea is used as a pedestrian walkway. Many piers jut out into the sea. Piers in San Pedro are valuable real estate: rents for a pier and a shack for a bar or dive shop can run US$1,000 or more a month. The patch of white you see a few hundred yards out is surf breaking over the barrier reef. Don't try swimming out to the reef from the shore. There is a lot of boat traffic inside the reef, and over the years several swimmers have been killed or injured by boats.

Middle Street, or Pescador Drive, the other main north-south venue, is also busy. It's home to the original location of Rock's Grocery, an oversized convenience store, and one of the island's four main supermarkets. Hungry? The Reef restaurant, just up the street, is one of the places where locals eat. You can enjoy a huge plate of stewed chicken or fresh snapper with rice and beans, perhaps with a Belikin beer, for under five bucks.

Around the corner, on Caribeña Street, is the island's only casino. The Palace is small and homey as casinos go, with some slots and a few live tables, where the maximum bet on blackjack is US$10. A new floating casino and nightclub, to be docked between the shore and the reef, has been proposed. Many locals hope the floating casinos idea goes the way of a Cancun-style swim-with-porpoises park proposed a few years back. It was canned. Another land-based casino, for a historic building on Front Street, reportedly also is in the works.

As you go farther north on Middle Street, San Pedro becomes more residential. You'll see the San Pedro Supermarket, the Belize Electric and Belize Telecommunications Ltd. electric facilities, a small high school, playground, and then the San Pedro River. Homes in this area, mostly

Belizean-style places occupied by long-time residents, go for US$15,000 and up. At least, that's the Belizean price. Foreigners might be asked much higher prices.

A hand-pulled ferry will take you across the river channel to the other side in about 60 seconds, for US$0.75. A narrow golf cart and walking path wends its way north, mostly on the backside of the island. Stop at Sweet Basil deli for picnic fixings, or some of the imported treats you miss, such as Stilton cheese or prosciutto. A bit farther north on the water is Capricorn, a resort with just three rooms and the best—and one of the priciest—restaurants on the island. For around US$30 to $40 a person, plus US$5 for a water taxi, you can enjoy a dinner of rosemary foccaccia, French crepes with seafood, and a decent wine. The cart path continues to Captain Morgan's Retreat, a resort where some of the thatched cabañas on the beach are gradually being replaced by two-story condo villas.

Everyone who comes up here asks about the Essene Way, just north of Captain Morgan's. Developed in the mid-1990s by an eccentric health food magnate from Orlando and originally designed as a US$7 million millennium retreat, these days the Essene Way is mostly deserted, its solar arrays idling, its tennis courts and swimming pool usually empty, its kitchy biblical statuettes in a Disneyesque Garden of Eden fading under the sun.

Toward the end of the developed part of North Ambergris is Rendezvous, a Thai-French fusion restaurant, one of the growing collection of sophisticated eateries on the island. It was opened by a couple who had lived for years in Thailand, Singapore, and elsewhere in Asia. Next door is Journey's

Avalon Reef Club (formerly Casa Caribe) condos on North Ambergris Caye.

Marty Casado

KILLER BEES IN THE GARDEN

John Lankford was a 37-year-old lawyer in New Orleans when he first visited Ambergris Caye in 1982. Intrigued by what he saw, he came back a second time six weeks later. "I found five acres with a house and bodega I couldn't afford, and on return to New Orleans called the owner and agreed to buy it on the Gringolian plan: There. I've bought it. Now how the hell do I pay for it?" It took him about 11 years to pay for it, he says, with periodic commutes to resample life on the island. John finally moved to San Pedro full-time in 1993–94.

Then, John says, he had to figure out how to keep himself in rice and beans. "There were things that would pay a living in San Pedro that I could do, if necessary. I made a list of about ten activities I thought I could handle and, with unwavering perspicacity, picked the one that would return the least money for the greatest effort—market gardening." He found growing bananas and papayas easy but boring. As he added specialty crops such as herbs, he had to work harder for less money.

But he enjoyed it, says John, "and it did wonders for my middle-aged physique. I remember one day, humping an 80-pound stalk of bananas down the street in mid-summer, barefoot, sweat streaming off of me, en route to a restaurant that had ordered them, I suddenly thought of my former colleagues in three-piece suits and an air-conditioned office. 'Poor guys,' I said out loud."

Then, one day, while riding on his tractor, he came upon a hive of Africanized bees, which are common in Belize. They had made their home in an old stump. "With a cloud of angry bees, irritated by the low-frequency vibrations and fumes of the tractor engine, around me, I resorted to the last-chance strategy: act innocent. Thereby I discovered the secret to 'killer' bees. So long as a person doesn't slap, run, or make frantic moves, they can't identify the enemy. They may land on you and walk around, but they don't sting. Killer bees let you get away with murder, and their products are routinely harvested by local people in the bush."

However, John adds one reservation about his way of dealing with Africanized bees: "It's like swimming with sharks, barracudas, or morays. It's almost completely safe, but remember that a bad day is always possible." These days, John spends his time reading philosophy and on the Internet.

End, at 90 rooms the caye's largest resort by far, and now owned by a family from Ghana who live in Texas.

Like a number of other North Ambergris resorts and restaurants, Capricorn, Captain Morgan's, Rendezvous, and Journey's End all had significant damage from Hurricane Keith. They were closed for weeks after the storm and had no electricity for several months, but all have now reopened.

Various plans have been announced to develop large new luxury hotels on North Ambergris, but so far these plans have proved to be mostly hot air.

Beyond the last resorts is a large, undeveloped tract. Over the years, many schemes have been floated for this part of the island. Much of this area has been saved from Cancunization thanks to establishment of the Bacalar Chico National Park and Marine Reserve. The park, which opened in 1996, comprises 12,000 acres of land and 15,000 acres of water. At present the park is accessible by boat from San Pedro, from the Belize mainland at Sarteneja and elsewhere, and from the Mexican port village of X'calak. The park is home to a surprisingly large population of birds and wildlife, including several of Belize's wild cats, and there are a number of Maya sites.

If you visit North Ambergris, be sure to take plenty of bug spray, and wear light-colored clothes, because away from the breezes or the mosquito control efforts of San Pedro Town, the "mozzies" can be terrible, especially in the late summer after the seasonal rains.

Had you headed south from town rather than north, you'd be on Coconut Drive, another sandy little roadway and the only route to the south of the island. Only about a hundred yards of the road, near the airstrip, and another short section at the Island Supermarket, the largest grocery on the island, have been paved. You'll pass clusters of small resorts and hotels, including Caribbean Villas, owned by a dentist from the United States and his wife, and Coconuts, a small hotel developed by a couple from Montana. The beachfront Island Academy (tuition US$250 a month), one of the better private schools in Central America, was founded by Barry Bowen, Belize's beer, soft-drink, and shrimp-farming magnate and one of the country's wealthiest power brokers, as a place for his young daughter to go to school. Barry Bowen has a little 100,000-acre farm in Orange Walk District, where he also owns Chan Chich Lodge and runs Gallon Jug Estates, the only commercial coffee producer in Belize.

To the lagoon side of the road is the San Pablo area, a mostly Belizean residential section, where homes are mostly in the US$40,000 to $200,000 range. There are 12 lagoons on the island, the largest of which is Laguna de San Pedro, just to the west of San Pedro and San Pablo. Considerable development continues along the sea south of town, including the deluxe Villas at Banyan Bay condotel. Two-bedroom condos sell from around US$230,000, or rent for US$225 to $275 a night in-season, if you just want to be a hotel guest. The beach here, Mar de Tumbo, is one of the best on the island.

St. Matthews, an offshore medical school, temporarily is next door to Banyan Bay. The school is building a permanent campus farther south on the island. Demand by medical students has driven up the price of apartment rentals. Some hotels rent out spare rooms to students. St. Matthews students, who pay US$7,000 to $8,000 a semester, occupy apartments at several condo units in the area, at rents of around US$600 to $1,200 a month. Most of the hotels end about two miles south of San Pedro Town. If you continue farther south, by foot or cart, on a you're back in a residential area, with a number of upmarket houses including one owned by musician Jerry Jeff Walker, along with shacks and other assorted digs. As on the north end of the island, mosquitoes are often a problem once you leave the more-developed areas in the south.

The San Pedranos

Maya Indians were the first residents of Ambergris Caye. Some of their history is told in small ruins still remaining, including the Marco Gonzales site near the south tip of the island and several sites in Bacalar Chico park in the north. There are few Mayas on the caye today, however.

The village of San Pedro was founded in 1848 by refugees from the Caste Wars in the Yucatán. The Castes Wars were a series of successful rebellions by the Maya against the Spanish, and the Indian armies drove thousands of Mexicans south to Belize. The Mestizos who settled San Pedro were mostly fishermen (hence the name of the village, after St. Peter) and farmers, and they continued this work on Ambergris Caye. Many native San Pedranos today can trace their ancestry back to the Caste Wars immigration. At home and among themselves, these families, with surnames such as Guerrero, Gomez, and Nuñez, speak Spanish, though they are equally fluent in English. They control the island's politics, along with many of its small businesses.

While there is occasional friction between the local and expatriate communities, usually connected with real estate development, most foreign residents have high regard for their local neighbors. San Pedranos are known for their friendly, easygoing ways, yet they don't fawn for the sake of a tip. Following years of good lobstering and growing tourism, many San Pedranos are financially comfortable, and a few who run successful businesses or who have sold beachfront land are well off even by American standards. Begging and beach hustling are virtually unknown on the island.

The Expatriate Community

Ambergris Caye has more foreign residents than any other area of Belize, but no one knows the exact number. It's somewhere between 500 and 1,000, although not all are full-time residents. The number is growing almost daily. The problem is, how and whom do you count? Are the snowbird couple from Michigan who own a condo on the island and spend winters in it residents or just visitors? Do you count the students at St. Matthews med school? Is the guy who has been here six months and tends bar on the side a local or a beach bum? How about the yachties with their catamarans tied up at a dock? Quite a large number of expatriates on the island are perpetual tourists, in Belize on a visitor's card and here until their money, or perhaps their livers, run out.

"Lots of people come and go with some regularity and it seems like there are new gringos everywhere, but its very hard to say how many actually live here," says San Pedro real estate investment counselor Jesse Cope. "It could be. . . maybe 1,000," he says. Diane Campbell, another real estate agent, puts the number of full-time expats at only about 200, but "most gringos here aren't full-timers—there are a LOT of part-timers."

Many of the island's resorts are owned and operated by expatriates from the United States or Canada. Fairly typical are Wil and Susan Lala. Back in the States, Wil was a dentist and Susan was an artist. They moved to Ambergris Caye, bought a piece of land south of San Pedro, and built two villas on the beach in 1991, which they operate in a hands-on fashion as a 10-unit suites hotel, with rates from US$65 to $225. Guests can swim or fish off the hotel's 325-foot pier or snorkel over a human-assisted minireef (the real barrier reef is a short boat trip away). A "people perch" allows guests to climb up a three-story observation tower and watch birds in the hotel's private birding sanctuary. Susan Lala's bird list has more than 250 species spotted on Ambergris Caye alone.

Tim Jeffers is another American who came to Ambergris Caye, in his case from Montana, to live the island life and to try to make a go of the hotel business. He first built Coconuts, a 12-room hotel on the beach, and then developed Banana Beach, a 36-unit condotel a little less than two miles south of San Pedro, on Mar de Tumbo beach, where one-bedroom suites go for around US$125 a night. Condos here sell for US$105,000 to around $143,000, with 20 percent down and 10 percent interest over 10 years, with a balloon at the end. Overall, hotels in Belize have averaged occupancy rates of less than 40 percent in recent years—in the United States an occupancy rate of under 60 percent is considered a bankruptcy risk—but Jeffers says that, thanks to close attention to

WHAT EXPAT ISLANDERS SAY THEY MISS

Here's a sampling of what Ambergris Caye residents say they miss from their previous life back in the United States:

"Live jazz and artichokes, BUT we got a flat of fresh artichokes for the first time last week. Now all we need is a personal visit by Tony Bennett."

"Actually, nothing."

"I enjoy prowling a big U.S. store or supermarket when I'm there, but don't miss it when I'm gone."

"The *New York Times* on Sunday."

"I envy very low-cost, unlimited Internet access."

"I miss Wal-Mart and Home Depot like you wouldn't believe."

"I can't find a good selection of quality women's lingerie for sale here."

"I would kill for an Arby's beef and cheddar right now. I was never a fast-food person, but now that I can't get it, I'm craving it!"

management, good marketing through both travel agents and the Internet, and competitive pricing, his Ambergris Caye hotels have annual occupancies above 80 percent. Condominium sales have been slow, however, Jeffers says.

Among the new arrivals is Tammy Martinez, an ex-Floridian who is married to a Belizean. She drove from Pensacola, Florida, to Belize in late 1999, in a 1988 Taurus with all her worldly possessions, plus her son and two cats. This is how she remembers it:

"The trip was a nightmare; I still have flashbacks. It took us six days to reach Chetumal. Crossing the Belize border was the most unreal feeling after four days through Mexico feeling totally intimidated by armed men. I wanted to kiss the ground." She ended up in San Pedro, where her husband, who joined her there, quickly found a job as a bartender. It took her a while to find anything, as a work permit for a professional job costs US$750 and employers are reluctant to spring for that much for a perhaps transitory employee. Her husband, as a Belizean, didn't need a work permit. Martinez eventually found work as a timeshare salesperson.

Other expatriates operate bars, restaurants, dive shops, gift shops, sailing charters, the island's ferry boat service, and other small businesses. Several of these businesses are owned by long-time island residents, who were grandfathered in before stricter laws were passed to make it more difficult for small retail shops to be run by non-Belizeans. Selling real estate has become a popular option for new arrivals.

Man wades in mangroves near Ambergris Caye.

Marty Casado

Daily Life

Most expatriates moved here to be close to the Caribbean, and daily life revolves around activities on the water. Depending on their interests, they go fishing or diving, or just they just swim or beachcomb. Cable television is available (under US$20 a month) with more than 40 channels, mostly from the United States.

San Pedro has dozens of shops and stores, but most of them target visitors. Due to high import taxes and to the extra cost of shipping goods from the mainland to the island, costs here for most goods are higher than you'd pay in the United States or in Belize City. The island's four largest groceries (Island Supermarket, Rock's, Rock's II, and San Pedro Supermarket), each about the size of a large convenience store in the United States, have small selections of imported canned goods, cereals, and other items, for generally around twice what you'd pay in a U.S. supermarket. Their selections of meats and vegetables are limited. A 15 oz. box of Kellogg's Raisin Bran cereal is $5.25, a 3 oz. box of Jello brand gelatin is $.90, and a bottle of Gallo Turning Leaf cabernet is $12.50. Belize-produced items are cheaper: a pound of kidney beans is around $0.50 cents, and a liter of One Barrel premium rum is $7.50. Street vendors and a couple of shops sell fresh fruits and vegetables, and seafood is available directly from fishermen. The island has branches of Belize's two local banks, Atlantic and Belize banks, several hardware and building supply stores, plus appliance stores, laundromats, and other stores.

There is a municipal water and sewer system serving San Pedro and surrounding areas, but those living on North or far southern Ambergris have to make do with cisterns, shallow wells, and septic systems. One resident says: "Our water is outrageous because of the process we have to go through to get it. My water bill has been between US$48 and $100 a month since I've been here. We only use it for baths and washing dishes and toilet flushing. There are three of us in the household. We drink rainwater or when it is dry, buy bottled water, which is another added expense."

Electricity, most of it supplied from Mexico, at around US$0.21 per average kilowatt—the more you use the more you pay—is about twice as expensive as you'd pay in the United States and is generally dependable although spot outages do occur.

Despite the relatively high cost of real estate, imported food, and electricity, the overall cost of living on the island is lower than in the United States, say many residents. In part, that's because you don't need all the things you do in the United States—no heating oil, no cars or auto insurance or parking fees, and no fancy wardrobe. Seafood and Belize-produced food are comparatively inexpensive. Medical care, cable television and basic telephone service, though not international long distance, are among the items that are cheaper than back home.

In one way, island residents can save a lot of money: there's little need for a car or high-priced gas. A number of native San Pedranos have brought cars to the island, too many for the limited infrastructure, spurring a moratorium on permits for cars, but few expat island residents have cars. Instead they usually depend on golf carts, which are available used on the island for around US$2000.

> *Most expatriates moved here to be close to the Caribbean, and daily life revolves around activities on the water.*

Ambergris Caye residents say island fever strikes from time to time. Most residents go into Belize City regularly to conduct business, shop for items not available on the island, or to get dental care. Many expats take vacations in the United States, or long weekends in Cayo District or elsewhere in Belize.

If you aren't busy selling real estate or running a hotel, the island offers some volunteer opportunities. Some expats help out at the local library, or do church work (there are two Catholic churches and several Protestant denominations on the island). The San Pedro chapter of the Lion's Club is the island's most active civic organization. Its weekly barbecue on Saturday nights is delicious, cheap (US$3.50), and a fund-raiser for the group's good works.

For those who can't find enough to occupy themselves, substance abuse is always a risk, more so in San Pedro's freewheeling resort atmosphere than in most other areas of Belize. "Booze is ubiquitous here, and barhanging quite the social custom. And, in San Pedro as much as most U.S. cities, you can now add other chemicals. If you're vulnerable, unimaginative, not a self-starter, passive-dependent, maybe Peoria would be a better bet," says John Lankford, an ex-New Orleanian who has lived on the island since 1994.

In the past, expats used to say that their hospitals were TACA, American, and Continental airlines. For top-flight medical care, Americans on the island may still fly to Miami or Houston, or at least pop over to Belize City, but there are now full-time physicians on the island, along with a medical clinic operated by the local Lion's Club. The Lion's Club also is raising money to build a hospital on the island.

Most residents say they feel safe on the island. Burglary and petty thefts are relatively common, but violent crime is rare. Probably the worst crime in modern island history occurred in 1994, when, late at night, American expat Ann Reilly, a gardening writer with some 30 books to her credit, and her British husband, Alan Dines, were attacked and brutally beaten to death in a dark area of beachfront south of San Pedro. The attacker, a

Belizean from Punta Gorda, was eventually caught, tried, convicted, and sentenced to hang.

Real Estate and Rentals

Real estate prices on Ambergris Caye are among the highest in Belize. As elsewhere, prices vary tremendously depending on location and on the specific property. Houses and lots in predominantly Belizean areas, mostly on the backside or lagoon/bay side of the island, tend to be much less expensive than seafront property preferred by foreign investors and residents.

Demand in recent years generally has been strong for beachfront lots and beachfront homes. Appreciation has run 10 to 20 percent per year, according to local real estate brokers. Agents point to beachfront property on North Ambergris, which went for US$450 a front foot in the late 1980s, that is selling for US$1,250 a foot now. Some agents expect that by 2002 seafront land will be US$1,500 a front foot. That, however, may depend on the state of the U.S. economy, as most buyers are Americans and few Belizeans are able—or willing—to pay the current prices.

Condo development continues hot and heavy on Ambergris Caye. A number of hotels are converting some or all of their units to "condotel" status. The idea is to sell now for immediate cash, then make 40 to 60 percent of revenues in management fees for running the hotel for absentee owners. Sales, however, have not always met expectations, as some investors are wary of condominium laws in Belize—condos are new to Belize and exist mainly in San Pedro—and some have been burned by disputes with developers. One-bedroom condos in particular have been in oversupply on the island for several years.

Many developers offer some type of financing, typically 20 percent down, with the balance payable over 10 years at around 12 percent interest. Usually there's a balloon payment at the end of the term.

Building Lots: Caribbean seafront building lots range from around US$800 to $1,250 per beachfront foot. Less-expensive lots generally are on North Ambergris, which is accessible only by ferry or water taxi. Waterfront lots on the lagoon or Chetumal Bay (backside of the island) start at around US$250 per waterfront foot, with backside lots in nicer areas south of San Pedro starting at around US$500 a front foot. Building lots not on the water are much less, starting at around US$12,000, with second-row back from water lots with electric service on North Ambergris running around US$25,000, and around US$30,000 south of San Pedro Town. In general, lots a row back from the sea are just 30 percent of those directly on the water. Buyers should be aware that some beachfront lots have mangroves, not sand, on the waterside, and a permit is required to cut mangroves. Recent offerings include a large tract with 525 feet of beach frontage and 500 feet deep on North Ambergris for US$630,000; a lot with 100 feet of beach frontage and 125 feet deep on North Ambergris for US$67,500; a lot with 150 feet of beach frontage about four miles south of San Pedro for US$185,000; a one-acre lot in a subdivision on the back side of the island, with 200 feet of bayfront footage, US$55,000.

Homes: Two- or three-bedroom modern houses on the beach on North Ambergris Caye (access via water taxi or ferry) range from around US$175,000 to $250,000, or US$130–$150 per square foot. Those south of San Pedro Town on the sea start at around US$200,000 or $150 per square foot. Homes not on the water but with sea views are available from around US$100,000. Homes with "sunset views"—that is, on the westside or lagoon-side of the island—start at around US$75,000 for a simple house on stilts. At the top end, deluxe, recently built beachfront three- and four-bedroom homes may go for US$300,000 to $600,000 or more.

Condos: One-bedroom condos near the water but without sea views start at around US$75,000, and those with sea views run about US$125,000 to $160,000. High-quality two-bedroom condos with sea views range from around US$200,000 to $275,000. Some recent offerings:

TWO-BEDROOM CONDOS:
White Sands Cove: from US$235,000
Royal Palm Villas: from US$150,000
Belize Yacht Club: from US$200,000

ONE-BEDROOM CONDOS:
Banana Beach: from US$105,000, or $142,500
Hotel Playador: from US$85,000
Royal Palm Villas: from US$125,000

Home construction: Building costs on Ambergris are relatively high, due to the need to dig deep foundations and install pilings for stability in the sandy soil, and to build with hurricane protection in mind. Bringing building supplies in by barge also adds to the cost. Expect to pay US$60 a square foot and up for quality reinforced concrete construction. As elsewhere in Belize, labor costs are lower than in the United States, but most building materials are more expensive. An exception is native hardwood lumber, which is beautiful and cheap.

Rentals: Demand is fairly tight for rentals on the island. A "North American–style" two-bedroom unfurnished house rents for from US$600 to $1,500 a month, and a one-bedroom US$400–$800, depending on location and length of lease. Small apartments start at US$250 a month, with modern one-bedroom furnished apartments going for about US$400–$600. A furnished one-bedroom condo rents for US$600–$1,200 a month, including utilities. Off-season rentals are cheaper than during high season (roughly Thanksgiving to Easter).

Real Estate Agents

Ambergris Seaside Real Estate, P.O. Box 163, San Pedro, Ambergris Caye; tel. 501/2-64223, email seaside@blt.net.
Diane Campbell, San Pedro, tel. 501/2-64032; email camp@btl.net.
Sunrise Realty, P.O. Box 80, Barrier Reef Dr., San Pedro, Ambergris Caye; tel. 501/2-63737, fax 2-63379; email sunrise@btl.net; www.sunrisebelize.com.
Triton Properties, Barrier Reef Dr., San Pedro, Ambergris Caye; tel. 501/2-63783, fax 2-62403; email triton@btl.net; www.triton-properties.com.

Weather and Climate

The climate on Ambergris Caye is similar to that in Southern Florida. In the summer, temperatures often rise into the 90s, with lows in the 70s. In winter, the temps are cooler, typically in the 80s by day, 60s at night. A near constant breeze from the water makes it seem cooler, however, and in winter a long-sleeved shirt or light sweater may feel good, especially after you've lived on the island for awhile.

The high season for tourists and snowbirds is from Thanksgiving to Easter; occasionally during this period *Nortes* or "Northers" can blow in, bringing several days of rain and rough seas. Like the rest of northern Belize, Ambergris Caye has a dry season in the spring, from around February to May. Winds usually kick up during this time, but water visibility is at its peak.

Tropical storm season begins in June and runs through November, yet during most of this period the weather is pleasant, and it's fairly rare to get rain for more than a few hours at a time. On average, Ambergris Caye receives about 50 inches of rain a year, about the same as Atlanta, Georgia.

As noted, hurricanes are relatively rare, though Hurricane Mitch gave the island a scare in 1998 and Hurricane Keith in 2000 did as much as US$150 million in damage on Ambergris Caye alone. Besides Keith in 2000, the most devastating hurricanes to hit the island were in 1931, 1942, and 1961.

Recreation

Surrounded by water and just a few hundred feet from the Belize barrier reef, Ambergris Caye offers water sports of every kind. You couldn't ask for better fishing. For sports fishing, shallow bonefish and tarpon flats are only a few minutes away. In deeper water around the reef, you can catch grouper, snapper, wahoo, mackerel, jack, barracuda, and more. It doesn't necessarily take a fancy boat or a lot of equipment to catch fish. You can drop your hook in off a pier and, chances are, pull in supper. Diving around Ambergris Caye is very good, though not quite as good as around the atolls farther out. Snorkeling, especially off Mexico Rocks on North Ambergris, and in the Hol Chan marine reserve, is world class. In the Shark-Ray Alley area of Hol Chan, you can snorkel with nurse sharks and huge stingrays. Don't worry—they're gentle, at least most of the time.

Maya Indians were the first residents of Ambergris Caye.

Few San Pedro families would be caught dead without a boat, which range from small mahogony skiffs to modern fiberglass speedboats with twin 125-horse Honda motors. Expats have sailed in on everything from island trawlers to big catamarans. The shallow waters, hidden coral heads, and tricky winds and currents mean, however, that boating around Ambergris Caye is not like boating on a calm lake back home. Even skilled sailors with years of local experience have gone aground on the reef, a sure way to rip the hull of the boat to smithereens, and something that doesn't help the fragile reef either.

Kayaking on the lagoon side of the island is popular, and windsurfing between the reef and the shore is a growing sport. January through April have the best conditions for windsurfing, with consistent 15+ mph winds.

Although there is no golf course on Ambergris Caye, there is one on Caye Chapel, about 45 minutes away by boat. Larry Addington, a wealthy Kentucky industrialist, is trying to turn Chapel into a center for corporate retreats. The Caye Chapel course, which opened in mid-2000, is a par-72 laying beautifully along the Caribbean, flat but long, playing to over 7,000 yards, with four par-5 holes. Between the back and front nines is a 23,000 square foot clubhouse, the equal of any at a tony country club in the United States. Plans also call for an Olympic-sized swimming pool, work-out center, tennis complex with lighted courts and a basketball arena, all to be located near the clubhouse. Accommodations on the island are limited to twelve 3,000-square foot villas, which go for a whopping US$1,000 a night. Current greens fees are US$200 for unlimited play for one day, cart, clubs, lunch and as many Belikins as you can drink.

Tennis buffs will find slim pickings on Ambergris. At present, besides courts at two island hotels, Journey's End and Essene Way, the only courts are those at San Pedro High School.

How to Get There

You can fly to San Pedro or go by boat.

Belize's two commuter airlines, Tropic Air and Maya Island Air, have flights at least hourly during daylight hours to San Pedro. It's cheaper to fly from the old Municipal Airport in Belize City (about US$26 one-way) than from Philip S. W. Goldson International Airport north of Belize City at Ladyville (about $47 one-way). However, if you're connecting from a flight from the United States, it's easier just to walk a few feet to the domestic terminal at the International Airport than to transfer by taxi (US$17.50) to Municipal. Arrival is at the airstrip at the south end of town. San Pedro hotels meet the flights, and taxis (US$5 or less to most destinations) also are available.

A number of small ferry and water-taxi boats connect Belize City with San Pedro. The cost is US$12.50 one way for the 75-minute trip. The most dependable boats are operated by the Caye Caulker Water Taxi Association and leave from the Marine Terminal on North Front Street, near the Swing Bridge, arriving San Pedro at the old Sharks Dock near the Holiday Hotel and Cannibals café. The fast, open boats, powered by twin outboard motors, currently make the trip to and from San Pedro three times a day.

Tarzan's, one of the island's night clubs

Lan Sluder

Other boats depart from the Court House Wharf and from the Texaco gas station, North Front Street.

Sources of More Information

By far the best source of information on Ambergris Caye is the AmbergrisCaye.com website. Operated by Marty Casado, an Oregonian who fell in love with the island, the website has more than 6,000 pages of information including detailed information on hotels, restaurants, diving, fishing, house rentals, and real estate. Of course, a lot of the information is paid advertising, so use it with a healthy dose of skepticism.

The *San Pedro Sun* is a chatty, casual weekly newspaper covering news and gossip about Ambergris Caye, published by U.S. expats Dan and Eileen Jamison. A six-month subscription outside of Belize is US$40. Contact information: P.O. Box 35, Ambergris Caye, Belize, C.A., tel. 011-501/2-62070, fax 2-62905; email sanpdrosun@btl.net. The newspaper has a Web edition at www.ambergriscaye.com/sanpedrosun.

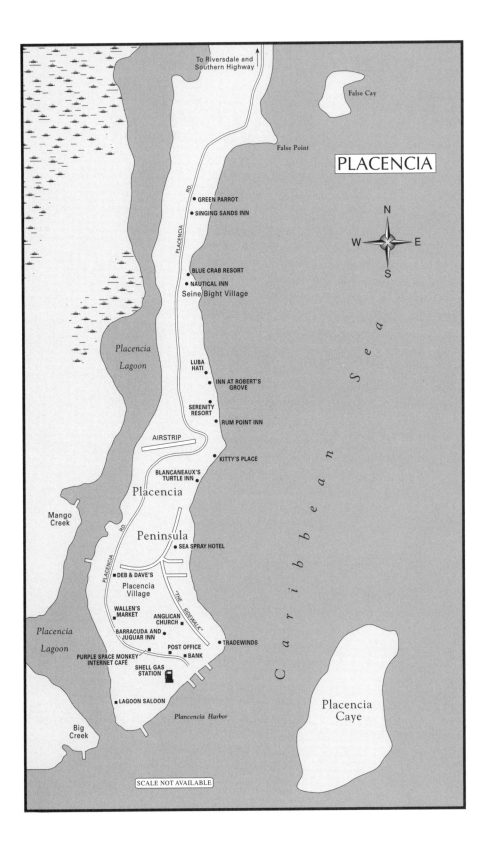

15 Placencia

If you're looking for a little bit of the South Pacific on the Caribbean coast of Central America, Placencia may be for you.

Indeed, film director Francis Ford Coppola, fresh from a visit to Bali and full of ideas about that beautiful island, in late 2000 bought Turtle Inn, a small hotel on the beach near Placencia village. The director of the *Godfather* movies, who also owns Blancaneaux Lodge in the Mountain Pine Ridge, brought in an architect from Indonesia to assess the beachside resort and to help plan its future development, which reportedly will be along the lines of hotels on Bali.

Placencia, in Stann Creek District, is a skinny peninsula on the southern coast of the mainland. The peninsula, only a few hundred feet wide at some points, lays between the Caribbean Sea on the east and the Placencia Lagoon on the west. The two main population centers are Seine Bight and Placencia villages, which combined have fewer than 1,500 people. While there are no other villages on the peninsula itself, a number of houses and small hotels dot the unnamed main road that runs down the spine of the peninsula; the largest concentration is in Maya Beach, about nine miles north of the southern tip of the peninsula. Across the lagoon—part of which is being used as a shrimp farm, to the dismay of environmentalists who worry about the impact on the native marine life—are several villages, including Mango Creek, Independence, and Big Creek, Belize's only true deepwater port. These mainland villages get few tourists, but they enjoy a modest prosperity from agriculture—mainly citrus—shipping, and shrimp farms.

Everywhere the land is low-lying and flat, although the hulking Maya Mountains are visible to the west.

Tourism boosters in Placencia brag that they have the best beaches in Belize. Not everyone would agree, pointing to rival stretches of sand on Ambergris and other cayes, and to the mainland beaches around Hopkins. But Placencia certainly has the longest beach in Belize, running with few interruptions some 16 miles along the sea. The beaches are narrow, rarely more than 15 or 20 feet wide, with toast-colored sand.

> *Placencia certainly has the longest beach in Belize, running with few interruptions some 16 miles along the sea.*

Like most beaches in Belize, these are only fair for swimming, as the water near shore is shallow and there's a good deal of sea grass, except where property owners have removed it around piers. You can snorkel here and there off the beaches, but for world-class snorkeling you'll have to take a boat out to the reef or to one of the small offshore cayes, a 10- to 20-mile boat trip. Several marine national parks and reserves are within an hour or two by boat, including Laughing Bird Caye and Port Honduras. The Caribbean is incredibly beautiful, above and below the surface. Above, the crystal clear water sparkles in the sun. Poke your head below, and you find a whole new universe of color and activity, from tiny tropical fish to dolphins and manatees.

Every year in the late spring, usually April through June, large groups of whale sharks *(Rhincodon typus)* appear in an area called Gladden Spit on the barrier reef about 25 miles from Placencia. These gentle giants—they can reach 40 feet or more in length but eat nothing larger than plankton or tiny fish—are occasionally sighted in much of the tropics and even in colder waters, but Belize is one of only about half a dozen places in the world where aggregations of them predictably appear year after year.

Placencia offers some of the best sports fishing in Belize. Anglers enjoy fly fishing in Placencia Lagoon and on the Monkey River south of Placencia, fly or live bait fishing around the cayes, and open water spinning and trolling inside and outside the reef. This also is one of the best areas in Belize for catching permit. There's world-class fishing for tarpon, snook, and bonefish. Inside and around the reef you can catch barracuda, snapper, king mackerel, wahoo, yellow- and black-fin tuna, just to name a few. Visitors should expect to pay about US$200 to $250 for two persons per day, including boat, guide, and equipment.

While there's little to do here beyond water activities, and the biggest store on the peninsula is about the size of your living room, Placencia has some of the best hotels and restaurants in Belize. All are small, personality places. The biggest inn on the beach has fewer than two dozens rooms, and a restaurant with 10 tables is considered a large operation.

This combination of easygoing resort atmosphere, myriad water activities, and plenty of beachfront has attracted a growing number of real estate buyers, although as yet few of the buyers have built homes or taken up residency.

Placencia's Two Villages

Placencia village, at the southernmost tip of the peninsula, is a predominantly Creole village of about 600 people. Most of the area's restaurants and shops, such as they are, are located here. To the west of the village is the lagoon, to the east the sea, and to the south a small harbor. A mile-long concrete sidewalk runs up the center of the village. A stroll up and down the sidewalk will give you a good introduction to life in the village, which centers around relaxing, tourism, and fishing, roughly in that order. Many of the residents in Placencia village are related to each other, and you'll hear the same last names over and over again, such as Cabral, Leslie, Eiley, and Westby.

Seine Bight is a Garifuna village of around 700 people located about five miles north of Placencia village. This is a village deep in cultural change, with the traditional Garifuna society under siege from tourists, developers, and general modernization. With no little irony, one of the most successful

The Nautical Inn on the Placencia Peninsula

Lan Sluder

businesses in the village, a combination restaurant, bar, and a place for tourists to experience Garifuna-style music and drumming, is named Kulcha Shak. It's pronounced Culture Shock.

Painted, ramshackle frame houses stand elbow to elbow with multimillion dollar resorts. Groups of uniformed Garifuna school children walk along the dusty or muddy road to the new school, a two-story concrete building that opened in 2000. In this matriarchal society, Garifuna grannies and moms run the homes and tend small shops, while the men fish or hang out at Sam's or Wamasa, two local bars.

The Expatriate Community

Until recently, the expatriate community in Placencia numbered in the single digits, and almost all of them were involved in running the peninsula's hotels, restaurants, bars, dive shops, and real estate agencies. Beginning in the late 1990s, a boom in real estate sales attracted more Americans and Canadians to this area. However, few have as yet built homes or settled in permanently, but an increasing number of retirees and the almost retired come down to spend a few weeks or months of the year clearing their lots and making plans to build. Enough construction is going on to keep a couple of building supply companies in business.

Most foreign residents still are involved in some way with tourism. Among the hotels owned by expatriates are Inn at Robert's Grove, Singing Sands, Luba Hati, Miller's Landing, Green Parrot, Blue Crab, Serenity, Blancaneaux's Turtle Inn, Xcape, Barracuda and Jaguar Inn, Nautical Inn, Mariposa, and Barnacle Bill's.

HOW TO MAKE IT IN BELIZE

Karen Cochran, an American who owns a house in Independence across the lagoon from Placencia, explains her views on how to get along in Belize: "To live in Belize, you need to have a sense of adventure. Also, you have to have some skills. You need to be able to change a tire, have some mechanical skills and some basic knowledge of how things work. I would be the first to admit that the only skill I have is I could walk 10 miles for help if I had to, but I possess none of the others. Good thing that I have my husband, Bob, because he knows all of these things. He knows cars, plumb-

ing, electricity, cement, fiberglass, boating, lawn mower repair, weed eater repair, cabinets, how to tile, just lots of things.

The Belize that I know is rough. Women still wash their clothes by hand, some of the homes have rats in the ceiling, and roaches are a whole other story. Only a handful of Belizeans that we know have hot water. Several still have outhouses. The bugs can be horrendous and the living conditions hard. One of the best seats in the house we stayed in for years was and still is a seat out of a truck. Thank God that plastic chairs made it to Belize."

Ben and Jane Ruoti, owners of the Nautical Inn, a 12-room seaside hotel in Seine Bight, moved to Placencia from Arizona in the early 1990s. He imported prefab octagonal buildings from North Carolina and had them constructed on his four acres in Seine Bight. "We were middle-aged crazy," says Ruoti. "I was making too much money and not having enough fun. We needed a change and a better lifestyle—things that money really couldn't buy, like waking up to a Caribbean sunrise and walking on your beach, or eating fresh food not loaded with preservatives."

While the inn has been a moderate success—over the years the Ruotis have expanded and added a swimming pool—as of this writing the hotel is for sale. That's not unusual in a market where hotel occupancies are highly seasonal, average less than 30 percent year-round, and drop to almost nothing in September and October. In 2000, at least a dozen properties on the peninsula were on the market, at prices ranging from less than $200,000 to more than $3,000,000.

Ruoti says his experience in Placencia has been well worth the occasional problems he and his wife have faced. "We would definitely do it again. The pluses are the wonderful weather and people. The minuses are the roads and finding special parts and skilled workers."

Maralyn Gill is one of the newcomers to Placencia, though not to Belize. She's a fair-skinned ex-Californian who once designed clothes for members of the Grateful Dead band. Her husband, Albert, is a Creole Rastafarian originally from Belize City. They met in Eugene, Oregon, where he was playing in a reggae band. Together they came back to Belize with their three children and started a spice and wine company. Later they opened a restaurant at a hotel in San Pedro, moved to a new location, and then moved to another spot. As it turns out, they're now packing up and leaving San Pedro altogether. Their neighbors objected to the loud reggae music, Maralyn says, and she tired of paying the high Ambergris Caye rents, as much as US$2,500 for a restaurant space. They hope to do better in Placencia. Albert Gill and his band play at Rum Point Inn, and Maralyn is cooking up new business ideas.

Karen Cochran a 48-year-old Ft. Myers, Florida, resident tells how she ended up in the Placencia area, across the lagoon in Independence: "For some unknown reason we just knew that we would not end up in the States. Back in 1989, we saw an ad in the local paper here in Fort Myers advertising land for sale in Belize. The deal was that you could buy a certain amount of acres and the developer would match this amount—put so much money down and make monthly payments. This development was north of Crooked Tree in Belize District and called the Revenge Lagoon. Part of the deal was that you had six months to go to Belize (pay your own way) and see if you liked the acreage that you had picked. If you did not and another plot was found and available that you like you could switch your choice. So we first flew into Belize March of 1989. At that time there were only two hotels listed, the Fort George and the Bellevue. We picked the Bellevue. It was horrible. First evening the air-conditioning in the room did not work and we went down to the desk to report the problem. A nice Belizean said to me, 'Well, Miss, perhaps you do not know how to run the air-conditioner.' The result was that about an hour later they showed up, took the wall unit away, and left. So there we sat with a hole in the wall.

The next day a representative from British American Cattle Co. showed up and took us to see the property that we had selected. He had a regular spiel about how this area would develop and so on and so on. We did see possibilities for the future development of the Revenge Lagoon area. We flew home and thought to ourselves, 'OK, we will keep making our payments and see what happens.'

Several months later a gentlemen came to our business in Fort Myers, and we happened to mention the word Belize. He said 'Hey, I have been to Belize. In fact I have a friend who has a Belizean woman visiting and I would you like to meet her.' Sure, we said, so off we went to visit. It turned out to be a delightful older woman named Mrs. Gertrude Mena from Independence. She said, 'Why don't you come south and visit us the next time that you come to Belize? Think you would enjoy our part of the country.' It turns out that she has seven children of her own plus one boy that boarded with her. We took her up on her offer, and my husband, Bob, and her oldest son formed quite a friendship. The first time down we stayed in small one-bedroom house and met the Mena family and wandered around the village. So that is how we ended up in Belize and the Independence area.

After about 30 visits to Independence over a five- to six-year period, we decided that perhaps we should consider building our own home. At that time there was nothing that you could buy and there really still is not. A friend was able to get a lot for us and we went about building our own home. Since Independence is not a town, there is no planning or building department. You just go ahead and do what you want. We at first thought that maybe we wanted to be down by the water. But after seeing the damage that the sand flies and bugs can do to you decided that was not a good decision. So we ended up with a lot over by the village water tower. Actually it is a big lot as lots sizes go in Belize. What started out as a plan to construct a cement house in a year and a half took three. The main problem was that when you show up most of the construction people are already working and you have to pull them off whatever job they are on and see if they will come and work on yours. Our house is a simple two-bedroom, one-bath with an eight-foot veranda surrounding half of it. It is elevated and has two rooms underneath. Currently, we try to go to Belize at least four times a year and usually spend from 10 to 14 days. The plan is to eventually retire to Belize and live there on a permanent basis."

Another American resident of Placencia is Mary Toy. In a previous life, she was an attorney in St. Louis. Now she helps run a fishing guide business with local Kevin Modera. Asked whether she would make the move again, if she had it to do over, she says, "Now that's a million-dollar question."

Toy says: "The first advice I give is come and live here first—for at least six months, but a year would be better. I think it takes that long for us foreigners to begin to develop an understanding of Belize. Belize is beautiful and very seductive for people seeking an escape from the first world rat race. I think the seductiveness stems in large part from its British culture and English as its official language, which makes Belize immediately seem to be a comfortable, safe, and 'just like home' tropical paradise. Trouble is, Belize is not just like home. The cultures, and governmental, political, and legal structures are very different. Most foreigners learn this the hard way, after being scammed a few times and finally realizing that they really have no effective redress, from the police, elected representatives, or the courts. Usually, unless the foreigner is really stupid or has a lot of money to burn, the scams are small—and are very valuable as lessons in how to survive life in Belize."

Indeed, not all expats find smooth sailing in Placencia. Doug Richardson is an American retiree who is building a home on the peninsula. His story in Placencia is a litany of problems and run-ins with Belize government officials and local residents, along with a series of misadventures with tenants of a hotel and restaurant building he owns.

The Caribbean Beach Bug

A couple from the United States come on vacation to Placencia and get nicked by the Caribbean beach bug. No, it's not an insect. It's a fantasy. This couple's fantasy is to run a little hotel while living the easy life by the Caribbean. They have some money saved, and they put it all in a hotel with five or 10 rooms, or they buy a big lot and build. The price they pay is far too high for them to ever earn a decent return on their investment. If they had listened to their accountant, they would have invested their money in a conservative mutual fund where over time they might earn 10 or 12 percent return. But they didn't listen.

With two-thirds or more of their guest rooms vacant most of the time, they struggle to get by. They don't go broke, but they don't make enough money to effectively market their property or to upgrade it to international standards. At first, it's all new and fun. After a while, they get burned out and tired. Maybe he hits the bottle a little too hard. She's angry much of the time.

They put their property up for sale. Years go by. It doesn't sell. Due to financial and business stress, their marriage flounders, and they talk about getting a divorce. Finally, they get an offer for their property. With beachfront property values rising, they do OK. The profit from the sale makes up for a lot of lean years. They take the money, split it, and go back to the United States. They invest their money in a conservative mutual fund. He retires in Florida; she ends up in California.

Happily, most visitors aren't bitten by this bug, or if they are, they recover.

Richardson, an investor and attorney, who lives part of the year in Malibu, California, says his home in Seine Bight, when completed, will be the "finest retirement house in Belize" and claims he has about one million U.S. dollars invested in the property. He had the home built "like a fortress," he says, with the main living area on the second floor, to offer protection from storms and burglars.

"[Anyone] contemplating retiring or other residing in Belize should be aware that public services, utilities, fees, etc. can cost the 'foreigner' as much as 10 times that charged for the same item to the Belizean," Richardson says.

Richardson goes on: "The police can break into your house at any time to search it without a warrant. If Belize Electric wants to run a pole line across your property, they just do it. If the Ministry of Works wants to build a road through your property, they just take as much of your property as they want without due process or compensation."

Daily Life

As in many coastal communities in Belize, daily life for both locals and expatriates revolves around the sea. If you like to dive or fish, this is paradise. Many of the foreign residents own a boat or at least small skiff to poke around the lagoon. The shallow Caribbean can kick up very rough chop, making just boarding a boat on a windy day an adventure. The lagoon side enjoys gentler waters, so if boating is a priority you'll want to have a dock on Placencia Lagoon.

If you don't catch your own, a fishing co-op in Placencia village is a source of inexpensive, ultrafresh fish. That's a good thing, because the local groceries have a limited stock of foodstuffs. The biggest and most popular grocery, Wallen's, is the size of a small convenience store in the United States. The owners, Harold and Lucy Wallen, moved to Placencia in 1974 from Evergreen, Colorado, just after Hurricane Fifi. Initially they sold vegetables and lobsters from their house, later expanding to a location in Placencia village across from the football (soccer) field. In late 1999, in what made headlines in the local monthly newspaper, Wallen's opened the first air-conditioned market in Placencia, adjacent to the old store, which now is used to service wholesale customers. The two-register grocery stocks basic canned foods, some frozen meats, and plenty of rum. During the busy tourist season, and especially around Christmas, the shelves get bare by late in the day. Prices, except for rum, are roughly about twice what you'd pay in a supermarket in the States. Wallen's and the area's two other groceries, Olga's and Placencia Grocery, don't usually have much in the way of fresh fruits and vegetables. Most expatriates buy produce from trucks that come down once or twice a week from Dangriga.

The Placencia area has several churches, including Anglican, Catholic, and Seventh Day Adventist. Sadly, the area also has its share of drug problems, and reputedly one or two crack houses are in operation. The lack of local industry, except for tourism, means that many locals lack gainful employment. Crime, including theft and burglaries, but mostly small-time pilfering from tourists or building sites, is on the increase. In 1998, an American tourist at a hotel in Maya Beach was murdered in a robbery attempt, but violent crime affecting visitors and resident foreigners is rare.

As there are no movie theaters, bowling alleys, or health clubs in Placencia, what social life there is for expats revolves around casual encounters in Placencia village, visits at each other's homes, or meals at local restaurants. The restaurants at Kitty's, Luba Hati, and Inn at Robert's Grove are among the best eating places in southern Belize. They are not inexpensive, however. Dinner for two with drinks and tip runs US$50 to $75 or more at these and similar spots. At casual, modest places such as Cozy Corners or the Pickled Parrot, dinner for two with drinks is usually under US$25. On Tuesdays, the popular Pickled Parrot, a sand-floored eatery run by a Canadian woman, Wende Bryan, in Placencia village, has pizza for US$1.25 a slice and rum drinks for the same price.

Ben Ruoti sets up the pins for "coconut bowling" at his hotel in Seine Bight.

Drinking is a popular pastime among expats, and not a few can be seen from morning to night at local water holes. At happy hour at the Lagoon Saloon, Belizean rum goes for US$0.50 a shot, and some of the regulars really take advantage of the bargain.

Lack of good medical care has long been a drawback for this area. The nearest hospital is a regional one 50 miles away in Dangriga, and until the late 1990s to get to a doctor you had to cross Placencia Lagoon to Independence. However, a full-time nurse, Nurse Reynolds, is now on duty at a medical center in Placencia village, and a

Lan Sluder

visiting Cuban doctor is on duty part-time. Seine Bight village now also has a clinic, with a part-time doc on duty. These days, the peninsula even has an acupuncture center and a massage therapist. Still, for serious trauma or illness, you'll need to go to Dangriga, Belize City, or farther afield.

Most of the peninsula is now on the power grid, and residents of both Seine Bight and Placencia villages enjoy good drinking water piped in from the Maya Mountains. Homes and hotels at the north end of the peninsula at present have to make do with well water or cisterns, along with septic systems for waste disposal. A new garbage dump been established off the peninsula, and along with regular garbage pickups this has improved the appearance of residential areas.

Due to the distance from one part of the peninsula to another, most expat residents find it necessary to have a car. Taxis are expensive, costing US$15 to $20 from Maya Beach to Placencia village. An off-and-on shuttle bus service charges—when it's running—US$2.50 from Maya Beach to Placencia village.

Real Estate

Placencia is in the middle of a real estate boom, at least by Belizean standards. Local property owners and foreign developers are trying to cash in on the demand for property on or near the Caribbean.

For beachfront land in Placencia, you'll have to pay as much as US$1,000 a front foot, though some lots are available for less and larger prime beachfront lots go for US$1,500 a front foot and up. Thus, a lot with 60 feet of beachfront and 100 feet or more deep (the actual depth has surprisingly little to do with the price) would run US$60,000.

Bill Wildman, British by birth, has four decades of experience in land surveying and developing in Belize, including 37 years of surveying on the Placencia peninsula. He's surveyed most of the land there, except in the villages, at least once during that time. He says that this area is finally starting to see some serious activity. With a few exceptions, he says, beachfront lot prices on the peninsula are now around US$600 to $1,000 per front foot. "We sold two waterfront lots at Maya Beach for US$60,000 each, no water or telephone, but with electricity," Wildman says. He continues: "We have a few seafront lots at Surfside just north of Seine Bight listed at about US$1,000 per front foot, but they are top grade, beautiful high sand, well treed, with water, electricity, and telephone. We have one large development tract in the middle of the peninsula running from sea to lagoon for sale at US$675 per front foot and another at US$700, both very good buys. Residential lots on the lagoon side are about one-third the cost of those on the seaside if they do not badly need filling." A resident of Consejo Shores

near Corozal Town, Wildman (tel. 501/4-38005, email blzland@btl.net)
spends part of most weeks in Placencia.

Several other developers are actively selling lots on the peninsula. Coming from the Southern Highway, The Plantation is the first sizable development on the Caribbean Sea. You'll recognize it by the large model home and office on the left. This is a planned resort community with a master land use plan and about three miles of beach. Beachfront lots are in the US$50,000–75,000 range. The contact is Bill Niderver (cell phone tel. 501/01-48363). The Plantation says it is putting in place an alternative energy generation system to provide electricity to the development.

Continuing south, the Maya Beach area is the next landmark and the next development is a subdivision offered by Regent Realty. The contact for this development is John Burk (tel. 501/2-73744 in Belize City).

Placencia offers some of the best sports fishing in Belize.

The next development south is Surfside, also offered by Bill Wildman. Surfside currently has one house under construction, with four sea-front and three lagoon-front residential lots for sale. The rest are strips of sea-to-lagoon lots and offered as resort development sites.

Then you come to a sign that simply says "For Sale." This is a narrow strip of properties, all set back from the beach. The beach itself is an area dedicated for the lot owners. They run about 80 x 120 feet and are in the US$35,000 price range. In addition, there are some lots on the lagoon side. The local contact for this development is Lionel Williams, though everyone knows him by his nickname "John B." His phone number is 501/6-24012.

About a mile south of Seine Bight village, you come to Buccaneer's Retreat, Playa de Piratas, and Smugglers' Landing. The developer of these properties is Ron Shivers (tel. 501/6-23180, fax 501/6-23203, email plyadpirat @btl.net). At Buccaneer's Retreat, the lots, not on the water but with beach access, are priced from around US$40,000 and up. Playa de Piratas, which was the peninsula's first subdivision, has smaller lots priced from US$30,000. Smugglers' Landing has six one-half acre lagoon-side lots starting at US$75,000. The developer promises a marina and a gated entrance for Smugglers' Landing.

Harbour Place (tel. 501/6-23145) is the last development before you get into Placencia village. Prices at this 51-lot subdivision on the lagoon side with planned marina start at around US$30,000 and range up to US$90,000. There's no residential building going on yet, but a lodge is being built. Individual residential lots within Placencia village, not on the water, typically go for US$10,000 to $30,000. Not many completed homes are available for sale on the peninsula. A new two-bedroom, one-bath, 800 square foot house completed in late 2000 near Placencia village was offered for

US$75,000. A small cement home in Maya Beach with 75 feet of beach frontage sold at around US$85,000.

Tourism is the number one industry on the peninsula, and quite a number of visitors dream about running a small hotel on the beach. *(See the Caribbean Beach Bug sidebar elsewhere in this chapter).* At any one time, there are usually eight to ten hotels actively for sale on the peninsula, and nearly all are for sale at some price. Recent sales suggest that hotels on the beach are going for around US$100,000 or more per room, a high price even by U.S. standards and higher still given the relatively low occupancy and room night rates in Placencia. Among recent offerings are Kitty's Place, 11 rooms and cabañas with 340 feet of beach frontage for US$1,500,000; Soulshine Resort, five units with swimming pool, for US$680,000; Sonny's, an eight-unit budget resort in Placencia village for US$800,000; and Nautical Inn in Seine Bight, 12 rooms with pool and beach for US$1,400,000. Several islands off Placencia are for sale. A 100-acre island about a mile south of Placencia village was on the market in 2000 for US$1 million. A 55-acre caye just off the tip of the peninsula was available for US$750,000.

In addition to the developers and agents shown above, Brian Yearwood, Yearwood Properties (tel./fax 501/6-23462, email brian@belizebeach-front.com), has a number of residential and commercial listings on the peninsula.

If you decide to build on the peninsula, residents say you can expect to pay from US$35 to $75 a square foot for construction. At the upper end, construction is concrete with some nice finishings and detailings; at the

The sales office and model home at The Plantation, a real estate development on the Placencia Peninsula

Lan Sluder

lower end, you'll get simple wood construction with the house raised eight to 10 feet on stilts to catch the breeze, reduce problems with bugs, and avoid water damage from storm surges. While the total number of homes under construction on the peninsula is small, it's enough to strain local building resources, and currently there is more demand for qualified builders than there is supply. Mennonites from Cayo District are actively building in Placencia at all price levels. A local company, Professional Building Supplies (tel. 501/6-23238, email pbs@btl.net) is a good source of building supplies and information, and the owner, Steve Christiansen, an American expat, also can help you with high-quality custom-made furniture.

There are few rentals on the peninsula, although off-season hotel owners often rent rooms or cabins on a monthly basis (off-season is roughly the period between Easter and Thanksgiving). When available, modest small houses in Placencia village go for US$250 to $500 monthly. More upmarket homes north of the village rent for US$400 to $1,000 a month, again with very limited availability.

Climate and Weather

Placencia enjoys a subtropical coastal climate. In this part of southern Belize, expect highs in the 80s most of the year, with lows in the 70s. Occasionally in the late fall and early winter, 'Northers blow down bringing chillier temps and rough seas. While it's humid year-round, prevailing breezes off the water make life more comfortable and keep the bugs in their places. Occasionally, mostly in late summer, the winds die down. At those times, the sand fleas and mosquitoes can make your life miserable. Sunny skies are the norm much of the year, but beginning in May or June seasonal rains usually dump a good deal of water on Placencia, continuing periodically until November. Even during the wet season, however, rainstorms usually last just an hour or two, and afterward the sunshine returns, so outdoor activities are practical nearly every day.

How to Get There

Placencia is about three to four hours by car from Belize City, depending on weather and which route you take. Going via the coastal road, a distance of about 115 miles, is shorter, but much of this route is on unpaved roads. After a heavy rain the road turns into mud, and occasionally bridges wash out. Going via the Hummingbird Highway, which connects Belmopan and Dangriga, is a few miles longer, but the Hummingbird is paved and the most scenic road in Belize. From the intersection of the Hummingbird Highway and the Southern Highway, it is about 22 miles to the turnoff to Placencia. Paving is under way on this section of the Southern Highway. Then, from the Southern Highway, it is about nine miles on a dirt/gravel road to Riversdale, the elbow point at which you begin to see the blue Caribbean. From here, it is another 16 miles or so to Placencia village and to the tip of the peninsula. The road down the peninsula is unpaved, and after summer rains it often becomes muddy and difficult to drive, even in a four-wheel-drive vehicle.

Maya Island Air and Tropic Air each have about five flights daily from Belize City. Fares are around US$140 round-trip from the international airport and about one-third less from the municipal airport. A small ferry, the *Gulf Cruza,* does a weekly run from Placencia to Puerto Cortes, Honduras, for about US$50.

By bus, Z-Line has two departures daily from Dangriga. You can make connections in Dangriga from various points north, including Belize City and Belmopan. Cost from Belize City is around US$8. If you are arriving from the mainland across the lagoon at Mango Creek, a little ferry—the *Hokie Pokie*—costs US$5 and usually runs twice a day.

Sources of More Information

Placencia has no radio station or weekly newspaper. The best source of information, besides word of mouth, is the monthly tabloid newsletter, the *Placencia Breeze.* An electronic version of the *Breeze,* along with listings for hotels, restaurants, and other tourist services, is online at www.placencia.com. A tourist information office is near the peninsula's only gas station, a Shell station, at the south end of Placencia village (tel. 501/6-24045, email placencia@btl.net.)

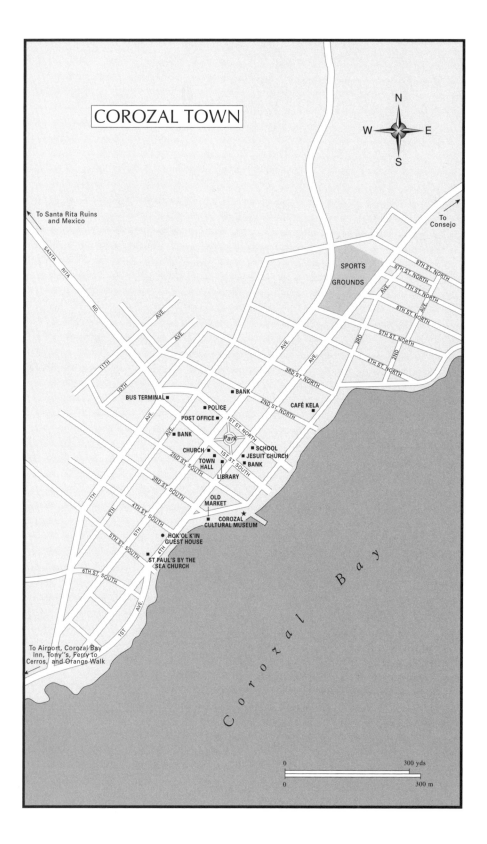

COROZAL TOWN

To Santa Rita Ruins
and Mexico

To
Consejo

SANTA RITA RD.

SPORTS

GROUNDS

8TH ST. NORTH
8TH ST. NORTH
7TH ST. NORTH
6TH ST. NORTH
5TH ST. NORTH
4TH ST. NORTH
3RD ST. NORTH
2ND ST. NORTH
1ST ST. NORTH

AVE.

11TH

10TH

AVE.

AVE.

3RD

2ND

AVE.

BUS TERMINAL ■

■ BANK

■ POLICE

POST OFFICE ■

CAFÉ KELA ■

■ BANK

Park

CHURCH ■

TOWN
HALL

LIBRARY

■ SCHOOL
■ JESUIT CHURCH
■ BANK

1ST ST. SOUTH
2ND ST. SOUTH
3RD ST. SOUTH

7TH
6TH
5TH
4TH

OLD
MARKET

★
CorOZAL
CULTURAL MUSEUM

● HOK'OL K'IN
GUEST HOUSE

■ ST PAUL'S BY THE
SEA CHURCH

4TH ST. SOUTH
5TH ST. SOUTH
6TH ST. SOUTH

AVE.

1ST

To Airport, Corozal Bay
Inn, Tony''s, Ferry to
Cerros, and Orange Walk

Corozal Bay

N
W E
S

0   300 yds
0   300 m

16   *Corozal*

orozal Town doesn't have much sex appeal. Unlike Placencia or some
of Belize's cayes, Corozal has no real beaches and no hot dive spots.
The shopping in Corozal Town is limited. Somewhat off the beaten
tourist track, it sports only a handful of small hotels and restaurants, and
those that are here don't compare with the
deluxe seaside resorts of Ambergris Caye or
the world-class jungle lodges of Cayo District. Aside from some unprepossessing
Maya ruins, there are few notable historical
or cultural sites.

> *Corozal is one of the best-
> kept secrets of Belize*

Yet, Corozal is one of the most pleasant
spots in all of Belize and should rank near
the top of your must-see list if you're thinking of retiring, relocating, or
investing in the country. To use a hackneyed but accurate phrase, Corozal
is one of the best-kept secrets of Belize.

Despite its lack of beaches, the Corozal Town area enjoys a beautiful setting on Corozal Bay (or, as it's referred to by Mexicans, Chetumal Bay.) The
waters of the bay are as blue as those elsewhere on the coast or cayes, and
the breezes from the water as cooling and constant as any in Belize. If
you're an angler, you'll find good fishing for tarpon, bonefish, permit, and
other fish, and boating is enjoyable on the protected waters of the bay. Next
door is Chetumal, capital of the Mexican state of Quintana Roo, with its

good, low-cost medical care and inexpensive shopping. *Corozaleños* are friendly, the crime rate is low, and the climate is sunny with less rain than elsewhere in Belize. Best of all, housing and real estate prices are a bargain. First, though, let's clarify the area we're discussing. Corozal Town is a town of about 12,000 people in northern Belize some nine miles south of the Mexican border. Corozal District is the northernmost district in Belize. It includes not only Corozal Town but also other parts of northern Belize including the Sarteneja peninsula. This chapter focuses on Corozal Town and the immediately surrounding areas only. (*For some information on Sarteneja, see chapter 18.*)

Corozal Town and Environs

Corozal District is 718 square miles in area. The largest town by far is Corozal Town. The town is laid out on a small grid with the most appealing part, with its colorful houses and market, along the bayfront. A nearly constant breeze off the bay cools the homes and businesses near the water, reducing the need for air-conditioning. The Corozal Cultural Centre and Museum, in a landmark building over 100 years old that features a clock tower, is in the waterfront park near the market. Among other interesting artifacts, the museum has hand-blown rum bottles, a traditional Maya thatch hut, and displays from the lighthouse that once stood on this site.

Nearby, on and near the Northern Highway, are "suburbs"—the small villages of Ranchito, Xaibe, Calcutta, San Antonio, and others. Consejo village and Consejo Shores, about 7 miles north of Corozal Town on an all-weather unpaved road on Corozal Bay, have attracted a number of expatriates.

Corozal Town is about 83 miles by road from the International Airport in Ladyville just north of Belize City and nine miles from the Mexican border. As you go north from Corozal Town to the border, you pass *La Laguna de Cuatro Millas* (Four Mile Lagoon) on the right and the Corozal Free Zone complex, a busy duty-free zone that attracts Mexicans for cheap gas and other shopping and which employs some 1,000 Belizeans. The border, marked by the Hondo River and the small village of Santa Elena, has on the Belize side a bustling little frontier station. The Santa Elena crossing processes about 300 arrivals to Belize on a typical a day, a few of them international tourists arriving by bus but most Mexicans coming to Belize for the day or Belizeans returning from shopping trips. Just north of the border is the city of Chetumal, with a population of more than 150,000, larger than any city in Belize.

Much of Corozal District is sugarcane country. It was once anchored by Libertad, the now-closed sugar cane processing plant south of Corozal

Town. Sugarcane has long been the leading industry in Corozal District, and while sugarcane fields still honeycomb the district, weak sugar prices have hurt the local economy. Smuggling, drugs, and also inexpensive beer and household goods from Mexico are important industries in the district.

Corozal History and People

The Maya have lived in what is now Corozal—the name is from the Yucatec Maya name for the *cohune* palm—since at least 2000 B.C. They established the Maya city of Chetumal, now represented by the Santa Rita archeological site in Corozal Town, around that time. Santa Rita, where only a few buildings remain visible today, was an important Maya center because it controlled trade routes up and down the coast and into the Petén. Only a small area has been excavated, and it is thought that much of the ancient city of Chetumal is now covered by the town of Corozal. Cerros, across Chetumal Bay, was a busy Maya maritime trade center from around 400 B.C. to A.D. 100. The site apparently suffered an economic decline and was abandoned in the Early Preclassic period after A.D. 250. Three main structures have been excavated, along with plazas and ball courts. One structure rises about 70 feet. The site is of special interest because of its location overlooking the Bay of Chetumal. Its waterfront location is reminiscent of the better-known Tulum site in the Yucatán. An American developer is trying to sell lots in a "subdivision" near Cerros, which is described as being "just 15 minutes from Corozal Town." It is, by boat.

Along the waterfront in Corozal Town

Lan Sluder

The Spanish arrived in the 16th century and eventually were successful in conquering the area that is now the Yucatán and northern Corozal District. Modern Corozal was settled mostly by Mestizo refugees from the Mexican Castes Wars of the mid-19th century, when Mayas fought to drive Mestizos from the Yucatán. Spanish is still the first language in Corozal District, especially in smaller villages. In Corozal Town, you can get by with only English.

In 1955, much of the town was destroyed by Hurricane Janet. It was rebuilt combining Mexican and Caribbean styles. Hurricane Keith in 2000 did not cause any damage to Corozal Town.

Expatriate Living

Most foreigners looking to live or invest in Belize dream about a beachfront spot on the Caribbean Sea, so they don't even consider the Corozal Town area. Only a few hundred foreigners presently live in Corozal. However, as each month passes more and more would-be expats who are looking at Corozal as a low-cost and remarkably appealing alternative to the Florida-level prices in San Pedro or Placencia. One first-timer to Belize who was looking for a retirement home, for example, said he was disappointed by the crowds and the "sky high" prices on Ambergris Caye and "couldn't wait to get out of there." He's now looking to buy around Corozal Town.

Shopping in Corozal Town is, well, limited. **U-Save Super** at 4th Avenue and 2nd Street South—locally called Mirna's after the owner, Mirna Gomez—is where most expats shop in Corozal. Mirna stocks items that are hard to find elsewhere, such as whole wheat bread. **Reyes** on 4th Avenue may be less expensive but doesn't have as wide a selection. The market in town on the water has stalls selling fresh fruit and vegetables and other items at modest prices. Corozal also has the usual small-town mix of hardware stores and small clothing and other shops. However, Chetumal has a **San Francisco** hypermarket, a Mexican chain of large supermarkets that also sell household goods, along with many other stores. Three of Belize's banks—Scotia Bank, Belize Bank, and Atlantic Bank—have branches in Corozal Town, and you can exchange money at better than bank rates at the border.

The town has a Rotary Club and a few other local organizations of interest to expats. Some foreign residents take courses at the area's two local schools—Corozal Community College and Corozal Junior College. Tuition costs are nominal. Corozal Town has a small public library. Local cable TV has more than 30 channels, some in Spanish but most in English, for around US$15 a month.

While Corozal does not have any support groups specifically set up for Americans or other foreign expats, all Corozal residents are eligible to join

How to Save Money on Purchases in Belize

Some tips from those who've made the move and adapted to the Belizean way of life.

- Ask a trusted Belizean friend to buy for you—the "Belizean price" is almost always less than the "rich foreigner" price

- If you are doing the buying yourself, buy in person rather than by computer or phone. Belizeans like to do business face-to-face

- Pay cash. Credit cards may be surcharged, and any credit price is usually much higher than the cash price

- If you are a resident of Belize, at hotels, museums, and other attractions (but not restaurants or stores) ask for the rate for Belizean citizens and residents, which may be one-half of the tourist price

- Bargain if appropriate—ask politely if there is a "discount"—but prices are fixed in most stores and shops

- Don't buy in haste—the longer you're in Belize, the better you'll understand the system and the lower the price you'll probably pay

local clubs including Rotary. Corozal area has a number of churches, including Anglican, Baptist, Catholic, Jehovah's Witness, Seventh Day Adventist, Church of Christ and several others. Here also are chapters of Alcoholics Anonymous and Al-Anon.

Residents can become involved with various volunteer programs, including efforts to protect the Maya sites in Corozal District. A plus for Corozal residents is the presence of two small colleges, Corozal Junior College and Corozal Community College.

Most residents consider Corozal one of the safest places in Belize. Even so, burglary and property theft are fairly common. It is a good idea to keep a dog, and if you're away from home you should have someone dependable look after your place. Corozal Town and surrounding villages are on the power grid and generally have municipal water supplies with potable water.

Real Estate

Real estate is a bargain in Corozal.

Belizean-style homes in and around Corozal Town sell for US$15,000 to $50,000, and attractive modern homes on or near the bayfront with U.S.-style amenities are available for US$50,000 to $150,000. In late 2000, a 2,200-square-foot concrete bungalow in Corozal Town was for sale for US$65,000, a 900 square-foot concrete house on three acres was available for US$43,000 (annual property taxes US$30), and a 2,000-square-foot, three-bedroom, recently constructed home on about 18 acres near Consejo village was on the market for US$155,000.

Thanks to low labor costs and proximity to Mexico, building costs in Corozal are about the lowest in Belize. In most cases, you will get more home for your dollar by building rather than buying.

Consejo Shores is a 350-acre planned development on Chetumal Bay, about seven miles north of Corozal Town. Several dozen homes have been built here so far, mostly occupied by retirees from the United States and Canada. Lots are large, most being about one-half acre or more. The land is higher than in most other coastal areas, an advantage during storms. There is electricity (typically US$75 to $150 a month), piped water (about US$8 a month), digital telephone and Internet service (full Internet service is US$20 a month for 10 hours, plus US$2 for each additional hour, supporting 56K modem speed) and even garbage pickup (US$10 a month). Building lots directly on the water go for around US$35,000–to $50,000 and those not the water sell for US$16,000–$25,000. Recently built two and three-bedroom North American–style homes sell for US$70,000–$125,000 or more.

Several other developments are in the Consejo area, though so far none has taken off. Most of the "subdivisions" here are still vacant land. For years, there has been talk of building a golf course near Consejo, but so far that's all it is—talk.

Rentals

Corozal has some of the lowest cost rentals in Belize. You can find an acceptable small home in Corozal Town for under US$100, and an attractive larger home on or near the water shouldn't cost more than US$350 or so and could be less. Upscale three- or four-bedroom homes in Consejo Shores or other residential areas around Corozal Town rent for US$400 to $800 a month. As elsewhere in Belize, you'll do best by spending some time here and finding your own rental, rather than trying to do it by phone, mail, or email. Foreign residents here say they generally have little problem finding a place to rent. For a short-term stay while looking at a place to live, consider **Corozal Bay Inn** (P.O. Box 184, Corozal Town, tel. 501/4-22691, www.corozalbayinn.com, email doug@corozalbayinn.com), which has a pool and nearly new two-bedroom suites near the bay for about US$300 a week. Smaller and far less appealing, but cheaper, is the **Central Guesthouse** (22 6th Ave., Corozal Town; tel. 501/4-22358; fax 4-23335), a one-story concrete building in the middle of town. Weekly rates are around US$50, monthly from US$150.

Real Estate Agents

The most knowledgeable real estate guy in northern Belize is Bill Wildman. He's a Canadian real estate surveyor and developer who has lived in Belize for going on four decades. Bill developed Consejo Shores, and he and his wife, Jenny, own a good bit of property in the area. Contact him at **Belize Land Consultants** (P.O. Box 35, Corozal Town, tel. 501/4-38005, fax 4-38006; email: blzland@btl.net; www.consejoshores.com or www.belizeland-consultants.com).

Weather and Climate

The climate in Corozal is similar to that of Central Florida. Rainfall is a moderate 50 inches or so a year. If you live on or near Corozal Bay, a brisk wind from the water—it usually dies down only in late summer—keeps you cool and also keeps the bugs away.

Dining and Nightlife

The Corozal area has several good restaurants, and many residents pop over to Mexico to enjoy that city's many fine restaurants. **Café Kelá** (First Avenue, tel. 501/4-22833) is by far the best restaurant in northern Belize. For a recent dinner, a total tab for a snapper filet sautéed in herbs with a

Part of the beautiful bayfront in Corozal Town

Lan Sluder

big serving of *pommes frites,* washed down with a couple of glasses of delicious fresh-squeezed lime juice, came to under five U.S. bucks. And this is no dive. It's a charming little bistro—there are only five tables—in a thatch *palapa* (hut) framed by bougainvillea across the street from Corozal Bay. The menu offers seafood, crepes, cassolets. Most items have a French twist, as co-owner Stephan Moerman is originally from France. His wife, Marguerite, is a Corozaleña. Café Kelá is named for the couple's children, Kevin and Lela. No alcohol is served, but you can bring your own bottle.

Casablanca (tel. 501/4-23452) is a restaurant and inn in Consejo, owned by an American couple, John and Beverly Tempte, which enjoys a nice setting with views of the lights of Chetumal across the bay. **Hok'ol K'in** a guest house in town run by a former American Peace Corps worker and a Belizean partner, has a nice little restaurant (tel. 501/4-23329), a good place to get a cheeseburger and a cold drink. **Tony's** (south end of town, tel. 501/4-23555) is where better-heeled gringos and Belizean government officials grab a good breakfast or hearty—if fairly pricey—dinner of lobster, steak, or chicken. In good weather, there's outside dining with a view of the bay. Several cheap Chinese and Mexican places favored by locals, including **Bayview**, are in or near the market. North of Corozal Town along Four Mile Lagoon are several small spots where you can get a soft drink or beer and relax by the lagoon. These get business mostly from Belizeans on weekends and from visitors passing through from Mexico. Among them are **Riverol's Cool Spot, Godfrey's Place**, and **Kich-Pam-Ham**, which is usually called Alcala's. However, with the development of the hotel-casino complex called Galleria Maya, this area may change.

Sailboat docked near Corozal Town, in northern Belize.

Lan Sluder

At least one casino is expected to open in the Corozal Free Zone, targeting wealthy Mexican visitors. Mexico does not permit casino gambling.

Recreation

There's no barrier reef here, so no diving and snorkeling, but you can swim in one of the lagoons or in the bay. Fishing is excellent, not only in Chetumal/Corozal Bay but also in Corozal District rivers and lagoons. The bay is known for its virgin bonefish flats, and you can also catch snapper, jack, permit, tarpon, and snook. Boating is popular on the relatively calm, shallow bay, and you can take your boat all the way to Ambergris Caye or to Mexico's Caribbean Coast with its wide, white sandy beaches at Akumal, Cancun, and elsewhere. There is a customs entry point at Chetumal, at Xcalak (a tiny Mexican fishing village near Ambergris Caye), and at several other points along the Yucatán coast. If you want to dive, take a day trip to Ambergris Caye or head to the Chinchorra Banks atoll off Mexico.

You can also take advantage of recreational opportunities in Mexico. About 15 miles from the border is Bacalar, a lagoon with excellent swimming. There's a public beach with a palapa bar serving drinks and snacks. The city of Chetumal has several museums and historical sites.

Medical Care

Corozal Town has a district public hospital (tel. 501/4-22076) although there has been talk of shutting it down and consolidating care in a regional hospital serving both Corozal and Orange Walk. Many residents go to Chetumal for medical and dental care, where there are modern hospitals and clinics and charges are only a fraction of that in the United States and even lower than in Belize City. Shipyard, a Mennonite settlement south of Corozal Town, has a low-cost dental clinic.

How to Get There

From Mexico: **ADO** (tel. in Mexico 525/133-2424, www.adogl.com.mex, email info@adogl.com.mx) and other Mexican bus lines serve Chetumal from various towns and cities in the Yucatán, including Cuidad Cancun, Mérida, and Playa del Carmen. Fares on first class and deluxe buses—with reserved seats, videos, and bathrooms—are around US$10 to $15 depending on the origin and class of service. It's about five hours from Cancun, six from Playa del Carmen or Mérida. At Chetumal, you change to a **Batty** or **Venus** bus to Corozal Town (fare US$.75). Buses leave Chetumal for Corozal Town and points south beginning at 4 A.M., and the last bus is at 6:30 P.M. Venus buses leave from the Nuevo Mercado station and Batty from the main Chetumal terminal. At the border, marked by a bridge over the Rio Hondo, you get off the bus to go through customs and immigration and then reboard for the 15-minute ride into Corozal Town. Money changers here pay a higher rate than the two Belize to one U.S. dollar you generally get in Belize. A taxi into Corozal Town from the border is about US$10. **AeroCaribe** (reservations tel. 52-98-84-2000 in Cancun or 501/2-77185 in Belize City, www.aerocaribe.com.mx, email info@aero-caribe.com.mix) flies daily from Cancun to Chetumal, and from there you can take a taxi to the border. AeroCaribe also has service several days a week from Cancun to Belize City. The Chetumal airstrip is modern and can take small jets.

> *The waters of the bay are as blue as those elsewhere on the coast or cayes, and the breezes from the water as cooling and constant as any in Belize.*

Note that there is now a US$10 exit fee for those leaving Belize by land, but you won't be charged this fee if you are an official Belize resident. Mexico also has instituted a US$17 fee for visitors entering Mexico, but this is not charged if you are only going a few miles into the country.

From points south in Belize: The Northern Highway is one of Belize's best roads. It will take you about two hours by car from Belize City. Batty

In rural areas of Belize, you can drive for miles and never see a soul.

Lan Sluder

(tel. 501/2-72025) and Venus (tel. 501/2-77390) are the primary Belize bus lines on the Northern Highway, with frequent service in both directions. Fares are US$4-5 to Belize City, depending on the type of bus. Most buses on this route are retired school buses or other older equipment, but a few express air-conditioned buses also serve it. **Maya Island Air** (tel. 501/2-31140, www.mayaairways.com) and **Tropic Air** (tel. 501/2-45671 or 800/422-3435 in the United States, www.tropicair.com) fly from Corozal's tiny airstrip to San Pedro, Ambergris Caye (20 minutes, about US$40 one way). Both offer two or three flights daily. The airstrip is about two miles south of town, a US$5 cab ride.

Sources of More Information

At present, there is no newspaper published in Corozal Town, and residents get most of their news from Mexican radio, TV, and other media. The website www.corozal.com, produced mostly by students at Corozal Community College and Corozal Junior College, provides an excellent introduction to the area. For a highly personal perspective on Corozal, see the website developed by an American resident at www.belizenorth.com.

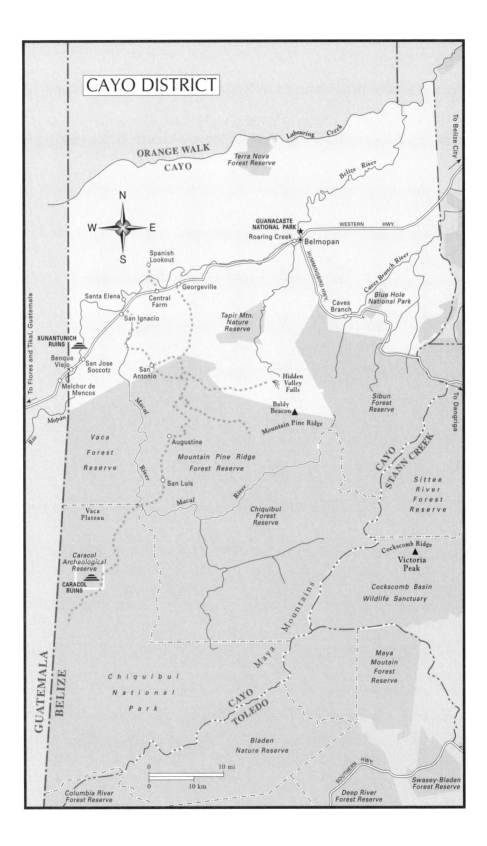

CAYO DISTRICT

ORANGE WALK

CAYO

Terra Nova
Forest Reserve

Labouring   Creek

Belize   River

To Belize City

N
W   E
S

GUANACASTE
NATIONAL PARK
Roaring Creek   Belmopan

WESTERN   HWY.

To Dangriga

Spanish
Lookout

Georgeville

Santa Elena   Central
Farm

San Ignacio

Caves Branch River

HUMMINGBIRD HWY.

Caves
Branch

Blue Hole
National Park

XUNANTUNICH
RUINS

To Flores and Tikal, Guatemala

Benque
Viejo   San Jose
Soccotz

Melchor de
Mencos

San
Antonio

Tapir Mtn.
Nature
Reserve

Hidden
Valley
Falls

Sibun
Forest
Reserve

Mopán

Rio

Macal

Vaca

Forest

Reserve

River

Augustine

Mountain Pine Ridge
Forest Reserve

Baldy
Beacon

Mountain Pine Ridge

CAYO

STANN CREEK

Sittee
River
Forest
Reserve

San Luis

Macal   River

Chiquibul
Forest
Reserve

Cockscomb Ridge

Victoria
Peak

Vaca
Plateau

Caracol
Archeological
Reserve

CARACOL
RUINS

Cockscomb Basin
Wildlife Sanctuary

Maya

Mountains

Maya
Moutain
Forest
Reserve

GUATEMALA

BELIZE

Chiquibul

National

Park

CAYO

TOLEDO

Bladen
Nature Reserve

SOUTHERN   HWY.

Swasey-Bladen
Forest Reserve

0   10 mi

0   10 km

Columbia River
Forest Reserve

Deep River
Forest Reserve

17 *Cayo District*

Cayo District, in western Belize bordering Guatemala, is an exception to most of the rules. Landlocked, it borders on no sea or bay. Instead of low-lying, bug-infested tropical vistas, in Cayo you'll find rolling hills, low mountains, and few mosquitoes or sand flies. While Cayo has some lush broadleaf jungle, it also has piney woods and red clay that may remind you of northern Alabama. It has both the hottest and the coldest weather in Belize. On summer days, temps can soar to over 100 degrees; on a winter's eve in the 3,000-foot elevations of the Mountain Pine Ridge, they can dip to near 40.

Belmopan, Belize's capital, is in the Cayo District, as is the largest town in Belize, San Ignacio, with a population of about 16,000. Along the Western Highway, which runs through Cayo District, are a number of small villages including Tea Kettle, Unitedville, and Esperanza. At the border is Benque Viejo del Carmen.

A Tour of Cayo

As you drive west from Belize City on the Western Highway, you gradually leave the flat savannas of the coastal plain. The savanna gives way to citrus groves and cattle ranches. You begin to see low limestone hills, some in striking formations, rising up out of the plain. The terrain becomes progressively more hilly and scenic as you go west.

Belmopan, at Mile 48 of the Western Highway, is hardly more than a sleepy small town. With its new block houses set in tidy rows with tiny lawns, it has the feel of a lower middle-class suburb in Florida. Most of the government buildings are low, ugly concrete structures of indifferent personality. The few lodging places here are modest motels, and the town's restaurants are equally modest. Belmopan does boast several modern stores, among them a branch of Brodies and a Courts appliance store. Belmopan's most appealing feature is that it is the northern access point to the Hummingbird Highway, Belize's most scenic roadway. The Hummingbird, recently resurfaced and now the best road in Belize, wings about 55 miles southeastward, through the Maya Mountains and into Stann Creek District, ending as the Stann Creek District Highway at the sea in Dangriga. Along the way are multivariate green hillsides, large orange and grapefruit groves, and, here and there, old railroad bridges, relics of a railway built in colonial times to transport bananas.

> *In Cayo you'll find rolling hills, low mountains, and few mosquitoes or sand flies.*

If instead of heading south on the Hummingbird at Belmopan you continue west, the land gets hillier and the Western Highway curvier. Most of the land has been extensively logged in the past, and sizeable areas are given up to citrus farms and Brahma cattle ranches. This is Belize's "Wild West." While occasionally you still see Mestizo cowboys on horseback, more often today the ranch hands here ride in the back of a Toyota pickup or drive a Land Rover.

About 70 miles from Belize City, you come to San Ignacio, which in early 2001 outpaced Orange Walk as the largest town in Belize. The Hawksworth Bridge, a 1949-vintage suspension structure over the Macal River, marks the entrance to San Ignacio. Nearby the Mopan and Macal rivers merge, forming the Belize River, which wends its way northeastward to Belize City.

San Ignacio, like Rome, is built on seven hills. Lovely are the views over the river valleys and into Guatemala from some of these hills. At the top of one of the hills, at around 900 feet, is a Pre-Classic and Classic period Maya site, Cahal Pech, a name that in the Mopan Maya language unfortunately means Place of the Ticks. I've not seen any ticks here myself, but occasionally on weekends the noise from the Cahal Pech Tavern is bitingly loud.

While it is not for those looking for a high-energy urban atmosphere, San Ignacio, with Corozal and Punta Gorda, is one of the three most appealing towns in mainland Belize. It's safe and easygoing with a kind of down-to-earth, folksy charm. The residents, mostly Mestizos with some Mayas and an occasional Creole or Anglo, are attractive and friendly. Not that there's a

HIGHLIGHTS OF CAYO DISTRICT

- **Belize Botanic Gardens:** On the grounds of duPlooy's Lodge, the gardens are a work in progress. Already there are some 450 trees and other plants, mostly collected by Ken duPlooy, the Zimbabwe-born co-founder of the lodge. The plantings are on about 45 acres. Most trees are identified, so you can do a self-guided tour. There's also an orchid house. The long-range plan is to duplicate six of the eco-zones in Belize a visitors center and a research lab.

- **Chaa Creek Natural History Museum:** At Chaa Creek Resort & Spa, this small museum has informative and expertly done displays on the Macal River Valley.

- **Rainforest Medicine Trail:** Formerly the Panti Trail, this small site next door to Chaa Creek has a self-guided trail with marked native medical plants. There is a small gift shop selling natural medicines.

- **Maya Villages:** Several small villages around San Ignacio are predominantly Maya. Among these are San José/Succotz, a vibrant Mopan Maya village, near Xunantunich on the Western Highway, and San Antonio, a Yucatec Maya village (population about 1,500) south of San Ignacio toward the Mountain Pine Ridge.

- **Spanish Lookout Mennonite Community:** Mennonites in this area are "progressive" and use modern farm machinery and vehicles. You'd think you were in Iowa.

- **Caving:** This is a fast-growing activity in Cayo. In most cases, no special equipment or training is needed to visit local caves. However, going with a trained guide or tour operator is highly advised. Barton Creek Cave has become one of the most-popular caves to visit in Cayo. You canoe about a mile through the cave, past colorful formations and Maya relics. Actun Tunichil Muknal is noteworthy because of a large amount of undisturbed Maya pottery. On Ek' Tun Lodge property, Flour Camp Cave is a collection of caves with multiple entrances and exits. There is considerable pottery from several periods.

- **Maya Sites:** Among the many Maya sites in Cayo District are Xunantunich, Cahal Pech, El Pilar, and, in the Mountain Pine Ridge, Caracol.

lot to do here. San Ignacio is mostly a place to stock up on groceries at Celina's Superstore or Cross Roads Supermarket, or to pick up some building supplies at a local hardware.

If you drive south from the San Ignacio area on either the Cristo Rey or Pine Ridge roads—they are equally bad, unpaved limestone roads—you soon come to the entrance of the Mountain Pine Ridge. "Ridge" in Belizean usage refers not to the geographic feature but to the type of tree common in the area. In this case, it's the mountain pine, which is similar to the Caribbean pine. Unfortunately an infestation of pine beetles is putting tens of thousands of acres of pine forest at risk. The beetles bore into the bark of the trees and eventually cause their deaths, creating a huge potential for forest fires. The elevations here range from about 1,000 to 3,000 feet. With the adjoining Chiquibul Wilderness, Vaca Plateau, and the northwestern part of this Maya Mountain range, this is the largest protected wilderness area in Belize. While the Mountain Pine Ridge is piney woods, the Chiquibul, Vaca, and Maya Mountains areas have broadleaf jungle. Here you'll find ironwood, cohune palm, sapodilla, and other exotic trees. This region is rough and wild. There are isolated waterfalls, clean mountain streams, and huge underground cave systems. Britain's Prince William spent some time here in mid-2000, training with the Welsh Guards.

Part of the Mountain Pine Ridge is privately owned, mostly in huge tracts once bought for a dollar or two an acre, and part is owned by the government. Controlled logging is allowed, and the roads in the Pine Ridge, many impassable after rains, are all former logging tracks. Except for a small settlement at Augustine/Douglas de Silva on the road to Caracol, four small jungle lodges and some isolated villages of Guatemalan immigrants, few people live in the region.

Northeast of San Ignacio, in and around Spanish Lookout, is one of Belize's Mennonite areas. Farms here, mostly run by the more liberal Mennonites who use tractors and other modern equipment, supply a large part of Belize's produce, chickens, eggs, and cheese. The well-tended, rolling farmland may remind you of parts of the American Midwest.

Cayo History and People

Maya Indians settled the Belize River Valley in what is now Cayo District thousands of years ago. By the time of Christ, sizable cities and large ceremonial and trading centers had been constructed. The Maya began building at El Pilar around 500 B.C. and at Cahal Pech even earlier. Duing the Maya Classic Period, A.D. 250 to 950, Caracol in the Chiquibul wilderness area beyond the Mountain Pine Ridge was one of the dominant Maya city-states in Mesoamerica. Xunantunich, located just west of present-day San Ignacio, was a major ceremonial center.

In the seventh century A.D., the warlords of Caracol even defeated mighty Tikal and Naranjo in what is now the Petén region of Guatemala (which borders the Cayo district). The Indians developed an immense agricultural system, complete with irrigation and drinking water sufficent to support a large population. Estimates are that 200,000 people lived around Caracol alone, nearly as many people as live in all of modern Belize. The area had so large a population, in fact, that archaeolologists think it may have suffered from the Maya equivalent of urban sprawl. Even today the tallest human-built structure in Belize is Canaa, a temple at Caracol, and the second-tallest is El Castillo at Xunantunich.

After the still-mysterious decline of the Maya civilization soon after the end of the first millennium, the number of Maya in the Cayo was much reduced, and it was further reduced when in the 18th century some Indians were forcibly removed to Guatemala by white settlers. The first modern settlements of any size were logging camps. Later chicle—used to make chewing gum—was an important revenue source.

Today citrus farming is the main industry in Cayo, and many local residents are employed in agriculture or in supporting industries. Nearly 60,000 acres in Belize are planted in citrus fruit. Much of this acreage is in Cayo District. Valencia oranges do particularly well in Belize. In 1998–99, the Belize citrus industry produced 5.7 million boxes of fruit, which were processed into both frozen juice concentrate and not-from-concentrate juice.

Some local entrepreneurs also are trying their hand at tourism. Several of the small hotels in San Ignacio and a few jungle lodges in surrounding areas are run by Belizeans. One of these lodges, Clarissa Falls, is a popular spot for Belizeans to come for weekend picnics and parties. Located on a working cattle ranch on the Mopan River, Clarissa Falls is run by Chena Chavez, a small woman with a smile that lights up her entire 600-acre ranch. Within 10 minutes of your meeting Chena, she'll be hugging you and telling you about her latest pet project. She's one of Belize's friendly ambassadors who make the country such a delight. Her sister, Anna, is also a great hostess and a good cook to boot. The resident parrot, Larry, loves to slurp coffee.

Boys play in the Macal River.

Lan Sluder

The Expatriate Community

Most members of the small expat community in Cayo, whose exact number is unknown but likely numbers in the several hundreds, also are involved in either tourism or agriculture. A few foreign retirees have moved to small farms and ranchettes, where they've built homes and piddle in their gardens and groves.

The pioneers of tourism in this area are Mick and Lucy Fleming (he's British, she's American), who started a lodge at Chaa Creek in 1980, when foreign tourists were almost unknown in this part of Belize. Over the years, they've expanded and fine-tuned the property on 330 acres on the Macal River, creating the queen of Belize's jungle lodges. Near Chaa Creek is duPlooy's, another top Macal River lodge developed by expatriates. Ken duPlooy came from Zimbabwe and wife, Judy, from the United States.

Farther up the Macal River on some 500 acres, two former Coloradans, Phyllis and Ken Dart, built the tiny—there are just two cabañas—but deluxe and delightful Ek 'Tun Lodge. The Darts have put their hearts and souls into the project, and they have a hard-earned, realistic view of the difficulties of making a go of it in Belize. "I've often thought of writing a book about Belize titled *The Other Side of Paradise* wherein reality is the focus, and the many frustrations are not overlooked," says Phyllis. "We've seen so many gringos give up and go home, and so many others still here that are burned-out and bitter, that you sometimes feel there is really something insidious underlying the friendly surface appearances. Maybe it's just that the brain drain has sapped all the thinking, ambitious, or hard-working individuals, and most that are left to deal with are nice, but a little crooked or don't really care enough. . . If we lived anywhere else in the country than Ek' Tun, I'm not sure we'd still be here, either," she says.

More recent comers to the bed-and-bush group are Pamella and Jay Picon, Americans who started Belize's first all-inclusive resort near Benque Viejo. Their Mopan River Resort opened in 1998. Jay first visited Belize in the 1960s to investigate cattle farming, but at that time went to Mexico instead. Pam's first visit was in the 1980s. They became citizens through the Economic Citizenship program in 1988 but only started living in Belize in the mid-1990s, first in Belize City and then in Benque Viejo.

Pam offers this advice for those thinking of starting a lodge or hotel in Belize:

"Don't do it unless you LIKE people. If you see it strictly as a business, you won't enjoy it. Belize has too many average, look-alike facilities. Be prepared to do something different. Be prepared to WORK! In order for your project to be successful, and to avoid cost overruns, you have to be on site, at least 99 percent of the time. It also helps if you know how to do a lot of things yourself—some construction or mechanical background. Do not be deluded into thinking that you can build something, and leave it for someone else to run. It can be done, but you won't make much money at it. As simple as it sounds, you have to really like Belize for what it is. You must be prepared to adapt your lifestyle to fit Belize—Belize will not adapt to you. The biggest misconception is that with money, you can do anything. Be prepared to accept the fact that some things just can NOT be done here and it will still cost you a lot.

"Although the government encourages foreign investment, many locals will see you only as unfair competition. Choose your type of business and its location with this in mind. Hire as many locals as you can, and be prepared to train them. Again, treat everyone with respect; support local causes nonpolitically."

The svelte 30-something Pam also offers a bit of contrarian advice for those thinking of moving to Belize to start a business: "Burn your bridges on the way here. You'll be a lot more successful if you work as though there's no going back. If you know your house and favorite chair are back there waiting for you, you're not as likely to have the dedication required to make it here. It's not necessarily easy, but it can be very rewarding if you're up to the challenge."

While there are no support groups specifically for American or other foreign residents, Rotary and other civic clubs have chapters in the area. In Belmopan, San Ignacio and elsewhere in Cayo are a number of churches, including Anglican, Bah'ai Faith, Catholic, Assembly of God, Church of Christ of Latter Days Saints, Mennonite and others.

JUNGLE LODGES

Around Belmopan are more of Belize's top jungle lodges. Most are located on one of the many rivers that cut through the country's midsection.

Banana Bank Lodge, run by a former Montana cowboy John Carr and his artist wife, Carolyn, is on the Belize River.

Jaguar Paw, run by two former Floridians, Cy and Donna Young, is on the Caves Branch River.

Pook's Hill Lodge on Roaring River is run by a couple, Ray and Vickki Snaddon, long-time Belize residents though both are from other outposts of the British Commonwealth.

Dining and Nightlife

The pickins' are slim in Belmopan, but you can get a good meal at Sanny's at the western edge of San Ignacio, where they take basic Belize dishes like pork chops with rice and beans and turn them into something spicy and exotic, or at Serendib, a Sri Lankan–run downtown restaurant with authentic curries, along with all the usual Belizean fare. If you have some extra cash in your jeans, try the Running W restaurant, specializing in steaks, at the

LAND OF THE FREE

O, land of the free by the Carib Sea,
Our manhood we pledge to thy liberty!
No tyrants here linger, despots must flee
This tranquil haven of democracy.

The blood of our sires which hallows the sod,
Brought freedom from slavery oppression's rod,
By the might of truth and the grace of God.
No longer shall we be hewers of wood.
Arise! ye sons of the Baymen's clan,
Put on your armour, clear the land!
Drive back the tyrants, let despots flee.

Land of the Free by the Carib Sea!
Nature has blessed thee with wealth untold,
O'er mountains and valleys where prairies roll;
Our fathers, the Baymen, valiant and bold
Drove back the invader; this heritage hold
From proud Rio Hondo to old Sarstoon'
Through coral isle, over blue lagoon;
Keep watch with the angels, the stars and
*   moon;*
For freedom comes tomorrow's noon.

San Ignacio Resort Hotel. Queen Elizabeth stayed at this hotel when she visited San Ignacio in 1994. Or head out to La Vie en Rose restaurant at the Green Heaven Lodge on the Chial Road west of San Ignacio. There Dominique Agius and Anne-Karine Chappaz, refugees from the South of France, serve French classics like beef Bourguignonne, and you can even get real French champagne.

Everyone, locals and tourists alike, eventually ends up at Eva's, a San Ignacio restaurant and bar cum cybercafé and community bulletin board, run by an ex-Brit soldier named Bob Jones, who married a local gal and stayed on. Bob claims his place was the first Internet café in Central America. For US$4.50 an hour you can surf the Net to your heart's content, and Bob says part of your fee goes to provide free Internet access to local schoolkids.

Nightlife in Cayo mostly involves loud music and booze. The Cahal Pech Tavern rocks on the weekends, and several downtown clubs in San Ignacio, including the Blue Angel plus Caesar's Place on the Western Highway, offer live music from time to time. Less savory is the local brothel, which, in this age of political correctness and AIDS, shall remain nameless.

Real Estate

Land is plentiful in Cayo, but the locals have seen you coming, and the cheap land of yesterday is hard to find. Still by U.S. standards land is inexpensive. Expect to pay US$1,000 to $2,000 an acre for citrus-growing land with good access. Rougher, more remote land goes for US$500 an acre or less. In late 2000, a 64-acre farm with about one-half planted in citrus fruit was on the market for US$125,000, with $25,000 down and the balance over five years at 12 percent. Another tract of 94 acres, of which 54 were planted in oranges, was for sale for US$170,000, with $60,000 down. A 10-acre tract in Esperanza village was on the market for US$25,000. In Benque Viejo, a 20-acre ranchette with two-bedroom cement home was offered for US$79,000. A 78-acre parcel near San Ignacio with creek and pond was on the market for an asking price of US$80,000.

Building lots with electricity and perhaps cable TV start at US$2,000 and go to US$10,000 or more. However, we know of foreigners who, after befriending local families have bought nice building sites for just a few hundred dollars. As elsewhere in Belize, you'll usually get a better price if you buy from the owner rather than a real estate agent, and the longer you're in Belize the lower the price you're likely to have to pay.

Land in small tracts in the Mountain Pine Ridge is not often for sale. When on the market it goes for US$2,000 an acre and up.

Homes around San Ignacio start at US$10,000 for small Belizean-style places and range up to $300,000 or more for deluxe haciendas. Most homes, however, are priced under US$100,000. On the market in early 2001 was a six-bedroom, two-story home on a hillside in the Santa Elena area for US$69,000, and several others were available around San Ignacio for under US$100,000.

At the top end of the market, a 7,000 square-foot, four-bedroom home on 6.5 acres in the Central Farm area near San Ignacio was on the market for US$348,000. The house is of concrete construction with a tile roof and has two "great rooms" and its own water storage system. About four acres of the land are planted in fruit trees.

Most foreigners moving to Cayo build their own homes rather than buy an existing one. Perhaps not so atypical is Louanne LaRoche. The Bluffton,

Cattle ranch in Cayo District

Lan Sluder

South Carolina, resident came to Belize on vacation, fell in love with the Cayo area, and decided to buy land and build a small bungalow. She intended to move to Belize and live in the little house. But the house plans grew like Topsy and construction ended up taking three years. "I built it as I had the money," says Louanne. She ended up with her "house of dreams" with touches like hand-carved doors and handsome tile floors. Then, back in the States, Louanne married and had a child and decided not to live in Belize full-time, so she is putting the house on the market.

Rentals

Rentals start at under US$150 for a Belizean-style house, with attractive North American–style homes available for US$400 to $700. Few rentals are advertised or listed with an agent, so you must seek them out yourself on the ground in Cayo.

Real Estate Agents

Most of the Belize City–based real estate firms, including Regent, Emerald Futures, and Belize Real Estate have listings in Cayo. Also, there are several small real estate companies in Cayo District, including the ones below. Some for-sale-by-owner notices can be found in Eva's in San Ignacio.

Citris orchard, growing Valencia oranges, near San Ignacio in Cayo District

Lan Sluder

Cayo Real Estate, 15 Burns Ave., San Ignacio, tel./fax 501/9-23739, email cayo-info@awrem.com.

Maxsell Realty Services P.O. Box 29, San Ignacio, tel. 501/9-23381, email info@maxsellws.com.

Tropic Real Estate, P.O. Box 453, Belmopan, Cayo, tel. 501/9-23475, fax 9-23649, email tropic@realestatebelize.com.

Climate and Weather

Cayo District is generally hotter by day but cooler by night than most other parts of Belize. From spring to late fall, daytime temperatures around San Ignacio and Belmopan commonly reach into the 90s and occasionally get over 100, with nighttime temps mostly in the 60s. In winter, it often drops into the 50s at night, cold for Belize, and in the higher altitudes of the Mountain Pine Ridge on winter evenings a fireplace feels good, with chilly 40-something temps. Year-round it is cooler by five to 10 degrees or so and also less humid in the Pine Ridge than in lower elevations. From February through May it is what locals call the dry season in Cayo, with hot dry weather and rarely any rain. Forest fires are common, especially in the Pine Ridge, where they leave acres of pines black and lifeless. Usually in June seasonal rains begin, with heavy black clouds sweeping in from Guatemala.

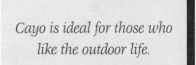

Cayo is ideal for those who like the outdoor life.

Recreation

Cayo is ideal for those who like the outdoor life. There's hiking, horseback riding, mountain biking, canoeing on rivers and absolutely world-class caving. The Mountain Pine Ridge and Chiquibul Wilderness are particularly exciting areas for outdoors types. There are waterfalls seemingly around every bend—with cool pools for a private skinny-dip—along with cave systems worthy of a *National Geographic* story. (Several in fact have been written on caves in this region.)

Medical Care

San Ignacio has two small hospitals, the public **San Ignacio Hospital** (tel. 501/9-22066) and the private **La Loma Luz** (tel. 501/9-22087). Belmopan also has a public hospital (tel. 501/-8-22264). There are pharmacies in San

Ignacio and Belmopan. Near Chaa Creek, Rosita Arvigo, a disciple of the late Don Elijio Panti, has a small natural healing center and spa. For dental care, most residents go to Belize City.

How to Get There

The main road to Cayo is the well-paved, two-lane Western Highway. From Belize City, Belmopan is about an hour by car, and San Ignacio is another three-quarters of an hour. Add another 15 minutes to get to the Guatemala border at Benque Viejo del Carmen. Novelo's, Batty's, and other buses run this route some 30 times a day each way. Between Belize City and San Ignacio the cost is around US$3 for an express bus. There is no scheduled air service to San Ignacio, although there are several private airstrips.

Sources of More Information

Destination Cayo is a small monthly free newspaper focused on tourism. An online edition is at www.belizex.com/cayotrader.htm. All sorts of information on Cayo District, including links to real estate companies, is available at www.belizex.com.

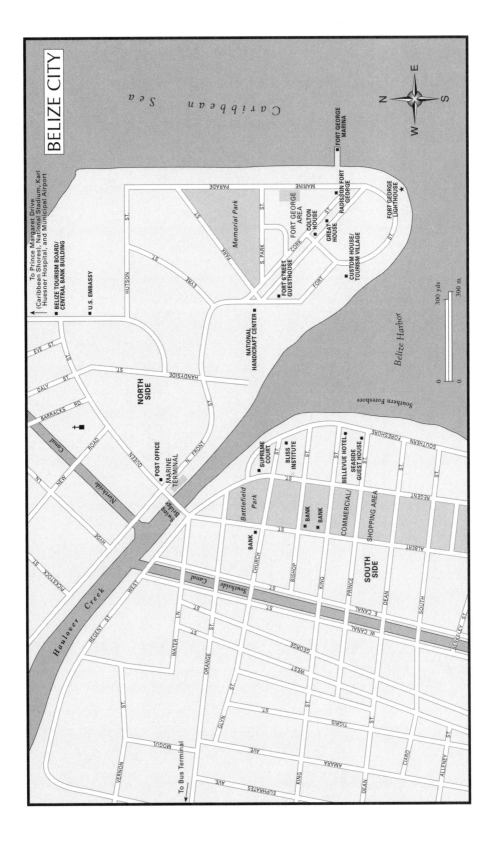

18 Other Prime Living Areas

esides the four areas—Ambergris Caye, Placencia, Corozal, and Cayo—that attract the vast majority of foreigners, and which are covered in individual chapters, Belize has a number of other areas that may appeal to retirees, investors, or second-home buyers. This chapter highlights these locations, organized geographically from north to south, with caye options at the end.

Sarteneja

Sarteneja is a village of about 2,000 mostly Spanish-speaking Mestizos on the Sarteneja peninsula in northeastern Corozal District. The original Maya settlement was built around the site of a well, which is said to have never gone dry. The Maya deserted the area before colonial times, but Sarteneja was resettled in the mid-19th century by Caste War refugees from the Yucatán. Most of the villagers make their living from the sea, fishing and lobstering in Chetumal Bay. Although on the water, with a postcard setting, the village has no real beaches. It doesn't have much else either—a school and several churches, two most empty guest houses, one vacant hotel that is for sale, a few little bars and eating places in local houses, and a handful of minimarts. At Easter and occasionally at other times, a sailing regatta is held with local boats—built by hand in the village—and others from Belize City and Ambergris Caye.

Near the village is the 22,000-acre Shipstern Nature Center, a preserve designed to protect the moist subtropical forest. One of Belize's six butterfly farms is here (see the butterfly sidebar below). The shore is lined with mangroves, and the water is shallow. Manatees are common in the Shipstern Lagoon, and more than 200 species of birds have been spotted.

This is a place for those who really, really want to get away from things. There is no airport, and the drive or bus ride from Orange Walk Town winds by the beautiful Progresso Lagoon and takes a couple of hours—it will seem longer—on a rough, unpaved road. Resident foreigners are few

BUTTERFLY FARMS IN BELIZE

Even the most sedentary can now see the Blue Morpho and other species of colorful butterflies at close range, without doing a jungle trek. As you tour the screened or netted butterfly rooms at Belize's Lepidoptera ranches, often the butterflies will land on your hands or head, as if posing for the camera. At any of the farms, you can learn about the life cycle of the butterfly. It's a metamorphosis which begins when the female butterfly lays eggs. From the egg hatches a caterpillar, or larva. The caterpillar is a small eating machine. As it eats, it grows, and because its skin cannot stretch, the caterpillar sheds its skin several times. The final molt produces the chrysalis, or pupa. Chrysalises, in some species green, and in others brown or variegated, usually hang from twigs or leaves. The butterfly slowly forms within the chrysalis, until the fully formed adult butterfly emerges, to begin the cycle anew.

Almost 800 species of butterflies have been recorded in Belize. That's as many types of butterflies as in all of the United States and Canada combined. Each butterfly ranch specializes in only a few types of butterfly, since different species require different host plants. A host plant is the food plant of the butterfly in its caterpillar stage. Usually the best time to view butterflies is mid-day, between about 11 and 4, as butterflies require the sun's heat to maintain their metabolism at an active level. On extremely hot and sunny days, the butterflies are more active in mornings and late afternoons. On cloudy or rainy days, they may be inactive. Three farms—Fallen Stones, Blue Morpho and Green Hills—are involved in the export of pupas to exhibitors, zoos, natural history museums and butterfly collectors around the world. The others are primarily educational facilities.

These six butterfly farms, listed in order of likely interest to visitors, are an easy way to see some of Belize's 600+ species of butterflies, including the strikingly beautiful blue morpho:

Green Hills Butterfly Farm, Mile 8, Pine Ridge Road, Cayo District

Fallen Stones Butterfly Ranch, near Lubaantun in Toledo District

Blue Morpho Butterfly Centre, at Chaa Creek, Cayo District

Tropical Wings Butterfly Center, near Xunantunich, Cayo District

Shipstern Butterfly Center, Shipstern Nature Preserve, near Sarteneja in Corozal District

Xochil Ku Community Butterfly Center, near Lamanai and Indian Church, Orange Walk District

and far between. A new hand-pulled ferry across the New River makes access from Corozal Town easier, but remote is still an apt description for this area.

In 2000, a modern 1,800 square foot house just 60 feet from the water was on the market for US$110,000. It had two master bedrooms, two baths, kitchen with built-in mahogany cabinets, a 10,000-gallon cistern for backup water, and many mature, bearing fruit trees. An RV that sleeps four even came with the property. Belizean-style houses are available in and around the village starting at under US$10,000, and rentals begin at well under US$100 a month. Another modern house on eight acres, including about 500 feet of frontage on Chetumal Bay, was offered for US$275,000.

> *This is a place for those who really, really want to get away from things.*

Also on the Sarteneja peninsula and nearby are a number of other small villages, including Copper Bank and Chunox (pronounced Shoo-NOSH). If you stop at Copper Bank—pronounced Copper BONK—which is another picturesque fishing village, be sure to have a bite or a beer at The Last Resort (tel. 501/4-12009), run by Donna Noland and Enrique Flores.

Mennonite farmers, mostly conservatives, are active in the area near the Progresso Lagoon called Little Belize. An American developer has been trying to sell, mainly via the Internet, waterfront lots near Cerros. *Caveat emptor*, pal.

Belize City

Belize City is the place nearly everyone loves to hate. Even some Belizeans dislike the city and go there only reluctantly. As one guidebook to Belize says, when you think of Belize City, the word "dump" comes to mind. In fact, Belize City is a lot nicer and safer than it used to be. A grant from Canada helped Belize replace most of the open sewers with a modern sewerage system. The addition of tourist police in 1996 in areas visitors are likely to be has reduced the number of cases of harassment and petty street crime. A new system of quick justice means that anyone apprehended for a crime against tourists or other foreigners can be tried within a few hours and if found guilty sentenced and taken off to prison the same day. Roads have been resurfaced and new directional signs have been put up, although even good signage can't help much with the city's rabbit warren of narrow one-way streets. Belize City's residential areas sustained a lot of damage in the hurricanes of 1931 and 1961, and many of the old wood-frame colonial houses have been replaced by ugly concrete structures, but there are still many interesting and photogenic buildings. Get out your cameras.

But keep a close hold on those cameras. Crime remains a serious problem in Belize City. And I do mean serious. Residents say they get used to it, but murders of shopkeepers, drive-by shootings, and machete choppings and knifings, not to mention burglaries and muggings and street thefts, are distressingly common. It is never a good idea to walk around in Belize City after dark, even in groups.

Nonetheless, Belize City, with a metro population of around 80,000, remains the business, transportation, cultural, and even political hub of Belize. Nearly all of the country's lawyers are in the city, and more than one-half of its doctors and other medical personnel. The largest stores are here, including the country's only big supermarkets and general merchandise stores. If you are doing business in Belize, you can't overlook it. As a Belize resident, you'll occasionally have to visit here for medical care or to take care of personal business.

For those who can afford it, the Caribbean Shores area and other neighborhoods along Princess Margaret Drive, where the hospital is, and Barracks Road near the waterfront are Belize's best residential areas. You will pay US$30,000 and up for a building lot in this area, or US$200,000 or more for a modern home. Rentals, catering to the international business crowd and the very affluent locals, are mostly US$1,000 and up. Marina Towers, a high-rise apartment building with water views near the Princess Hotel & Casino, is a prime address. Another good area is Fort George, home to a

A West Indies-style colonial house in Belize City

Lan Sluder

number of colonial mansions and most of the city's best hotels. Prices here also are high. In more modest areas, prices are much more affordable, but security is a big concern. You can almost be guaranteed that your property will be broken into at least once every year or two.

Some expats prefer to live in the "suburbs," either west of the city along the Western Highway, or north along the Northern Highway. Both areas have secure houses and apartments starting at US$100,000, but the fancier properties can easily cost US$500,000 or more.

If you are just visiting, I recommend that you stay in the Fort George area, with its old British Honduras ambiance, good hotels, and restaurants. (*See chapter 3, Planning Your Fact-Finding Trip, for details.*)

Hopkins/Sittee Point

The Hopkins area, 10 miles south from Dangriga on a now-paved section of the Southern Highway, and then four miles east on an unpaved road to the Caribbean, is a lot like Placencia of 10 or 15 years ago. It's just now beginning to blossom as a tourist center and location for retirees and vacation-home buyers. Like Placencia, Hopkins village and the Sittee Point area just south of Hopkins have good beaches. Hopkins, like Seine Bight on the Placencia peninsula, is a Garifuna village, while some of the area's other villages are Creole. Hopkins didn't get telephone service until the mid-1990s, and even today its biggest shops are just little shacks. Village restaurants and bars are usually in someone's home.

To the south of Hopkins village is a growing collection of resorts and real estate developments. Jaguar Reef Lodge, developed by a Canadian, was the first upmarket resort in this area, but it has been followed by several new places, including Kanantik, a high-end all-inclusive resort with rates of US$300 per person per day, along with several other small upscale beach inns.

Resort operators hate anyone to mention it, but sand flies are a major problem in this area. These little no-see-ums can make life your life miserable, and they can even get in the house through screens and tiny openings under a door or window.

An Austin, Texas-based outfit called the British American Cattle Company (4600 Spicewood Springs Rd., Suite 102, Austin, TX 78759, 512/346-7381, email baccbelize@cs.com, www.bacc.com) is developing a seafront area south of Hopkins. British American has been marketing building lots on the seafront in Sittee Point for around US$1,000 a front foot, with lots with 50 feet of beachfront going for US$50,000. Lots not on the water but with sea views are around US$25,000. British American Cattle Company provides financing with 20 percent down, with the balance over 20 years at

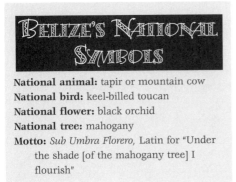

BELIZE'S NATIONAL SYMBOLS

National animal: tapir or mountain cow
National bird: keel-billed toucan
National flower: black orchid
National tree: mahogany
Motto: *Sub Umbra Florero,* Latin for "Under the shade [of the mahogany tree] I flourish"

10 percent interest. There's a 5 percent discount for cash purchases. The company is now selling "estate-sized" lots for about US$90,000; lots available in late 2000 included several with 75 feet of beach frontage and a minimum of 450 feet of depth, connecting with a canal. Although scores of lots have been sold on and near the beach, so far few homes have actually been constructed in this area. A few that have been built and put up for sale are in the US$150,000 to $200,000 range. Given the local real estate boom, some owners of houses in Hopkins are asking US$20,000 for shacks they would have sold for US$2,000 a few years ago. Only a sucker would buy some of these places for anything more than a fraction of the asking price.

Away from the water, land in small tracts around Hopkins is affordable, with prices similar to that in other rural areas in Belize.

The Hopkins area has no real inventory of rentals, although you may be able to find a small Belizean-style house for US$200 or less. A few beachfront houses and cabañas that are rented to the tourist trade go for US$500 to $1,500 a week.

Coast South of Placencia

The remote and isolated coast of southern Belize—roughly from Monkey River to Punta Negra and then south beyond Punta Gorda to Barranco and the Guatemala border—is the new frontier for real estate development and rugged retirement living in Belize. Large tracts of coastal seafront are "in play," as the real estate guys say (meaning they are on the market). The eventual paving of the Southern Highway is supposed to bring all kinds of development opportunities to this area.

True, it is mostly virgin territory, very lightly populated. And the price is right. But you can't get there from here—or from anywhere, except by sea. There is a seasonal dirt track from the Southern Highway to Monkey River, and a few other tracks run, at least in the dry months, to coastal areas, but the only dependable access is by boat, a two-hour ride south from Dangriga or about half that or less from Punta Gorda or Placencia. Once there, don't expect electricity, telephone, or services of any kind.

The only settlements of note are Monkey River, once a thriving banana town but now a Creole village of a few hundred souls living off the tourist overflow from Placencia; Punta Negra, a small Garifuna fishing village; and Barranco, another Garifuna village that is cut off from most of the rest of civilization. Offshore are some of the most pristine of Belize's cayes—the Snake Cayes and Moho Caye and others—and the Port Honduras Marine Reserve, rich with manatees and many other types of undersea life.

Our guess is that it will be many years, if not decades, before this area gets the accoutrements of modern life, but if you're the adventurous type with a yen to get away from everything, and if you know your way around a boat, this could be your place. In late 2000, plenty of beachfront acreage was on the market, with asking prices from under US$200 a front foot. For example, a 10-acre tract near Punta Negra with 400 feet of beachfront was available for US$75,000. But even here, the real estate yahoos are out doing their thing and don't expect dirt-cheap bargains. Near Punta Ycacos south of Punta Negra, lots are being marketed for US$100,000, albeit these are big—of up to three acres with about 150 feet of beachfront. The developers claim a road and airstrip will be in place "within two years."

For information on real estate in this area, try contacting Yearwood Properties, General Delivery, Placencia, tel./fax 501/6-23462, email info@belize-beachfront.com, www.belizebeachfront.com.

Punta Gorda

Punta Gorda, or PG as locals call it, is a small, untouristy, and colorful frontier outpost in the far south. Two things have worked to keep it that way. The first has been the Southern Highway, a highway in name only. More accurate nomenclatures would have been the Southern Mudway or Southern Dustway, depending on whether you were traveling its 100 unpaved miles in the rainy or dry season. In wet weather, bridges would wash out and even four-wheel drive vehicles sometimes would get stuck. In dry weather, big eighteen wheelers driving along the road kicked up a cloud of red dust so thick you'd have to drive with your lights on to be able to see. But, miracle of miracles, parts of the Southern Highway are now paved. Thanks to loans from various international agencies and several foreign countries, about 25 miles at the south end of the road near PG are surfaced, and by the time you read this most of the 35-mile northern section from near Dangriga to Independence should be paved. That still leaves some 40 miles in between that are still mud or dust, but within another couple of years the entire highway may be as good as the Hummingbird or Western highways.

The other factor even foreign loans can't mitigate: rain. It's wet down here. PG and most of Toledo District get 100 to 200 inches of rain a year. That's two to four times what the Southeastern United States gets. The rainy season in PG stretches from May until January or February. You haven't seen a real rainstorm until you've seen the black clouds roll in from Guatemala and the skies open up, pouring water by the buckets.

With so much rain and high humidity year-round, this part of Belize has real tropical rainforests, with giant bromeliads lining roadways, ceiba, monkey apple and Santa Maria trees in the lowland jungle and everywhere the deep green, unruly bush. Rice grows in flooded fields. Mosquitoes and all kinds of tropical creepy-crawlies await you.

The town of PG, population around 3,500, enjoys an attractive setting on the Gulf of Honduras. There are no beaches to speak of, but a nice breeze usually blows from the water. Front Street, newly resurfaced, winds along the waterfront and is home to several good small hotels, including the Sea Front Inn, run by Larry and Carol Smith, expats who have been here for 20 years. The town's five main streets run parallel to the sea, and a clock tower in the main plaza welcomes you in four languages: English, Garifuna, and Ketchi Maya and Mopan Maya. On market days, Wednesday and Saturday, the town's Garifunas, Creoles, and East Indians are joined by Maya from the surrounding countryside and from Guatemala.

Some of the best fishing in Belize is here, both in the sea and in Toledo's many rivers.

The few visitors and prospective retirees who make it this far south by car or bus, or who come on one of the Maya or Tropic Air flights, likely are attracted by the exotic countryside around PG. Here Maya Indians live in small villages much as they have for thousands of years, in thatch-roof huts with dirt floors. Bare-breasted Maya women wash their clothes in the rivers, beating them on rocks. In these remote villages, usually the only telephones are community telephones, and the only running water comes from a community pump. Several guest-house and homestay programs allow you to stay in a village and see the daily Maya life up close. Also near PG are a number of interesting Maya ruins, including Nim Il Punit and Lubaantun.

Offshore are numerous cayes, including the Sapodilla Cayes where snorkeling is excellent. Some of the best fishing in Belize is here, both in the sea and in Toledo's many rivers. Underground are extensive cave systems and, at Blue Creek, Belize's only aerial walkway through the jungle canopy, a swaying platform built some 80 feet above the jungle floor.

In the early and mid-1800s, Garifuna from Honduras settled in Punta Gorda, Punta Negra, and Barranco. After the American Civil War, they were followed by Confederate gunrunners seeking a new life. Sugar became the dominant cash crop, and by 1870 a dozen sugar mills, all owned by the North American immigrants, were in operation. But the price of sugar began to drop, and tired of fighting the rain and bugs, most of the North Americans returned home. In modern times, religious missionaries have flocked to PG, seeking to convert the heathen Maya. Hotels in PG, with occupancies averaging less than 15 percent, would be almost completely empty if it weren't for the missionaries who rent rooms.

Living is not cheap in PG. High transportation costs and lack of competition mean that cost of groceries and everyday items are higher than in Belize City. Rents for Belizean-style homes are modest, but clean, modern North American–style housing is dear. One expat is renting apartments for US$600 to $800 a month, about what you'd pay for a similar place in Miami.

If you're in PG for more than 10 minutes, you'll hear about somebody who has a piece of land for sale. We're not sure why, but everybody seems to think their land, stuck out on a remote hillside, is worth a small fortune. US$1,000 an acre is the going rate for most small tracts. Our only guess is that everybody is hoping to take advantage of what may happen in the future, that someday when the Southern Highway is paved this area will explode with development. Our view: It'll never happen. Even with good road access, the low population density, rainy climate, and lack of good beaches mean that PG will remain much the way it is today, a sleepy little outpost, colorful and quaint, near the Guatemala border. If you like PG, then buy, but don't do it as an investment.

Real estate brokers in PG are all kitchen brokers, part-timers who work out of their home or hotel hoping to sell a property now and then. One is Bonita Mommé (tel. 501/7-22270). Some Belize City real estate companies also have listings in PG. But if you're seriously interested in living in PG, the only way to get the real lay of the land is to visit, stay a spell, and do your own prospecting for a piece of land.

Bay of Honduras at Punta Gorda

Lan Sluder

Caye Caulker

Located just south of Ambergris Caye, Caye Caulker is about four miles long and a few hundred yards wide at its widest point, with a village population of about 1,000. It, like many other parts of northern Belize, was settled by Mestizo refugees from the Yucatán Caste Wars of the mid-1850s. The close-knit families of Caulker lived by fishing and lobstering. The local fishing cooperative has a contract to sell spiny lobster to the Red Lobster chain. In the 1960s and 70s, Caulker became a part of the hippy trail, one in a string of laid-back, low-cost, warm-weather destinations stretching from Thailand to Greece, where the living was cheap and the grass was too. Budget hotels sprang up to serve backpackers, where for US$5 a day young people could crash and dream.

Today Caulker, also sometimes called Caye Corker or Caye Cocker, is struggling to go upmarket. While there are still many inexpensive hotels, newer properties like Iguana Reef Inn offer suites for as much as US$100 a night. Simple wooden houses on stilts are slowly being replaced by concrete buildings. In late 2000, Hurricane Keith slammed Caulker with winds over 120 miles per hour, destroying dozens of homes. Most of the island has now recovered, and, except for coco palms stripped of their fronds, Caulker looks much as it did before the storm, or even better, thanks to insurance payments.

Windsurfing is excellent here, especially in the spring when the offshore breezes are consistently brisk. Fishing, diving, and snorkeling on and around the barrier reef are all wonderful.

Beach with sea-grass debris and wind-blown palm trees

Lan Sluder

Good beaches aren't one of Caulker's assets, although a recent beach recla-
mation project widened the sand on the front, or Caribbean, side. Many
small homes, painted in Caribbean pastel colors, dot the water's edge only a
few hundred feet from the barrier reef. With most of the island land controlled by local families, there are few homes or building lots for sale on
Caulker. A handful of expats take life easy here, mostly running hotels and
guest houses. A small number of waterfront lots are available from
US$35,000 to $60,000 each. Rentals also are in short supply, but some simple
apartments and small frame houses are US$300 to $700 or more a month.
Off-season, several hotels rent rooms by the week for US$100 to $200.

For information on Caye Caulker real estate, it's best to visit the island
and see for yourself. You can also contact the folks at **Eden Isle** (P.O. Box
37, Caye Caulker, tel. 501/2-22170, fax 2-22119, email keycocker@btl.net)
who have some residential and commercial lots for sale.

You can take a water taxi to Caye Caulker from the Marine Terminal in
Belize City for US$7.50 one-way, or fly Maya Island Air or Tropic Air for
around US$47 from the international airport, or US$26 from municipal.

Remote Cayes

Besides buying an entire island, it's also possible on a few remote Belizean
cayes to buy a building lot or a home. These are options only for those who
are seriously inclined toward isolated living. All of these cayes are tiny, at
most a few hundred acres, and none has amenities such as shopping or a
choice of restaurants. About all there is to do is eat, sleep, dive, and fish.
Getting to these islands can cost several hundred dollars or more one-way
by boat, and once on the island, in most cases there are no facilities, not
even drinking water.

Because everything has to be transported to these remote islands by
boat, including workers, building costs can be as much as twice as high as
on the mainland. Tropical storms and hurricanes are a threat in summer
and fall, and any construction should bear that in mind. These small, low-
lying islands may be covered in many feet of water during a storm.
One island where lots are being sold is Long Caye, a 650-acre island at
Lighthouse atoll, about 45 miles or three hours by boat from Belize City.
According to the developers, the island "has its own fresh water source."
Tiny interior residential lots start at US$5,000, with sea-view lots from
US$9,000 and beachfront lots with at least 50 feet of beach frontage from
around US$18,000. Financing with about one-third down is available at 10
percent over one to 10 years. The seller pays closing costs, including the
10 percent stamp tax and 2 percent attorney's fees.

An "eco plan" has been developed for the island calling for reviews (at a fee of US$200) for any proposed building. Electricity must be solar or wind generated, only composting toilets are permitted, and there are many detailed restrictions on buildings, setbacks, and requirements.

Quite a number of these lots already have been sold, in most cases to buyers who have never seen the island or even been to Belize. One wonders what will happen when these installment-purchase buyers finally start to build on the island!

For information on Long Caye, contact **Pitts and Eltrington, Attorneys**, 50 No. Front St., Belize City, tel. 561/488-5524, email www.longcayebelize .com, or www.longcayebelize.com.

Support groups specifically set up to assist Americans and other foreign expats don't exist in Belize. However, foreign residents are welcome to join Rotary and other civic clubs which have chapters in most Belize towns. Community volunteer activities are possible everywhere—just ask where your help is most needed. Even the smallest Belize village is likely to have a Catholic church, and larger communities have a variety of churches.

PART V

Earning a Living

19. WORKING IN BELIZE

19 Working in Belize

Imagine you're living beside the blue Caribbean Sea. You spend your days snorkeling, diving, fishing. Now imagine you get paid to do this. You pay your way through paradise by working as a dive master, or guiding tourists, or tending bar in a little thatch hut.

Reality check! Reality check!

In reality, Belize has an unemployment rate in the double digits. The few good jobs that are available are mostly reserved for Belizeans. Many occupations, including tour guiding and waiting tables and barkeeping, are reserved for Belize citizens. Residents under the Qualified Retired Persons Incentive Act can't work for pay at all. Even if you were able to legally get a job, salaries in Belize are far below those in the United States, Canada, or Western Europe, and even physicians, college teachers, and other professionals may earn under US$15,000 a year.

After all, it's the United States that is the mecca for job seekers and entrepreneurs. Millions of people around the world vie to get a green card to let them live and work in the States. More than 100,000 Belizeans have left Belize to work and find their fortunes, legally or illegally, in the United States.

So you're going to leave the United States with all its opportunity, capital, and huge base of consumers and set up shop or find a job in poor little Belize, with its tiny population and economic resources of a small American town? What's wrong with this picture? Fact is, if you can't make it in the United States, your chances of success in Belize and slim and none. There are good reasons why someone might decide to move to Belize and work or invest there, mostly having to do with quality of life, but economic rewards and an easy road to fortune are not among them.

Working in Belize

In theory, unless you are a Belize citizen or a permanent resident under the regular permanent residency program you cannot work in Belize without a work permit from the government. (As a permanent resident under the Qualified Retired Persons Incentive Act program you can't work for pay.) In practice, we know of a few foreigners without work permits who have part-time jobs and take in-kind or cash payments. One foreign resident of Corozal said: "I spent last semester teaching without a work permit, and nobody noticed—wink, wink, nudge, nudge. My next door neighbor is [a high-ranking official] in the Ministry of Labour and he said 'don't worry about it.'" Maybe there's no need to worry, but if you're caught working without a permit both you and your employer could be in trouble. Rules for work permits were tightened in 1999, due to concern about illegal aliens from other countries in Central America taking jobs from Belize citizens. Fines are imposed on employers found with illegal workers.

Alan Colton, a former British soldier, runs a guest house with his wife, Ondina.

Lan Sluder

We know, however, quite a few expatriates who have carved out a comfortable niche for themselves in Belize, either working for an established Belizean company or running their own business. It is possible to do so, but it's not easy.

There are two types of work permits for employees. One is a permit that is obtained by an employer in Belize. The employer has to prove that he or she can't fill the job with a Belizean and has exhausted all avenues for finding a qualified

WHAT IT PAYS: SALARIES AND WAGES IN BELIZE

As in most other countries, salaries and wages in Belize vary widely, even for the same position. Overall, wage levels in Belize are about one-fourth of those in the United States, or lower, although a few business people and entrepreneurs in Belize make as much or more than their American counterparts. In general, wages are highest in Belize City and San Pedro and lowest in remote rural areas. All figures are in U.S. dollars:

Maid/Domestic Worker	$8–$10 per day
Day Laborer	$10–$15 per day
Carpenter or Mason	$20–$25 per day
Nurse	$6,000 per year
Doctor in Public Health Care	$10,000–$20,000 per year
Primary School Teacher	$4,800 a year
High School Teacher	$6,600 a year
Sixth Form or College Professor	$13,000 a year
Shop Clerk	$75–$90 a week
Office/Clerical Worker	$75–$100 a week
Secretary	$100–$150 a week
Lodge/Resort Workers	$10–$15 a day
Minimum Hourly Wage	$1–$1.15 an hour

Belizean applicant, including advertising the position for at least three weeks. Examples of jobs that may require a foreign applicant are hotel restaurant chef or a specialized computer software engineer. Application must be made to the Immigration Department with proof that the foreign employee is qualified, three passport photos, a valid passport, and US$5. A foreigner employed under this permit must have lived in Belize for at least six months before employment can begin.

Another type of work permit is the temporary self-employment certificate. This category applies to foreign investors and others seeking self-employment or who are starting a business in Belize, where it is assumed that the venture will lead to the creation of jobs for Belizeans. The applicant has to show proof of adequate funds for the proposed venture—for example, a bank statement. Also, the applicant has to have a reference from the relevant government ministry or other organization showing that the venture is reasonable. For example, if opening a tourist operation a reference from the Ministry of Tourism or the local village or town council where the operation is to be located may be required. For the temporary self-employment certificate, the six-month residency period is waived. The fee for either type of certificate is US$750 for professional and technical work, a category that covers almost any kind of work a foreigner is likely to do. For general workers the fee is US$100. Permits must be renewed annually and new fees paid. With rare exceptions, work permits are not granted for waiters, domestic workers, farmhands and anyone involved in retail or other types of sales. For information and application forms, contact the Immigration and Nationality Department, tel. 501/8-22611, or the Labour Department, tel. 501/8-22204.

If that sounds like a lot of red tape, it is. The Belize government is trying hard to discourage foreigners from working in jobs in Belize that Belizeans can perform. Tammy Martinez, who moved to Ambergris Caye from Florida, says, "It was very hard for me to find work. My husband found work as a bartender at Fido's the first week we were here, but he is Belizean, so he didn't have the problem of a work permit to deal with. I found that businesses are reluctant to hire you if you don't already have a permit in hand. The problem is, the price of work permits has gone up to US$750 for professional permits, which encompasses most jobs. None of the employers want to spend that amount of money when they don't know if you will stay or go. So basically, you could be the best qualified person for the job and not get it because you don't have the permit in hand."

Another American, Katie Volk, who was an executive in the music business in New York City before moving to Belize, recalls the frustrations of trying to get a work permit: "It was not at all difficult adjusting—Belize was a perfect fit for me. Finding work wasn't a problem for me either. Getting a work permit was, however, and it took a tremendous amount of stick-to-it-ness, patience, and energy. But I finally got that, then my residency, and now I'm seconds away from being a citizen."

Starting and Running Your Own Business

With good-paying jobs few and far between, most foreigners who want to generate an income in Belize will be looking at operating a business. In theory, the Belize government welcomes investors who can contribute to the Belize economy and provide work for Belizeans, particularly in tourism, agriculture, and manufacturing. But, theory in Belize is about as worthless as a Belize dollar outside Belize. It's rarely simple or easy to do business in Belize.

A timeworn saying in Belize is that if you want to make a small fortune in the country, better start with a big one. Belize's small domestic market, inefficient distribution and marketing systems, heavy-handed government red tape, and other factors make it difficult for entrepreneurs to achieve great success in Belize.

Here's the story of a California couple who were interested in relocating their small business, an embroidery shop, to Ambergris Caye: "We spent three years researching Belize. We wanted to restart our business in San Pedro. We contacted all we could in reference to moving our equipment, housing, waiting time to set up, residency, business costs, etc. Boy, did we get a shock. We were told it was VERY hard to do business in Belize. So many hidden costs and surprises! This came from current business owners in Belize. We just were not sure that our business would be welcome. After getting the cost of duty, shipping of our equipment, and tax on all of our business stuff just to start was a shocker. Then came duty and tax on all the items we wanted import and all the supplies we would need. WOW!" As of 2001, the couple are considering moving to Corozal Town.

On a somewhat larger scale is the story of Cy and Donna Young who came to Belize and started Jaguar Paw Jungle Resort near Belmopan. In the early 1990s, the Youngs were living in Florida. Cy had been a beer distributor and owned several video rental stores. Donna was a food and beverage manager for a greyhound racetrack. They were looking for something different and heard about Belize. Eventually they bought a 200-acre tract of land in the jungle for US$45,000 and began planning for an upscale jungle lodge, one that would have air-conditioning and gourmet food—adventure by day, comfort at night. Although both were experienced in business, they weren't prepared for the red tape and special problems of Belize. They initially thought the lodge, located in a remote area near the Caves Branch River, could be built for under US$500,000. They reportedly ended up investing more than three times that amount, spending close to US$100,000 a room for the 16-room project, similar to costs for a luxury hotel in the United States. The government, according to the Youngs, didn't live up to its promises to extend power and a road to the property, so the Youngs had

The Cannibal Café, now called Cannibal's, is run by an ex-pat American couple.

Marty Casado

HOTELS FOR SALE

Ever wanted to be an innkeeper? Here's a sampler of hotels advertised for sale in Belize in early 2001. Figures shown are asking prices, in U.S. dollars.

Don Quixote Hotel near Corozal Town, six suites plus additional rooms, swimming pool, on 4.5 acres with more than 1,000 feet of frontage on Chetumal Bay, $1,200,000

Coconuts Hotel, 12 rooms on the beach, Ambergris Caye, $850,000

Lillpat Resort, Sittee River, six rooms, pool, 7 acres, two boats included $725,000

Nautical Inn, Seine Bight (Placencia), beachfront, 12 rooms, pool on 4 acres, $1,400,000

Soulshine Resort, Placencia, five cabañas, pool, $680,000

Luba Hati, Seine Bight (Placencia), 400 feet of beachfront, 12 acres, 8 deluxe rooms, and 4 casitas, pool, $2,500,000

Howler Monkey Lodge, Community Baboon Sanctuary, 20 acres, 6 cabañas, $350,000

Kitty's Place, Placencia, 340 feet of beachfront, 3 acres, 3 cabañas plus rooms, $1,500,000

Kinich Ahau Lodge, near Maskall village on Old Northern Highway, 1,360 acres, 4 cabañas, horses, $750,000

Little Water Caye Resort, 3 acre island with 3 cabañas, $1,300,000

Beaches and Dreams, Sittee Point, 4 units, 110 feet of beachfront, $500,000

Windy Hill, San Ignacio, 97 acres, 25 units, plus tour company, $3,000,000

to buy and run large generators. Officials lost the import paperwork for equipment and materials, which sat in a Belize City warehouse accruing thousands of dollars in storage fees. In the early stages of getting the project going, the Youngs ran into killer bees, poisonous snakes, and reportedly even got kidnapping threats from Guatemalan bandits who came across the border. The hotel turned out beautifully and since its opening in 1996 has ranked as among the top lodges in the country, but according to several reports it never achieved the consistent large revenue stream it needed to provide a competitive return on the investment. In 2000, the Youngs put up the hotel up for sale, though they continue to operate it and the lodge and restaurant still get rave reviews from visitors to Belize.

Another hotelier, Judy duPlooy, shares her views on running a business in Belize. Judy and husband, Ken, started one of the first lodges in Cayo, duPlooy's Lodge, and have continued to expand their operation. "Starting a business and actually making a profit is difficult. We are fortunate to have a good location and reputation, so we do quite well. Always, your market is small due to limited numbers of tourists and limited local population."

The difficulty of making a go of tourism in Belize is shown by the number of hotels that are actively on the market at any one time. In Placencia, for example, while writing this book probably one-fourth of the properties were actively for sale, and other owners would have quickly sold for the right offer. In the 1990s, hotel occupancies in Belize averaged only about 27 percent, though by 2000 occupancy reached 40%, and at that low rate (hotels in the United States typically have occupancies in the mid-60s), it is difficult to earn an adequate return. Only in San Pedro, which gets a regular flow of tourists year-round, do hotels appear to be more consistently profitable. According to a study done for the Belize Tourist Board, the typical Belize hotel has just 11 rooms. With average room prices in Belize at US$63 a night, and occupancy of 27 percent, that means the total revenue for an average hotel in Belize is only US$68,000 a year, not including revenue for any meals, tours, or other sales. Thus, the typical small hotel in Belize can't afford to do the international advertising and marketing necessary to compete with larger, better capitalized resorts in other parts of the Caribbean.

John Lankford, a former New Orleanian who now makes his home in San Pedro, puts the situation bluntly: "As to 'investing,' first realize that when Belize's government or general population speaks or thinks of foreigners 'investing in Belize,' they mean bringing money and handing it over. They also contemplate a long-term, possibly permanent, commitment. They are not so solicitous of your expectations to realize a RETURN on your investment, and in some cases tend to think it craven of a 'rich' first-world person to try to make money off poor Belize. The approved motivation for investing in Belize is for the benefit of Belize. The investor's benefit is gratification at helping Belize advance, and any other motivation may be seen as *exploiting* rather than *investing*. As a general rule, don't even dream of investing in Belize unless you plan to be present with your eyes on your investment every day."

Types of Businesses That Might Succeed

Once again, in theory non-Belizeans can invest in or open almost any kind of business in Belize. In practice, though, several types of businesses require special permits or licenses, and these may not be granted to non-Belizeans. Again, the idea is to avoid permitting non-Belizeans to take jobs from Belizeans. The following businesses, in varying degrees, may not open to foreigners:

Commercial fishing
Sugarcane cultivation
Restaurants and bars (not associated with a resort)
Legal services
Accounting services

Bee-keeping
Retail shops
Beauty shops
Internal transportation
Sight-seeing tours (only Belizeans can be tour guides)

Businesses that are most likely to succeed in Belize are those whose main markets are outside Belize. The Belize market itself is small and spread out, and with a per capita income of under US$2,600 the average Belizean doesn't have the income to buy much beyond the basic necessities of life. Opportunities include any kind of export-oriented business, from agriculture to manufacturing. Niche products such as specialty or organic agricultural products may have a future. They also include businesses that target international tourists to Belize, although this market is much smaller. There are probably opportunities to supply products to tourist businesses—for example, to sell specialty herbs, fruits, and gourmet vegetables to larger resorts.

Besides the small size of the market and large doses of red tape, entrepreneurs in Belize face several problems related to the labor market.

Bob and Risa Frackman are former New Yorkers who now run one of the most successful beach resorts in Belize, the Inn at Robert's Grove.

Lan Sluder

Unemployment in Belize is stubbornly high, yet many of the best-trained and ambitious Belizean workers have moved to the United States. This brain drain means that it's difficult to find skilled, motivated employees. In rural areas, many Belizeans have never held a regular job. Training must start with the basics like showing up on time and coming to work every day. Another problem is that the cost of labor in Belize, while low compared with the United States, is relatively high compared with other third-world countries. The minimum wage in Belize is under US$1.15 an hour, but that's several times the minimum wage of workers in Honduras or Nicaragua. The minimum wage in Mexico is under US$4 a day, one-half that of Belize. Belizean workers also have comparatively strong workplace protections, including mandatory two weeks' paid vacation and participation in Belize's Social Security system, mostly funded by employer contributions of about 6.5 percent of wages, 16 days of sick leave annually and a required two weeks' notice or pay in lieu of that notice should the employee be terminated after having been on the job at least a year. In 2001, Belize was reviewing its Social Security system, and higher employer and employee contributions are expected. By American standards, the average wage of about US$10 a day for unskilled workers and an average salary of under US$100 a week for office and clerical workers may not seem high, but by standards of Belize's poorer neighbors these are princely sums. Businesses in highly competitive export industries may be at a disadvantage if they are located in Belize.

Tax Concessions

Belize has several incentive schemes designed to encourage investment in the country, including the Fiscal Incentives Act, the International Business and Public Companies Act, Export Processing Zone Act, and Commercial Free Zone Act. However, as a U.S. Commerce Department advisory notes, "[M]any foreign investors have complained that these investment promotion tools are rarely as open and effective as they are portrayed."

The programs of most interest to those thinking of starting a business in Belize are the Export Processing Zone Act, the Commercial Free Zone Act, and the Fiscal Incentives Act. The International Business Companies Act (IBC) makes it possible for foreign companies to get tax exemptions on all income of the IBC, all dividends paid by an IBC, all interest rents, royalties to non-Belizean residents, and capital gains realized. There are several thousand companies registered as IBC's in Belize. However, IBCs are not available to residents of Belize (only to those who reside outside of the country).

An **Export Processing Zone (EPZ)** is an area where goods destined for export are manufactured, process, packaged, or distributed. Three locations have been designated as EPZs. The San Andres EPZ is on about 29 acres north of Corozal Town, near the Mexican border. The other two zones are both located near Belize City. The EPZ adjacent to the Philip Goldson International Airport covers a tract of 4 acres, while the Price Barracks EPZ has 14 acres.

Businesses in an EPZ receive a Belize tax holiday of 20 years. During the tax holiday period, an EPZ business is exempt from income tax, withholding tax, capital gains tax, or any new corporate tax. Losses incurred during the tax holiday may be carried forward. There are a number of other benefits, not the least of which are reduced red tape and the fact that a business in an EPZ doesn't have to use Belize's monopoly telephone or electrical system but can use alternative suppliers. For example, businesses in the EPZs can get high-speed Internet access from Internet service providers other than Belize Telecommunications, Ltd. Several Internet casino operations have set up shop in Belize's EPZs, but the going has been rocky, and most have scaled back operations or left the country entirely.

Some resort operators and other investors have taken advantage of the Fiscal Incentives Act. For those who invest a minimum of US$125,000 in a Belize business, the Act provides for tax holidays of at least five years plus duty exemptions for 15 years on equipment and supplies, including automobiles, brought in to Belize. The exact benefits depend on the size of the investment. A fee of US$2,500 to $3,500 must accompany the application. For more information on tax concessions and EPZs, contact Belize Trade and Investment Development Service (BELTRAIDE), 14 Orchid Garden St, Belmopan, tel. 501/ 8-23737, email beltraide@belize.gov.bz.

Another government economic program of possible interest to business people is the **Commercial Free Zone (CFZ)**, created by the CFZ Act of 1994. The first CFZ was developed at Santa Elena at the Mexican border north of Corozal Town. A CFZ is a place where visitors to Belize (but not Belize citizens or residents) can shop for duty-free goods.It also is similar to a Export Processing Zone in that goods can be manufactured, processed, or stored duty-free if they are destined for export. All imports into and exports out of the zone are tax and duty free; the government charges a fee of 1.5 percent on general merchandise and 10 percent on fuel sold in the zone. Businesses in the CFZ also enjoy a reduced Belize income tax rate.

The Santa Elena Free Zone consists of 295 acres of which about a third currently are currently developed. More than 200 companies are doing business in this CFZ, mostly in the import/export sector, but there also are restaurants and retail businesses. Large numbers of Mexicans enter the Free Zone to do duty-free shopping, and many Mexican vehicles come in daily to buy low-cost gasoline. A casino targeting Mexican visitors—Mexico does not permit casino gambling—is planned. Currently, the Santa Elena CFZ employs some 1,000 Belizeans. The government of Mexico also has indicated an interest in starting its own CFZ on the Mexican side. The impact of this on Belize's CFZ is unclear, but it likely would mean an overall increase in tourist traffic to the entire northern Belize area. Another Belize CFZ for Cayo District near the Belize-Guatemala border is in the works. For information, contact the Corozal Free Zone Management Agency, Santa Elena, Corozal, tel. 501/4-23643, fax 4-22341.

PART VI

Appendix

20. USEFUL RESOURCES

20 Useful Resources

The information below may be useful in helping you learn more about Belize. The inclusion of any organization or firm does not imply a recommendation, nor does the omission suggest the opposite. Note that mailing addresses for some government offices in Belize do not have street addresses.

Emergency Telephone Numbers

Police: 911
Fire and Ambulance: 90

Time Difference

Belize time is the same as U.S. Central Time. Belize does not observe Daylight Savings Time.

Belize Government Offices

Ministry of Finance
New Administration Building, Belmopan
Tel: 501/8-22362
Fax: 501/8-22886
Email: finsecmof@btl.net

Ministry of Foreign Affairs
New Administration Building
P.O. Box 174, Belmopan
Tel: 501/8-22322
Fax: 501/8-22854
Email: belizemfa@btl.net

Ministry of Natural Resources and the Environment
Belmopan
Tel: 501/8-22630
Fax: 501/8-22333
Email: lincenbze@btl.net

Ministry of Public Utilities, Transport & Communication
Belmopan
Tel: 501/8-22435
Fax: 501/8-23677

Ministry of National Security & Immigration
Belmopan
Tel: 501/8-22423
Fax: 501/-8-22615

Ministry of Budget Planning & Management
New Administration Building, Belmopan
Tel: 501/8-22526
Fax: 501/8-20158
Email: primeminister@belize.gov.bz

Ministry of Economic Development
New Administration Buildin
Belmopan
Tel: 501/8-22526
Fax: 501/8-23111
Email: econdev@btl.net

Ministry of Investment & Trade
New Administration Building
Belmopan
Tel: 501/8-22218
Fax: 501/8-22195
Email: investment@btl.net

Ministry of Sugar Industry, Local Government & Latin American Affairs
Belmopan
Tel: 501/8-22167
Fax: 501/8-22854
Email: belizemfa@belize.gov.bz

Ministry of Public Services & Labour
Belmopan
Tel: 501/8-22204
Fax: 501/8-22206
Email: publicsvc@btl.net

Ministry of Human Development, Women & Youth
Belmopan
Tel: 501/8-22161
Fax: 501/8-23175

Ministry of Agriculture & Fisheries
Belmopan
Tel: 501/8-22241
Fax: 501/8-22432
Email: mafpaey@btl.net

Ministry of Works
Belmopan
Tel: 501/8-22136
Fax: 501/8-23282
Email: peumow@btl.net

Attorney General and Minister of Housing and Urban Development
Belmopan
Tel: 501/8-22110
Fax: 501/8-23390

Ministry of Education & Sports
Belmopan
Tel: 501/8-22380
Fax: 501/8-23389
Email: educate@btl.net

Ministry of Tourism
Belmopan
Tel: 501/8-23393
Fax: 501/8-23815
Email: tourismmdpt@btl.net

Ministry of Health
Belmopan
Tel: 501/8-22325
Fax: 501/8-22942

Ministry of Rural Development & Culture
Belmopan
Tel: 501/8-22444
Fax: 501/8-20317
Email: ruraldev@btl.net

Ministry of Industry & Commerce
New Administration Building, Belmopan
Tel: 501/8-22199
Fax: 501/8-22923
Email: mintrade@btl.net

Official Information and Embassies

Your best source of free official visitor information about Belize is the **Belize Tourist Board (BTB)**. Ask for *Destination Belize*, an annual magazine (there may be a US$5 charge for this). Belize Tourist Board, New Central Bank Building, Level 2, Gabourel Lane, P.O. Box 325, Belize City, Belize, C.A.; tel: 501/2-31913, fax 501/2-31943 or toll-free from the United States or Canada 800/624-0686; email: info@travelbelize.org; www.travelbelize.org. The BTB also is responsible for implementing the Retired Persons Incentive Act designed to attract retirees to Belize.

The **Belize Tourism Industry Association (BTIA)** is an organization representing tourism operators and hotels. It maintains, in cooperation with the Belize Tourist Board, helpful tourist information offices in Placencia,

San Ignacio, and elsewhere. BTIA, 10 N. Park St., P.O. Box 62, Belize City, Belize, C.A. tel. 501/2-75717, fax 2-78710.

The **Belize Audubon Society**, besides being an active environmental organization, manages many of Belize's national parks. Belize Audubon Society, 12 Fort St., Belize City, Belize, C.A., tel. 501/2-34985; email bas@btl.net; www.belizeaudubon.org.

The **Belize Embassy** in Washington is overworked but may be able to supply some information on investment and official matters. Belize Embassy, 2535 Massachusetts Ave., NW, Washington, DC 20008, 202/332-9636.

The **Embassy of the United States** in Belize is at 29 Gabourel Lane, Belize City, tel. 501/2-77161, fax 2-30802. Hours are 8 A.M. to noon and 1–4 P.M. Monday–Friday. Email embbelize@belizwpoa.us-state.gov. The embassy's website at www.usemb-belize.gov/ provides some useful information.

Canada has only an honorary consulate in Belize. It is at 83 North Front St., Belize City, tel. 501/2-31060, fax 2-30060. The **British High Commission** to Belize is in Belmopan, tel. 501/8-22146, fax 8-22761.

Builders, Contractors, and Construction Materials

BUILDING CONTRACTORS
Fabro's Industries, Ltd.
27 Victoria St., Belize City
Tel. 501/2-35798

H L C Engineers, Ltd.
2 1/2 Mls Northern Hwy, Belize City
Tel. 501/2-45480

Johnston International
Civil Engineering & Building
Mechanical & Electrical Contractors
116 Cemetery Rd., Belize City
Tel. 501/2-73322

BUILDING MATERIALS
Baraka, Ltd.
565 Buttonwood Bay Blvd., Belize City
Tel. 501/2-35806

Belize Aggregates, Ltd.
116 Cemetery Rd., Belize City
Tel. 501/2-73109

Benny's Homecenter
38 Regent/Prince Sts., Belize City
(also on Freetown Rd. and on Northern Hwy.)
Tel. 501/2-73347

Bradstar Construction Supplies
37 Forest Dr., Belmopan
Tel. 501/08-22162

Caribbean Depot
San Pablo, San Pedro
Tel. 501/2-62619

Gush and Emy, Ltd.
5 Mapp/Cleghorn Sts., Belize City
Tel. 501/2-45953

Koop Sheet Metal
Baltimore Dr., Spanish Lookout
Tel. 501/8-30118

Midwest Steel & Agro Supplies
Center Rd., Spanish Lookout
Tel. 501/08-30131

Professional Building Supplies
Placencia
Tel. 501/6-23238

Rick's Block & Tile Factory
7 Progress St., Orange Walk
Tel. 501/3-22421

Buildings—Prefabricated

Midwest Lumber Mill, Ltd.
Spanish Lookout
Tel. 501/8-30308
Tel. 501/08-38000

Tropical Wood
Edental Spanish Lookout
Tel. 501/8-38041

Contractors—General

Anderson, Rudolph O.B.E., J.P., C.S.C.
28 B Nurse Seay St., Belize City
Tel. 501/2-44195

Blue Creek construction, Ltd.
2 Blue Creek, Orange Walk
Tel. 501/3-30464

Graniels
San Pedro, Ambergris Caye
Tel. 501/2-62707

Johnny's Construction
Santa Elena Rd., Corozal
Tel. 501/4-22222

Johnston International
116 Cemetery Rd.
Tel. 501/2-73322
Fax: 501/2-73320

Modern Civil Engineering, Ltd.
3 1/2 Mls Northern Hwy., Belize City
Tel. 501/2-31763

Pristine Development
138 Newtown Barracks, Belize City
Tel. 501/2-34648

Robert M. Usher Construction
13 South St., Belize City
Tel. 501/2-71738

Real Estate Agencies

Belize Land Consultants, P.O. Box 35, Corozal Town, tel. 501/4-38005, fax 4-38006; blzland@btl.net.

Belize Real Estate (W. Ford Young Real Estate, Belize City, and Langdon Supply, Ambergris Caye), 160 N. Front Street (P.O. Box 354), Belize City, tel. 501/2-72065, fax 2-31023, email bzreal@btl.net.

Diane Campbell, San Pedro, Ambergris Caye, tel. 501/2-64032; email camp@btl.net.

Cayo Real Estate, 15 Burns Ave., San Ignacio, tel./fax 501/9-23739, email cayo-info@awrem.com.

Emerald Futures Real Estate, 13 Cork Street, #3 (P.O. Box 1442), Belize City, tel. 501/2-36559, fax 2-36559, email realgem@btl.net.

Maxsell Realty Services, P.O. Box 29, San Ignacio, tel. 501/9-23381, email info@maxsellws.com.

Regent Realty, 81 N. Front St., Belize City, tel. 501/2-73744, fax 2-72022, email regent@btl.net.

Southwind Properties, P.O. Box 1, San Pedro, Ambergris Caye, tel. 501/2-62005, fax 2-62331, email southwind@btl.net.

Sunrise Realty, P.O. Box 80, Barrier Reef Dr., San Pedro, Ambergris Caye, tel. 501/2-63737, fax 2-63379; email sunrise@btl.net.

Triton Properties, Barrier Reef Dr., San Pedro, Ambergris Caye, tel. 501/2-63783, fax 2-62403; email triton@btl.net.

Tropic Real Estate, P.O. Box 453, Belmopan, Cayo, tel. 501/9-23475, fax 9-23649, email tropic@realestatebelize.com.

Yearwood Properties, General Delivery, Placencia, tel./fax 501/6-23462, email info@belizebeachfront.com.

Belize's Media

Belize has no daily newspapers. The most reliable independent weekly "national" newspapers are *Amandala* and *The Reporter,* both published in Belize City. The People's United Party (PUP) and the United Democratic Party (UDP) political parties also have weekly newspapers. The *San Pedro Sun* is a chatty, informal weekly that does a good job covering Ambergris Caye. The best television news is on Channel 5. LOVE-FM is an "easy listening" radio station with a good news department. Many Belize hotels have either satellite or cable TV, usually with a full complement of U.S. networks. *Belize First Magazine* (www.belizefirst.com) covers travel, life, and potential retirement in Belize. On the Web, www.BelizeNews.com is a handy source for Belize journalism, as most of the Belize media are linked to the site.

Getting Married in Belize

Marriages in Belize are conducted in the tradition of British common law and are recognized worldwide. You must be in Belize for three days before you can apply for a license. Marriage licenses can be obtained in Belize City at the General Registry office or Belmopan at the Solicitor General's office, during normal working hours. Cost is US$100. No blood test is needed; parental consent not needed if over 18.

You need proof of citizenship. A valid passport will do, or a certified copy of birth certificate, which includes father's name, signed by a notary public. Proof of divorce is needed if applicable—bring original or certified copy of divorce decree. If widowed, you'll need a copy of the partner's death certificate.

A Justice of the Peace can conduct the ceremony at a magistrate's office; in Belize City, the Registrar General can conduct the ceremony at the Registry office. If you prefer a religious ceremony, most ministers in Belize can perform the ceremony at a church or at a hotel or private home.

Hotels on Ambergris Caye, in Placencia, Cayo, and elsewhere can assist with wedding details, including help with obtaining a minister or JP and getting the license, if you are staying at the hotel. Some Belize tour operators also provide wedding assistance.

Further Reading

ARCHAEOLOGY

Coe, Michael D. *The Maya.* New York: Thames and Hudson, 1993, 5th. ed.,
224 pp. First published in 1966, this is the best general introduction to
the subject.

Foster, Byron, Ed. *Warlords and Maize Men, A Guide to the Maya Sites of
Belize.* Cubola Productions, Belize, 1992, 82 pp. The first popular guide
focused entirely on Maya sites in Belize. Dr. Foster, the author of several books on Belize, was murdered by rampaging thugs at his farm in
Cayo. Maps, color photos.

Henderson, John S. *The World of the Ancient Maya.* Ithaca, New York:
Cornell University Press, 1981, 271 pp. Solid overview of the Maya in
Central America.

Kelly, Joyce. *An Archaeological Guide to Northern Central America: Belize,
Guatemala, Honduras, and El Salvador.* Norman: University of
Oklahoma Press, rev. ed. 1996, 352 pp. Includes coverage of many
smaller sites. Photographs by Jerry Kelly.

BOATING

Rauscher, Freya. *Cruising Guide to Belize and Mexico's Caribbean Coast.*
Stamford, Connecticut: Wescott Cove Publishing, 2nd. ed., 1996, 304
pp. with 119 charts and 133 photos. Comprehensive cruising guide,
the best available to this region. Includes general charts of Belize's
coast and Mexico's Caribbean Coast.

COOKBOOKS

Belizeous Cuisine, Delicious Belizean Recipes, by members of the Los Angeles
Belizean Educational Network Los Angeles: LABEN, 1997, 102 pp.
Good selection of Belizean recipes in all categories.

FICTION, DRAMA AND POETRY

Edgell, Zee. *Beka Lamb.* London: Heinemann, 1982, 192 pp. Classic novel
about ordinary life in British Honduras.

Ellis, Zoila. *On Heroes, Lizards and Passion, Seven Belizean Short Stories.*
Cubola Productions, Benque Viejo del Carmen, Belize, 1994, 130 pp.
"White Christmas an' Pink Jungle" is one of seven deliciously
Belizean stories, from a distinguished Belizean/Garifuna writer.

Miller, Carlos Ledson. *Belize, A Novel.* Philadelphia: Xlibris Corp., 1999, 402
pp. Fast-paced saga of father and sons over four decades, beginning
with Hurricane Hattie in 1961.

Theroux, Paul. *The Mosquito Coast.* New York: Houghton-Mifflin, 1982, 386 pp. Obsessed American drags his family to Central America. Actually set in Honduras, not Belize, but the movie of the same name was filmed in Belize.

Westlake, Donald. *High Adventure.* New York: Mysterious Press, 1985, 289 pp. Dope, dummies and deliverance in Belize, by popular adventure writer.

Young, Colville. *Pataki Full.* Benque Viejo del Carmen, Belize: Cubola Productions, 120 pp. Collection of short stories by noted Belizean writer and scholar.

GUIDEBOOKS

Eltringham, Peter.. *Belize, The Rough Guide.* London: Rough Guides, 2nd. ed., 2001, 265 pp. Thoroughly researched guide by knowledgeable writer who has lived in Belize and Guatemala.

Hennessy, Huw, Ed. *Belize Insight Guide.* London: Langenscheidt Publishing Group, 3rd. ed., 2000, 328 pp. Unmatched photos and good general background on the country.

King, Emory. *Driver's Guide to Beautiful Belize.* Belize City: Tropical Books, 2001, 56 pp. Mile-by-mile guide to most roads in Belize, with good maps. Updated annually.

Mahler, Richard. *Belize, Adventures in Nature.* Santa Fe: John Muir, 1997, 360 pp. Reliable source of eco-travel information

Mallan, Chicki and Lange, Patti. *Moon Handbooks: Belize.* Emeryville, California: Avalon Travel Publishing, 5th. ed., 2001, 372 pp. Favorite of many Belize travelers, with good maps and solid information.

Meyer, Franz O. *Lonely Planet Diving & Snorkeling Belize.* Oakland, California: Lonely Planet, 2nd. ed., 1998, 124 pp. Best diving and snorkel guide to Belize.

Sluder, Lan. *Belize First Guide to Mainland Belize.* Asheville, North Carolina: Equator, 2000, 288 pp. Focuses on the mainland of Belize, with more than 75 photos and maps.

HISTORY AND CULTURE

Barry, Tom with Vernon, Dylan. *Inside Belize.* Alburquerque, New Mexico: Resource Center Press, 2nd. ed., 1995, 181 pp. Useful overview of history, politics, media, education, economy and the environment.

Foster, Byron. *The Baymen's Legacy.* Benque Viejo del Carmen, Belize: Cubola Productions, 2nd. ed., 1992, 83 pp. A history of Belize City.

King, Emory. *The Great Story of Belize, Volume 1.* Belize City: Tropical Books, 1999, 53 pp. The first in a planned four-volume set, this volume covers the history of Belize from 1511 when the first Europeans arrive until 1798, when the Baymen won the battle of St. George's Caye.

—*The Great Story of Belize, Volume 2.* Belize City: Tropical Books, 1999, 87 pp. Volume 2 tells the history of Belize from 1800 to 1850, the period which shaped Belize's history for generations to come.

—*1798 The Road to Glory.* Belize City: Tropical Books, 1991, 348 pp. Fictionalized and somewhat glorified account of the Battle of St. George Caye's.

Merrill, Tim. *Guyana and Belize Country Studies.* Washington, D.C.: Federal Research Division, Library of Congress, 2nd. ed., 1993, 408 pp. One in the Area Handbook series sponsored by the U.S. Army; nevertheless, the historical, cultural and economic information is first-rate.

Shoman, Assad. *Thirteen Chapters of a History of Belize.* Belize City: Angelus Press, 1994, 297 pp. Somewhat left-wing interpretation of Belize's history.

LIVING IN BELIZE

Gallo, Roger. *Escape from America.* Portland, Oregon: Manhattan Loft Publishing, 1997, 352 pp. Devoted to living/retiring abroad. Includes chapters on Belize.

Gray, Bill and Gray, Claire (pseudonyms). *Belize Retirement Guide.* Pine Valley, California: Preview Publishing, 4th ed., 1999, 140 pp. Guide to "living in a tropical paradise for $450."

Belize First Magazine, edited and published by Lan Sluder, covers travel, life, and retirement in Belize. Our goal, rarely reached, is to publish quarterly. In any event, you are guaranteed to get four book-format, ad-free issues, even if you get some of them on Belize time. Cost for four issues plus a Belize Traveller's Map, in full color, is US$29 in Belize, Mexico, the United States and Canada, and US$49 elsewhere. Subscriptions and back issues are available from 287 Beaverdam Road, Candler, NC 28715, fax 828/667-1717, email bzefirst@aol.com. Web editions are at www.belizefirst.com.

MEMOIRS

Conroy, Richard Timothy. *Our Man in Belize.* New York: St. Martin's, 1997, 340 pp. Fascinating, readable memoir of life in former British Honduras in the late 1950s and early 60s.

NATURAL HISTORY

Arvigo, Rosita with Epstein, Nadine and Yaquinto, Marilyn. *Sastun, My Apprenticeship with a Maya Healer.* San Francisco: HarperSanFrancisco, 1994, 190 pp. Story of Arvigo's time with Don Elijio Panti, Belize's most famous bush doctor.

Beletsky, Les. *The Ecotravellers' Wildlife Guide, Belize and Northern Guatemala.* London: Natural World Academic Press, 1999, 488 pp. Lavishly color-illustrated guide, oriented to the amateur, to the most commonly spotted mammals, birds, amphibians, reptiles, fish and corals.

Cutlack, Meb. *Belize, Ecotourism in Action.* London: Macmillan Education, 2nd ed., 2000, 105 pp. Basic overview of Belize by an Australian who moved to Belize in the early 1980s.

Edwards, Ernest Preston, illustrated by Butler, E.M. *A Field Guide to the Birds of Mexico and Adjacent Areas: Belize, Guatemala, and El Salvador.* Austin, Texas: University of Texas Press, 1998, 288 pp. This is used by many local guides in Belize.

Rabinowitz, Alan. *Jaguar.* New York: Arbor House, 1986, 368 pp. Story of effort to establish the Cockscomb Preserve.

Travel

Chaplin, Gordon. *The Fever Coast Log.* New York: Simon & Schuster, 1992, 229 pp. Couple sets sail aboard the Lord Jim to sail the Caribbean Coast. You know it's all going to end badly.

Stephens, John L. *Incidents of Travel in Central America, Chiapas and Yucatán.* New York: Dover, 1969, reprint, two volumes. The great classic of early Central American travel books, originally published in 1841.

Wright, Ronald. *Time Among the Maya: Travels in Belize, Guatemala, and Mexico.* New York: Henry Holt, 1991, 451 pp. A modern classic.

Maps and Atlases

Atlas of Belize, 20th ed. Cubola Productions, 1995. 32 pp. with 11 maps and 80 photographs. Prepared for use in schools.

Belize Traveller's Map. ITMB, 1998. The best general map of Belize.

Map of Belize. Macmillan. Wall map with laminated coating.

British Ordnance Survey, Topographical Map of Belize. 1991. Two sheets, with maps of Belize City and towns on reverse. 1:250,000-scale.

British Ordnance Survey, Area Topographical Maps, various dates, 1970s–1990s. Country is divided into 44 sections, each 1:50,000-scale.

Videos

Anyplace Wild: Jungle Hiking in Belize. 60 min. PBS Home Video.

Belize, A Little Piece of Paradise. 45 min. Bill and Claire Gray, 2000. Interviews with expats who have retired to Belize.

Belize: The Sea, The Land, The People. 30 min. Naturalight Productions. Overview of Belize in 30 minutes.

Best of Belize All Over, vols. 1 and 2. Great Belize Productions. Collections of Channel 5 television shows from 1987–89.

Land of Belize. Great Belize Productions. Host Therese Rath guides an ecological and geographic tour.

Maya Heritage. Great Belize Productions. Host Froyla Salam looks back at Belize history from Maya times to the arrival of the first Europeans.

National Geographic's Tropical Kingdom of Belize, 1996. Re-released as *Belize, A Tropical Kingdom.* 59 min. Questar Video, 1998. Mostly devoted to land and sea animals of Belize. Slick, but not one of National Geographic's best efforts. Narrator mispronounces "caye."

Samples of Belize & Tikal: A Video Tour. Del and Pat Trobak, 1998. Covers about 20 areas of Belize, plus Tikal.

Sea of Belize. Great Belize Productions. A look at the barrier reef and Caribbean Sea.

Index

**AVALON
TRAVEL**
p u b l i s h i n g

How far will our travel guides take you? As far as you want.

Discover a rhumba-fueled nightspot in Old Havana, explore prehistoric tombs in Ireland, hike beneath California's centuries-old redwoods, or embark on a classic road trip along Route 66. Our guidebooks deliver solidly researched, trip-tested information—minus any generic froth—to help globetrotters or weekend warriors create an adventure uniquely their own.

And we're not just about the printed page. Public television viewers are tuning in to Rick Steves' new travel series, *Rick Steves' Europe*. On the Web, readers can cruise the virtual black top with *Road Trip USA* author Jamie Jensen and learn travel industry secrets from Edward Hasbrouck of *The Practical Nomad*.

In print. On TV. On the Internet.

We supply the information. The rest is up to you.

Avalon Travel Publishing

Something for everyone

www.travelmatters.com

Avalon Travel Publishing guides are available at your favorite book or travel store.

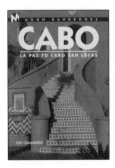

MOON HANDBOOKS provide comprehensive

coverage of a region's arts, history, land, people, and social issues in addition to detailed practical listings for accommodations, food, outdoor recreation, and entertainment. Moon Handbooks allow complete immersion in a region's culture—ideal for travelers who want to combine sightseeing with insight for an extraordinary travel experience in destinations throughout North America, Hawaii, Latin America, the Caribbean, Asia, and the Pacific.

WWW.MOON.COM

Rick Steves shows you where to travel and how to travel—all while getting the most value for your dollar. His Back Door travel philosophy is about making friends, having fun, and avoiding tourist rip-offs.

Rick has been traveling to Europe for more than 25 years and is the author of 22 guidebooks, which have sold more than a million copies. He also hosts the award-winning public television series *Rick Steves' Europe*.

WWW.RICKSTEVES.COM

ROAD TRIP USA

Getting there is half the fun, and Road Trip USA guides are your ticket to driving adventure. Taking you off the interstates and onto less-traveled, two-lane highways, each guide is filled with fascinating trivia, historical information, photographs, facts about regional writers, and details on where to sleep and eat—all contributing to your exploration of the American road.

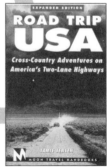

"[Books] so full of the pleasures of the American road, you can smell the upholstery."
~**BBC radio**

WWW.ROADTRIPUSA.COM

FOGHORN OUTDOORS guides are for campers, hikers, boaters, anglers, bikers, and golfers of all levels of daring and skill. Each guide focuses on a specific U.S. region and contains site descriptions and ratings, driving directions, facilities and fees information, and easy-to-read maps that leave only the task of deciding where to go.

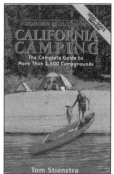

"Foghorn Outdoors has established an ecological conservation standard unmatched by any other publisher." ~Sierra Club

WWW.FOGHORN.COM

TRAVEL SMART guidebooks are accessible, route-based driving guides focusing on regions throughout the United States and Canada. Special interest tours provide the most practical routes for family fun, outdoor activities, or regional history for a trip of anywhere from two to 22 days. Travel Smarts take the guesswork out of planning a trip by recommending only the most interesting places to eat, stay, and visit.

"One of the few travel series that rates sightseeing attractions. That's a handy feature. It helps to have some guidance so that every minute counts." ~San Diego Union-Tribune

CiTY·SMaRT™ guides are written by local authors with hometown perspectives who have personally selected the best places to eat, shop, sightsee, and simply hang out. The honest, lively, and opinionated advice is perfect for business travelers looking to relax with the locals or for longtime residents looking for something new to do Saturday night.

About the Author

an Sluder has been banging around Belize for more than a decade and has visited every corner of the country. A former newspaper editor in New Orleans, he is editor and publisher of *Belize First Magazine.* Sluder also is the author of several books, including *Frommer's Best Beach Vacations, Carolinas and Georgia* and *Belize First Guide to Mainland Belize.* His articles on Belize and other travel destinations have appeared in *Caribbean Travel & Life, Chicago Tribune, The New York Times, Bangkok Post, Honduras This Week, Miami Herald, St. Petersburg Times, Chicago Tribune, Where to Retire, The Globe & Mail* and many other publications. He also updated the Belize sections of the *Fodor's Belize and Guatemala Guide* and *Up Close Central America.*

Brooks Lambert-Sluder